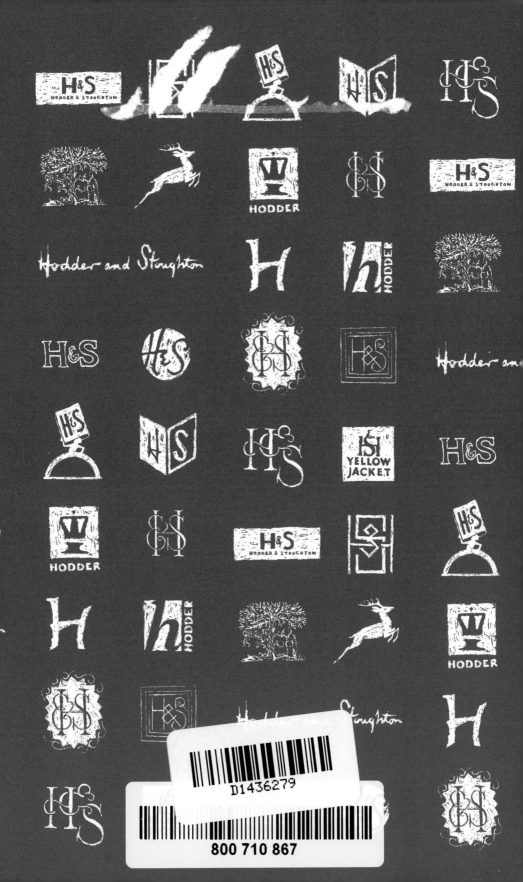

The Publishing Game

The Publishing Game

Adventures in Books:
150 years of Hodder & Stoughton

EDWARD STOURTON

HODDER &
STOUGHTON

First published in Great Britain in 2018 by Hodder & Stoughton
An Hachette UK company

1

Copyright © Edward Stourton 2018

The right of Edward Stourton to be identified as the Author of the Work has been
asserted by him in accordance with the Copyright, Designs and Patents Act 1988.

A CIP catalogue record for this title is available from the British Library

Hardback ISBN 978 1 473 67117 1
eBook ISBN 978 1 473 67118 8

Typeset in Bembo by Hewer Text UK Ltd, Edinburgh
Printed and bound in Great Britain by Clays Ltd, Elcograf S.p.A.

Hodder & Stoughton policy is to use papers that are natural, renewable
and recyclable products and made from wood grown in sustainable
forests. The logging and manufacturing processes are expected to conform
to the environmental regulations of the country of origin.

Hodder & Stoughton Ltd
Carmelite House
50 Victoria Embankment
London EC4Y 0DZ

www.hodder.co.uk

'Talk about navigators and explorers, we publishers get more fun out of life than they ever did. The books we pledge our hopes to that never come off; the other books with only a fighting chance for which we strived that become best-sellers! There's joy in the game, and it's the biggest game in the world.'

Sir Ernest Hodder-Williams

Contents

Introduction

For the first ten weeks of my working life I was paid to paint the sitting room and drink beer. I joined Independent Television News as a graduate trainee in 1979, just as the technical unions took ITV off the air for the duration of an epic pay strike. ITN's journalists were not asked to cross picket lines, but we were required to be contactable and available for work – thus the big painting job. And once a week the NUJ chapel met in the Green Man pub behind ITN's Wells Street headquarters – thus the beer drinking. When the strike was settled we all got a whopping rise. 'Trebles all round,' to use the slang of the day.

I was reminded of this extraordinary episode in Britain's industrial history because it played a minor role in the Hodder & Stoughton story; ITV's silence drove up the audience for John le Carré's *Tinker, Tailor, Soldier, Spy*, which was airing on the BBC, and so helped Hodder sales.

There were reports that some viewers stayed faithful to ITV despite the strike – switching on the telly to stare at a blank screen. It is difficult to imagine oneself back into that world; even when ITV, BBC1 and BBC2 were all on air, viewers faced a very limited choice of fare when they sat down for an evening's entertainment.

It meant that those of us making programmes enjoyed the near certainty of vast audiences. At ITN we took pride in being nimbler and less stuffy than the BBC; we were told that our reports must be pitched at a mythical viewer known as 'Mum in

Wigan', and the art of storytelling was highly prized. But I do not remember having to worry too much about seducing an audience; it was a given that millions of people would tune into *News at Ten* each night.

I did not realise what a privilege that was until, in my forties, I started writing books. The first one was such a thrill that I did not worry very much about the sales figures – simply seeing my name on the cover of a book that could actually be bought in the shops was validation enough. But about halfway through the second – which was published by Hodder & Stoughton – I was struck by the awful reality that it would only be read if people were willing to pay good money for it.

The book was based on a BBC Radio 4 series about a journey I made round the eastern Mediterranean in the footsteps of the apostle Paul, and the series had benefited greatly from the clever way my producer used the sounds of the journey and the people we met along the way. Somehow, I realised, I had to replicate that on the page, to persuade people that the story I had to tell was, of course, important, but also one they would enjoy reading. And ever since then I have tried to think about the reader with every sentence I write.

And that, of course, has made me wonder about the mechanism that connects me to readers – the complex, sometimes mysterious business we call publishing, the alchemy by which a manuscript bashed out in my writing shed becomes an artefact on the bedside table of someone I have never met. So when Hodder & Stoughton invited me – flatteringly – to write the firm's history, it was not difficult to make up my mind; this book has been something of a treat.

It has, inevitably, involved an extended conversation with the last Hodder history – John Attenborough's *A Living Memory*, which was published in 1975. It is a heroic piece of research work, and has been an invaluable resource. Attenborough was descended from Matthew Hodder, one of the firm's founders, and his book is written with both great pride in the family firm and, occasionally, irritation with some family members. It is, like all history, a distinctive perspective that reflects the author's time and character – just as this book is bound to reflect my own assumptions and, no doubt, prejudices.

Fortunately, a substantial amount of archive material from the firm's history has survived; the truest witness is borne by documents – like Matthew Hodder's American diaries – that were written very soon after the events they describe. But part of the fascination of a story like this is the way the telling of it changes over time. John Attenborough's decision to omit, edit or stress certain aspects of the narrative is itself part of the story. The history of a publishing house is one way of telling the history of a nation, because publishers live or die by their success or failure in discerning – and sometimes moulding – the tastes, customs and opinions of their age.

I claim one stroke of real genius in the writing of this book; when Hodder offered me some help with research I immediately thought of Sarah Harrison, a BBC producer I have worked with on some big Radio 4 and BBC television programmes. She is married to Jamie Hodder-Williams, so she too is a member of the Matthew Hodder clan, the family that have run Hodder & Stoughton for most of its history. The combination of BBC rigour and family connections has made her an unbeatable asset.

Hodder staff past and present have been generous with their time and memories, and a number of their best-known authors have talked or written to us about their relationship with the firm.

I have had most fun, however, from the books. Sir Ernest Hodder-Williams, probably the greatest of the publishers in the century and a half covered here, advised publishers to 'travel books yourself'. This project has been an excuse to do exactly that, and in the course of it I have met or renewed acquaintance with a wonderfully varied list of authors. The shelves of my writing shed now groan under the weight of my new friends – great mountains of Hodder & Stoughton material I have read, half-read, skipped through, simply handled and admired or, most excitingly, marked down for future pleasure.

I

Not slothful in business,
fervent in spirit, serving the Lord

The first book on the first Hodder & Stoughton list sounds a little worthy, but *The Beggars; the Founders of the Dutch Republic* is in fact a ripping adventure story. The Beggars of the title are an underground brotherhood of sixteenth-century Dutch Protestants and patriots struggling to throw off the yoke of Catholic Spain. The villains are an enjoyably wicked and wily bunch – Jesuits, Inquisitors and the like – while the hero is a clean-cut, brave, open-hearted fellow, a literary ancestor, indeed, of later Hodder heroes like Bulldog Drummond and the Saint. The Spanish are vanquished, the hero gets the enthusiastically Protestant girl, and the two are married by a pastor who has ministered to the rebels during their campaign. The triumph of Reformed Religion crowns their union. 'That their marriage was a happy one will scarcely be doubted,' the final paragraph declares, 'and their happiness was all the greater because Wouter Barends [the pastor] lived with them, and openly preached the reformed doctrines, no longer in the barn of Van Alphen, but in the cathedral.'

Matthew Hodder read those words on board ship while returning from the United States, and judged the book 'capital' in his diary. He was fighting his own religious crusade at the time. He had met a couple on board who were what he called 'backsliders'; they had been converted to Christ but subsequently lost their way. With their failings in mind he preached to the ship's company on the theme of the Prodigal Son, but 'one man, I presume a Catholic' was 'disposed to be troublesome', and had to be silenced by the captain. Mr Hodder was undaunted. He soon had the passengers in steerage singing hymns, and he handed out improving literature – 'little books, which were gratefully received'.

The Beggars went through several editions and sold solidly into the twentieth century; my edition (the seventh) of 1891 has a touch that was characteristic of the marketing enthusiasm of the young publishing house; opposite the title page there is a puff for the latest work by the author, J. D. De Liefde, promising a 'handsomely bound' historical novel, a 'story of Heroism and Adventure'. Many of the books offered by the new partnership of Matthew Hodder and Thomas Stoughton were inherited from the list built up by the firm of Jackson, Walford and Hodder, where Matthew had served his apprenticeship, and they reflected a vigorous religious tradition. Three of the five on that first list, which was advertised in the *Publishers' Circular* of 1 July 1868, were explicitly religious, and one of them, a translation of C. Tischendorf's *The Origin of the Four Gospels*, was a landmark work of nineteenth-century biblical scholarship.

Matthew Henry Hodder, the senior founding partner of the firm that is the subject of this book, began his publishing career in 1844. He arrived in Fleet Street by stagecoach on 5 August that year, and walked up Ludgate Hill to the great cathedral of St Paul's. Half a century later, at the celebration of his jubilee year in publishing, he recalled how, 'I travelled from Windsor to London to take up my duties with Messrs Jackson and Walford, whose premises were 18 St Paul's Churchyard. The firm were publishers of the Congregational Union.'

The term 'Dickensian' is much overused, but the world Matthew Hodder describes really could have come from the pages of *Nicholas Nickleby* or *Great Expectations*; 'There was only one other assistant in the house beside myself,' he remembered. 'During my apprentice days I wore a blue coat with brass buttons, and used to sit on a stool waiting for customers. We did not close till 8 p.m., and there was no Saturday half-holiday. An hour was allowed for dinner, but we had no break for tea.' It sounds like the beginning of a great Victorian adventure story – and it was.

The book trade had been flourishing around St Paul's since the late Middle Ages; manuscripts were copied, bought and sold there – and sometimes stored in the cathedral itself – even before Caxton printed *The Canterbury Tales* at Westminster in 1476. A printer called Julian Notary set up shop in St Paul's Churchyard – just next door to Matthew Hodder's new place of business – at some point between 1510 and 1515, and after the Dissolution of the Monasteries the Crown sold many of the buildings in the cathedral precinct to booksellers.

By the mid-sixteenth century, thirty-seven booksellers' signs – with names like 'The Row Greyhound' and 'The Black Boy' – could be seen hanging in the churchyard. Many early editions of Shakespeare's works and those of his contemporaries were published there; the frontispiece of a 1600 edition of *The Merchant of Venice*, for example, states that it was 'sold in St Paul's Churchyard at the sign of the Greene Dragon'. The area became, according to James Raven in his essay *St Paul's Precinct and the Book Trade*, 'one of the greatest publishing centres of Europe. From here, booksellers despatched books, magazines and other print to the country towns of England but also to the colonies in North America, the Caribbean, India, Africa, Australasia, and the Far East.'

So Matthew was entering a world soaked in tradition, and in later years he enjoyed describing the leisurely daily routine of one of the old school partners, Mr Jackson; he would, Matthew told a colleague, 'come to the office at little after eight. He spent the time till eleven poring over the morning papers. Then he began to tackle the correspondence of the firm. His labours were interrupted by luncheon, which occupied a considerable time. After that the letters were resumed along with other affairs, and this went on till eight at night.'

But the London of the mid-nineteenth century was also a city on the move, and for the thousands of young men who arrived from the country seeking their fortune change meant opportunity. Matthew quickly lost patience with the gentle ways of an earlier era. 'Young Hodder reacted violently against this waste of time,' wrote his friend and colleague. 'To the end he could not bear delays, or long interviews, or protracted negotiations.'

The life stories of Matthew Hodder and some of the close friends he made in the capital are a testament to the extraordinary social mobility of the period. Matthew's background certainly was not privileged; his father was a chemist with a shop in Staines. Hodder Senior's papers suggest that his real talents lay in the direction of marketing rather than medicine. A modern chemist might raise an eyebrow at the idea of treating gonorrhoea with a mixture of gum arabic, balsam and castor oil, but Mr Hodder's own-brand Aperient Antibilious Pills sound truly amazing; they could treat, according to the bill he had printed, 'Costive and Bilious Complaints, Attacks of Fever, Disorders of the Stomach and Bowels, Gout, Acute and Chronic Rheumatism, Cutaneous Eruptions, Indigestion, Dimness of Sight, Pain and Giddiness of the Head, Worms, Piles and Dropsical Complaints'.

The recipes and remedies preserved in the Hodder family archive suggest a small businessman of energy and commercial ambition, and all three of his sons seem to have been determined to grasp the opportunities for advancement the Victorian world offered. Their lives would take them a very long way from the high street in Staines. Reginald travelled furthest in a geographical sense – all the way to New Zealand, in fact, where he established a new branch of the family, and became a successful writer (his *Daughter of the Dawn* was described in an obituary as 'a remarkably imaginative New Zealand novel of Maori lore and magic'). Edwin was also an enthusiastic traveller as a young man, but settled back in Britain as a civil servant; he too became a writer – a prolific one – with a strong line in religious biography.

8

And Matthew founded a publishing dynasty. It took him seventeen years to amass the capital to buy himself into partnership, but in 1861 he was able to pay £6,335 to acquire a share in the business, and Jackson and Walford became Jackson, Walford and Hodder. During his time as a partner, the firm took over another long-established business, Thomas Ward & Co., which was 'a celebrated theological business issuing many cheap editions of the Puritans, and for many years *The Evangelical Magazine* and the *Eclectic Review*'. Ward's list also included a French textbook that 'was yielding £500 a year' and was still earning good royalties half a century later – a success story that Hodder & Stoughton would build on with its ventures into educational publishing. Mr Jackson retired in the year that Matthew Hodder bought into the partnership, and Mr Walford was also looking forward to an easier life. By the end of the decade Matthew Hodder was ready to complete his transformation from country boy and chemist's son to entrepreneurial publisher.

But the Victorian world that offered so much opportunity was also shot through with moral jeopardy. The Hodders were Nonconformists, pious Christians who refused to 'conform' to the teachings and practices of the Established Church, and to any godly young man the temptations of London could be truly terrifying. Matthew's brother Edwin painted a revealing picture of the moral landscape ambitious young men faced in a novella called *Life in London; or The Pitfalls of a Great City* (published, of course, by the family firm).

It tells the story of a young man called George Weston, who is forced to leave his boarding school on the sudden death of his father, and seeks employment in the City. His uncle secures him an interview for a position as a clerk, and when he is asked to demonstrate the neatness of his handwriting he chooses a passage from St Paul's Letter to the Romans, 'Not slothful in business, fervent in spirit, serving the Lord'. This proves a passport to a good position, and, by dint of diligence and clean living, George flourishes at the firm, earning his employer's trust, promotion and a good salary.

But a chance encounter with an old school friend changes everything; the primrose path to perdition begins with a glass of wine at his friend's smart lodgings in south London, progresses, shockingly, to a trip to the theatre, and within a couple of chapters George is gambling at cards, stealing from his employer to pay his debts and cooking the books to conceal the crime. When he is discovered he flees to Plymouth with the intention of seeking a new life in South Africa, but at the last minute he attends a chapel service at which he experiences a new conversion: 'That night there was joy in the presence of the angels of God over a new-born soul', Edwin Hodder wrote. 'As George listened to the voice of the preacher, there fell from his eye as it had been scales, and he saw the Father running to embrace the returning prodigal, and felt the kiss of His forgiving love.' George was rescued and also forgiven by his mother and some of his friends, and the story has a happy ending, but, as the title suggests, the book was clearly designed to serve as a warning about the moral perils of city life.

Matthew's friend George Williams (who would find fame and title as the founder of the YMCA), took an even more bracing view; he was of the opinion that 'the first twenty-four hours of a young man's life in London usually settle his eternity in heaven or hell'. He was not speaking metaphorically; for Christians of this cut the threat of eternal damnation was all too real (which is why Matthew was so concerned about the souls of the 'back-sliders' and that troublesome Catholic he encountered on board ship). 'In those days a young man was either burning hot or ice-cold', wrote one of Williams' biographers, 'was utterly and completely possessed of God or just as completely given over to the power of darkness. There was no middle road between the saint and sinner.'

The key to Matthew Hodder's approach to publishing lies in that powerful conviction that day-to-day life is lived in the shadow of eternity. In his *History of British Publishing*, John Feather argues that the connection between evangelical Christianity and the book trade can be traced right back to the Reformation: 'Protestant reformers had argued that since personal salvation was to be obtained only by a personal understanding of religion, and this could only be acquired by reading the Bible,' he wrote, 'literacy was an essential element of religious faith.'

In the late eighteenth and early nineteenth century that idea underpinned the Sunday School movement, which was also driven by a philanthropic ambition to better the lot of the urban working class created by the Industrial Revolution. One of the Sunday School pioneers, Hannah More, founded the Religious Tract Society, producing cheap but morally sound reading material for the newly literate readers who emerged from her schools – those 'little books' Matthew Hodder handed out on board ship were part of the tradition she established.

Most of the books and pamphlets published under the imprint of her *Cheap Repository Tracts* were written and also bought by middle-class philanthropists who gave them to the poor, but their huge success suggested a significant untapped commercial market. 'The lesson was not lost on publishers whose interests were far from the high-flown moral principles of Mrs More,' Feathers writes. 'The penny-a-part novel of the 1840s and yellowback of the 1870s are both direct descendants of the Religious Tracts of Hannah More.'

The Religious Tract Society gave birth to the British and Foreign Bible Society (now more generally known simply as the Bible Society), which is one of the great publishing stories of Victorian Britain. It was inspired by the experience of a young Welsh girl, Mary Jones, who was unable to find a copy of the holy book in her native Welsh language; this moved the secretary of the Religious Tract Society to propose the creation of a new society that would make good the deficit, and he famously declared, 'If for Wales, why not for the Empire and the world?' The BFBS was duly established in 1804, with the support of William Wilberforce and the so-called Clapham Saints who drove the campaign to abolish slavery, and the widespread distribution of Bibles very soon became a symbol of the civilising mission of nineteenth-century Britain.

In 1810 a pamphleteer and Bible Society supporter contrasted the image of 'Great Britain standing in the attitude of presenting the Bible to all the world' with Napoleonic France and 'the tyrant of the continent wielding his bloody sword'. He went on, 'I confess I derive more hope of salvation to my country from Britannia in this posture, than from Britannia in her posture of *defence*, with her trident in her hand, and surrounded by fleets and armies. Let Britons only study, and practise, and circulate the Bible, and we have nothing to fear.' In his study *Cheap Bibles*, Leslie Howsam writes, 'This institution [the BFBS] consisted not only of the bricks-and-mortar of Bible House, or the paper-and-ink, leather and glue of the books, but of the Bible transaction itself, the powerful idea that this was the secret of England's greatness, the way to avoid revolution at home and to disseminate English values abroad.'

The Society represented itself as a charity, and it was supported by donations and subscriptions, but it was also a highly successful commercial operation. Its business model was to sell – not give away – cheap Bibles in Britain, and to use the income to finance the production of foreign-language Bibles for free distribution in far-flung corners of the Empire. And the appetite for cheaply produced Bibles in Victorian Britain appears to have been almost inexhaustible. During the decade from 1837 to 1847 the three main printers of Bibles – Oxford and Cambridge University Presses and the Queen's Printer – churned out nearly eleven million copies between them, and the combination of missionary zeal and market dominance had a profound impact on the publishing industry and the way it worked. 'The single-minded tenacity of these men and women [of the BFBS] – dedicated as they were to the production of a single text, in durable volumes, at low prices, in massive quantities – transformed the book trade at large', he writes.

Matthew Hodder took his first steps in publishing at the high point of this national mania for printing Bibles. In mid-Victorian Britain the production of books was seen by many people as a religious mission and a significant contribution to social reform. It was often closely associated with the Temperance Movement; the early Hodder & Stoughton lists include F. Sherlock's *Virtuous Abstainers* and a book called *Sunlight and Shadow – a Temperance Gift Book for the Christmas season*. The firm also distributed *Cook's Tourists' Handbooks*; Thomas Cook, who established a shop in Fleet Street in 1865, had begun his career as a travel agent by organising trips for Temperance supporters.

And like the new fashion for tourism, religious publishing was, of course, also big business.

2

A partnership 'of the Lord'

The friendship between Matthew Hodder and George Williams was long and consequential. Its enduring impact on Hodder & Stoughton is reflected in the fact that, at the time of writing, more than a century and a half later, the head of the firm, Jamie Hodder-Williams, bears the surname of both men. Their shared beliefs and ideas are part of the Hodder & Stoughton DNA.

They both arrived in London in the early 1840s, and Williams' chosen trade also brought him to St Paul's Churchyard; the premises of the drapers' firm of Hitchock and Rogers, which he joined as an assistant in 1841, were at nos. 72–75. Williams came from a Devon farming family, and had served as a draper's apprentice in the town of Dulverton, so the two young men were of similar social standing. And both were animated by a deep, Dissenting Christian faith that drew them to one of the most prominent features on the London religious landscape, the King's Weigh House church.

It took its name from its original (seventeenth-century) location above a customs house in the City where the goods of foreign merchants were weighed. After the appointment of Thomas Binney as minister in 1829, the congregation soon outgrew the meeting house, and a new one was built on Fish Street Hill, which runs up from the river and the site of the old Billingsgate market. Binney remained as minister for forty years, earning himself the popular title of the 'Archbishop of Nonconformity' (a curious nickname, since Congregationalists like Binney did not believe in bishops). The deacon of the Weigh House described Binney thus: 'tall, thin, eloquent, natural, with a feeble voice and very rapid'. He used that feeble voice to develop a distinctive style in the pulpit, establishing a reputation as one of the most seductive preachers in London – no small achievement in the religion-soaked society of the Victorian age.

And Binney was a powerful advocate of a link between evangelical Christianity and middle-class commercial enterprise. 'How the devil must chuckle at his success,' he once told his congregation, 'when he gets a fellow to think himself wonderful because he can dress in scarlet or blue, and have a sword by his side and a feather in his hat; and when he says to him (the poor fool believing it), "Your hands are far too delicate to be soiled by the counter and by the shop."' Matthew Hodder and George Williams would have found plenty of business contacts as well as soulmates in the pews; two scions of another great publishing dynasty, Daniel and Alexander Macmillan, were also members of the church. 'To ambitious countrymen the Weigh House was a gateway to every prospect . . . the church had great business standing, some social standing, and increasing political standing', writes Clive Binfield in *George Williams and the YMCA – a Study in Victorian Social Attitudes*. And he argues that there was a certain clannishness at work in both Dissenting Religion and the business world where the two young men were making their way. 'The freshness and self-sufficiency of self-made men' was, he argues, 'balanced by a host of connections. It was almost a freemasonry.'

The conditions George Williams endured at his drapers' house, which employed 140 assistants, were tougher than those faced by Matthew Hodder at his small firm of publishers. At some shops, assistants were required to work for seventeen hours out of twenty-four. Hitchcock and Rogers was more enlightened than many, but the first team of assistants had to be at work by seven, dusting down the warehouse, and in the summer months the shop might not close until eleven in the evening. Meals were snatched on the run; a campaigning pamphlet published in 1843 complained that 'while the mechanic or day labourer has half an hour allowed him for breakfast, and an hour for dinner, out of his twelve hours of labour, the assistant draper has no fixed time for either . . . We may assert that at nineteen shops out of twenty the average time spent at the *three meals* – breakfast, dinner and tea – is not more than half an hour.'

Williams' great-nephew Ernest Hodder-Williams (of whom much more later) wrote the earliest biography of the YMCA founder, and he reflected that 'Young men engaged in shops do not differ from their fellows in their craving for some kind of recreation and amusement. Their late hours prevented them from the enjoyment of what little rational and wholesome recreation was available at that time in London.' The inevitable result, he observed, was that they sought 'gratification in the lowest form of sensual enjoyment. When at last they were free they turned, by an irresistible impulse, to the tavern, to strong drink, to the grossest forms of immorality.'

Hitchcock and Rogers exercised a strict curfew at 11 p.m., and the outer door of the establishment was banged shut – Oxbridge college style – when the cathedral clock chimed the hour. But there was plenty of opportunity for wickedness after lights out; a pub called the Goose and Gridiron – which Christopher Wren had used as an office when he was rebuilding the cathedral – stood at one end of the premises, and one of Williams' contemporaries recalled that 'One or two bedrooms having windows overlooking the Goose and Gridiron were occupied by young men who had an understanding with the landlord, so that when he heard a whistle he was to be on the *qui vive*, and, the coast being clear, a Wellington boot was lowered at the end of a string, and bottles of beer having been placed in it, another whistle was the signal to heave it up again.'

At Hitchcock and Rogers there were two or three beds crammed into even the smallest rooms, and two assistants were crammed into each bed. This led Ernest to speculate – in a roundabout way – about the possibility of even greater depravity: 'The effect upon a boy fresh from the country of being compelled to live and work, to share a bedroom, and in many cases the bed itself, with veterans of vice – men so sunk in debauchery that they took hellish delight in contaminating and defiling all around them – these things are best left to the imagination', he wrote.

There was no danger of George Williams becoming caught up in the Wellington boot carry-on, as he had 'signed the pledge' before coming up to London; a handwritten note on the flyleaf of a volume of sermons records, 'January 30th, 1839, Signed the teetotal pledge after hearing a convincing lecture from G Pilkington, at the Friends Meeting House, Bridgewater'. He was twenty when he arrived in the capital, and 'found no means of grace of any kind' among his fellow assistants. So he set about converting them.

'Going to bed at night was an undertaking calling for much careful scouting on the part of those who had attracted his attention', according to Ernest's biography, 'and they must carefully examine the passages leading to their bedrooms to make sure of the coast being clear, for their zealous comrade was often lying in ambush, and, given the opportunity, would not be denied.' As well as trying to save souls he campaigned for better working conditions, and became involved in the Early Closing Association (originally known as the Metropolitan Drapers' Association), which campaigned for shorter working hours. And it was from these twin impulses – religious and philanthropic – that the Young Men's Christian Association was born.

The foundation of the YMCA is generally dated to a meeting at the Hitchcock and Rogers premises on 6 June 1844 – two months before Matthew Hodder arrived in London. The meeting was held in a bedroom where a group of young men had gathered for prayer, and in later tellings of the story much was made of the echo of the biblical 'upper room' where Christ broke bread with his disciples on the eve of his Passion. One of those present recorded in his diary, 'Met in G Williams room for the purpose of forming a society the object of which is to influence young men (Religious) to spread the Redeemer's Kingdom amongst those by whom they are surrounded.' There is some controversy over whether it is right to identify George Williams as the sole inspirer of the movement, but he did two things that made him a natural Victorian hero, and they help explain why his name has become irrevocably linked with the movement: he proved an extremely successful businessman, and he married the boss's daughter. His wedding to Helen Hitchcock took place on 9 June 1853. He ended his life as a knight and was buried in St Paul's Cathedral, close to where his remarkable upward journey through Victorian society began.

Matthew Hodder slipped easily into this world of Dissenting Religion, commercial ambition and kinship ties, and it had a decisive impact on his personal life and the firm he founded. He met his wife, Frances Ann Biddulph, through the King's Weigh House where he and George Williams both worshipped, and his daughter Mary married George Williams' nephew John. And it seems likely that it was the YMCA connection that brought Matthew Hodder into contact with his new partner, Thomas Wilberforce Stoughton. Thomas's father, Dr John Stoughton, a minister at a chapel in Kensington at the time, appears on the first list of YMCA Vice-Presidents, and when the organisation sponsored the series of hugely popular public meetings that became known as the Exeter Hall Lectures, Dr Stoughton, who was a distinguished church historian as well as a minster, was invited to address the first event.

In his history of Hodder & Stoughton, John Attenborough, a member of the extended Hodder family, speculated that the first meeting between Henry Hodder and Thomas Stoughton 'may have taken place at the Young Men's Christian Association, which had begun to provide Matthew Hodder with a very congenial circle of friends and which was to play a central part in his life, or it may have started with a casual meeting between the two young publishers at Dolly's Chop House in Paternoster Row.' Thomas Stoughton was working at another St Paul's publisher, James Nisbet & Co. The Stoughtons were a notch above the Hodders on the social scale; Attenborough describes them as 'a yeoman family of ancient lineage. They had owned land both in Surrey and East Anglia at various periods of their long history, supplying their quota of men in the service of Parliament, the Law and the Church.' John Stoughton was a literary powerhouse who generated hundreds of thousands of words. Hodder & Stoughton published the first of his many volumes of English Church history in 1870, and he kept the printing presses busy for much of the rest of the century.

And his contacts would have been extremely useful to his publisher son: John Stoughton knew everyone who was anyone in religious circles, and his cultural reach extended into the more free-thinking areas of late-Victorian intellectual life too. When he joined the Athenaeum, that great bastion of lunching bishops and public servants at the heart of London's clubland, his proposer was Matthew Arnold, the author of *On Dover Beach*, one of the nineteenth century's most powerful evocations of the 'melancholy long withdrawing roar' that marked the end of the universal sway of Christian faith.

A twentieth-century researcher into the company's history remarked that John Stoughton 'in fact wrote so much that one cannot imagine how he found time to do anything else'. The younger Stoughton was a surprisingly unbookish son to such a father. He loved cricket, and 'used to be found at Lord's whenever a great cricket match was on, watching with the keenest joy'. In fact, he seems to have very much preferred the great outdoors to the book-lined world where his father spent his time;

a friend and contemporary wrote that he 'was keenly interested in horses and the open-air life generally'.

He enjoyed making the journey from his home in Norwood to St Paul's by driving his own horse and carriage, and, although he 'took a legitimate pride' in his own firm's books, he was 'not a great reader'. Like Matthew Hodder, he had 'very strong and fundamental' religious convictions, and he was a fellow disciple of Thomas Binney's. But the stern world view projected from the pulpit of the King's Weigh House does not seem to have dimmed his sense of fun; an obituary recorded that 'His great strength was a certain childlike delight in everything. Life was always full of wonderful things for him.'

Matthew Hodder and Thomas Stoughton made a good team. One of those closely involved in the firm's early days wrote that 'Mr Stoughton was considerably younger than his partner, but had much experience in the publishing business, and the two men made a remarkable combination. They were essentially of the same mind in many things, but in many ways complementary.' And it was a propitious time to start a new venture. 1868 was a year of change and challenge to the old order; it saw the election of a reforming Liberal government, the abolition of the practice of buying commissions in the army, the introduction of competitive entrance to the Civil Service and the admission of Dissenters – Christians outside the Established Church – to Oxford and Cambridge. The same writer recorded that 'When they started, the quiet little firms with which they were surrounded were gradually fading', but new opportunities were there for the taking. An 1890s letter to the *Publishers' Circular*, which is preserved in the Hodder archive, provides a flavour of the optimism of the era: 'I have found in book-selling what I could not find in any other business', wrote 'a Provincial Bookseller'. 'I succeeded from the first. And now my profits average about £15 a week. Book-selling to me has always been comparatively easy. Why, as a grocer I used to work ten times as hard.'

Messrs Hodder & Stoughton established themselves and their families in the newly popular London suburbs – Matthew Hodder in Bromley and Thomas Stoughton in Norwood – and their homes became local hubs for networks of kinship and religious relationships, which in turn fed into the way they ran their business. Carisbrooke, the Hodder home by Bromley Common, was said to be 'imposingly Victorian in its simple grandeur'. The Canadian publisher George Doran, a frequent visitor, recorded that 'one of the chief features was a huge room looking out over the lovely gardens and arranged as a chapel for the services conducted each week by Mr Hodder. From Carisbrooke there was dispensed real English hospitality. Here had been entertained many of the great evangelicals.' The establishment was presided over by 'a Victorian in the manifestation of an indomitable will' in the person of Mrs Hodder, and their only child, Mary, lived just across the lawn with her husband, John Williams, George Williams' nephew. One of their grandsons, Ernest, who was to be a hugely influential figure in the publishing world, made his first home in a Gothic lodge next door. 'That family would have provided Galsworthy with yet another saga,' Doran remarked.

He was less kind about the Stoughton establishment in Norwood, which he characterised as 'the perfection of Victorian austerity and discomfort'. Thomas Stoughton did not build quite such an extensive family fiefdom, but his enthusiastic religious activism provided him with a local network of suitable employees. After studying the firm's early records John Attenborough noted that 'the nominal roll of the firm bears record that in those early days almost every member of staff came from the Norwood area'. These included two stalwarts of the firm, Cuthbert Huckvale and Joseph Apted, who both gave half a century of service to Hodder & Stoughton. Huckvale was in charge of the counting house (as the accounts department was then called), and Joseph Apted became – in Attenborough's judgement – 'one of the greatest and most daring production managers in London publishing'. The two recruited other young men from the Norwood area, and Attenborough writes that 'These two young men from Mr Stoughton's bible class . . . formed the local nucleus around which was developed a corporate belief in the firm's destiny which was to remain a constant and vital factor in many future vicissitudes.'

There is a touching letter from Matthew Hodder to Thomas Stoughton preserved in the archives, which gives a flavour of the way business, family and God were inextricably bound up in these late-Victorian minds. It was written on the day of Thomas's marriage; 'I cannot refrain from adding a few words to those already spoken', Matthew Hodder begins, 'in wishing you on the morning of the consummation of your <u>third</u> partnership the earnest blessings which shall be rich and increasingly precious. You have already long enjoyed that union with our Divine Master which is of endless duration, and which I desire may be vividly realised now that you enter upon a relationship which is second in importance to it. I do not by any means think lightly of the minor relationship, in which I am personally concerned, and therefore most heartily desire that <u>each</u> may increasingly prove a source of much happiness to you. I am perfectly satisfied that our partnership is "of the lord", and I already know sufficiently of you to assure me that the same is the fact in reference to your marriage. May God bless you both, and may you find, as I have found, an increase of blessing with an increase of the years! I feel that every year brings with it an additional and more substantial happiness. In proportion to our <u>conscious nearness to Christ</u> will our happiness and prosperity be in relation to Home, business and all the duties of life.'

The premises at 27 Paternoster Row, just north of St Paul's, had been acquired with the takeover of Ward & Co, and the new partners set about smartening them up. Memories of those early days were recorded in a trade journal many years later. No. 27 had one foot planted in Matthew Hodder's Dickensian past and the other very firmly in the future. The original St Paul's publishers sold books directly from their offices, so there was 'The old double-fronted shop with its window displays, rigorously changed and daily dusted, though in fact the books could only be seen from outside by pressing one's nose to the glass.' The activity within, however, reflected Matthew's restless energy; on the office floors 'the proprietors and their executive people carried on conferences and interviewed authors, contributors, printers, engravers, binders and other frock-coated gentlemen who reeked of literature'.

There were soon touches of modernity too: 'On the first landing was a telephone, a wall instrument and very public; a great privilege and a great nuisance to use'. The article continues, 'Presently there came another great innovation. A typewriter arrived, and with it a lady – the first one to join the staff.' The attic was used to store files, and 'a terrifying and dusty mix-up it seemed to small boys ordered to search for some document required'. But, the article adds, 'the boys were happy and busy enough, so too must have been the partners and directors, conscious that their great enterprise was flourishing'.

They did not, perhaps, foresee one persistent problem the new enterprise would face. Even today, 150 years later, the correct pronunciation of the second partner's name remains a challenge for many people. In the 1970s a member of staff devised a rhyme to help, and it is worth quoting so that we can settle the matter before we set off on the Hodder & Stoughton journey.

> *The Tale of a Stoat*
> For those who pronounce the name Stoughton
> (qua Hodder),
> We offer this rhyme as mnemonic fodder:
> It's not Stough as in rough.
> It's not Stough as in bough.
> We've heard quite enough of this kind of rough
> (sorry) row.

And, perish the thought, it's not even stort.
But it's O as in proton,
To push out the boat on,
The name authors dote on,
And merchant banks float on,
As in, sow a wild oat on,
Or go to deep throat on,
So button your coat on,
And pray make a note on:
IT'S (UNISON PLEASE) Hodder and STOAT on.

3

Like Cerberus, three gentlemen at once

'The two men might be described as Imperialists in publishing', wrote one of those who watched the founding partners in action. They were both enthusiastic travellers, and, in the best imperial tradition, carved out complementary spheres of influence. As the Canadian publisher George Doran put it, 'It appeared that Messrs Matthew Hodder and Thomas W Stoughton as individuals had divided the world geographically for purposes of intense cultivation and operation, for in addition to being evangelical publishers they were, each in his own way, evangelists and propagandists.' They were also, he added, 'ever the shrewd merchants'.

Matthew Hodder took the new markets of the United States and the Empire, while Thomas Stoughton fished in waters closer to home. He had been partly educated in Berlin, and before taking up publishing he had considered a career in the diplomatic service, but, according to an obituary, 'For some reason never quite comprehended, Stoughton appeared to be happier in Scotland than anywhere else.'

The piece continued, 'He published for many of the chief Scottish divines, and cultivated their friendship and was very proud of it. He used to travel for his firm in Scotland, and there was no part of his work he enjoyed so much. He was happy for weeks before in the anticipation, happier when he was there and triumphant when he came back.' It conjures up an engaging image of this outdoors-loving publisher as a Victorian sportsman, heading north for the season and returning with a healthy bag of new books.

He was of course selling as well as buying. His son Cecil remembered that 'my father took Scotland as his parish and so built up our Scottish connection, which became in those days a very important market'. His business trips to Scotland, Cecil said, 'gave him a wide knowledge of Scottish booksellers. He could sell whole editions before they were published.' And George Doran confirms that 'Comparatively small in population, it [Scotland] was great and important from the publisher's standpoint. Not only did Scotland purchase and read a vast quantity of religious books, she was also the source of the authorship of the most important books of that day.'

It was the new talent Thomas Stoughton recruited in Scotland that had the greatest impact on the development of the firm. On a trip in 1884 he was scouting for an editor for its theological journal the *Expositor*. The incumbent, a Dr Samuel Cox, was said to be a 'skilled Hebraist', but had apparently veered some way off the theological rails, and the partners had been forced to recognised that his 'views on eschatology and inspiration offended and alarmed a section of his readers, who included clergy and ministers of all churches'.

Stoughton's search took him to the market town of Kelso in the Scottish Borders, where he spent a couple of days at the manse as the guest of a young preacher and minister called William Robertson Nicoll. He was deeply impressed, and offered his host the job. The heterodox Dr Cox was sent on his way with a lump sum of £1,000, and in January the following year Nicoll moved into the editor's chair at the *Expositor*. It was the beginning of a relationship that would continue until his death nearly four decades later – a relationship that was almost as important to the future of Hodder & Stoughton as that between the firm's founders.

Nicoll's biographer, T. H. Darlow, borrows a phrase from Sheridan to describe his complex and hyperactive subject: 'like

Cerberus, three gentlemen at once'. He writes that 'People were baffled by a man in whom such contrasting faculties could unite. Here was a powerful editor, continually hampered by frail health; a stalwart politician, steeped in literature; a deeply read theologian, who outstripped his rivals in business; a mystic who had mastered the whole craft of journalism; a catholic-minded humanist, who kept his fervid Puritan faith.' It is worth devoting a little space to Nicoll's background, because it was not just his talent that made him such an influential figure in Hodder & Stoughton's history; he brought a whole world with him, and it was a world peculiar to a particular time and place.

Nicoll was himself a son of the manse, and his childhood was about as spartan as a religious childhood in nineteenth-century Scotland could be. In 1843 the Church of Scotland split in what became known as 'The Disruption', and Nicoll's father, Harry, sided with the so-called Free Church – the 'Wee Frees', to use the common shorthand (which they dislike). By doing so he condemned his family to something very close to poverty. The leavers lost all the privileges they had enjoyed as representatives of the established church, and had to build a new church network without any financial assistance from the state.

For Harry Nicoll, leaving the established church meant giving up his job as a schoolmaster, and he became the first Free Church minister of the ancient parish of Auchindoir, in Aberdeenshire, 'primitive, russet, remote country' as his son later described it. The family lived in Lumsden, 'a bleak, lonely little village', where 'the scent of peat-smoke clings around its cottages, and the nearest railway station is eight miles away'. Looking back on his childhood, Nicoll wrote that 'it is the winter that strikes me as the dominant influence of the region. It was very long and very rigorous. The countryside was famous for its snowstorms, the huge drifts they left behind them often impeding traffic for days.' The manse 'stood exposed to fierce gales sweeping down from the hills', and was rendered 'sombre and damp' by the trees that had been planted to protect it. William's mother – whom he remembered as a 'bright, warm-hearted, eager girl' – died when he was eight, and he and his three siblings spent most of their days in the care of a Highland servant. William complained in later life that he felt 'defrauded of my youth – there was so little sunshine in it – far too little'.

As a Free Church minister Harry Nicoll could count on a very modest income indeed – between £100 and £200 a year. And yet he managed to pursue the 'ruling passion of his life', which was 'to read and collect books'. By the time he died he had managed to acquire some 17,000 volumes, including about a hundred different editions of the New Testament in Greek. It was said to be the 'largest private library of any minister in Scotland', and William Robertson Nicoll's biographer believed Harry's bibliomania made his children's pinched lives even bleaker: 'Their comforts were stinted to pay for the volumes he was continually buying', Darlow wrote, 'and they would have been better nourished if he had refrained from buying so many.'

But Harry's passion was inherited by his son. Years later, when his career with Hodder & Stoughton had brought him fame and fortune, a visitor to his house in Hampstead found him ensconced in a bibliophile's paradise that would surely have made his father proud; 'Never before have I seen so characteristically individual a library', wrote George Doran, 'it occupied the full top floor of a very large house. Two rows of shelving all around the walls – standards like those in a public library – occupied the available open floor-space. Every other inch of the floor was carpeted with books, backs upwards, save for a narrow path through this maze of letters which led to the seat of the mighty. This seat was a leather-covered ingle on one side of an old-fashioned marble fireplace. On this seat, with legs folded under him in true Oriental fashion, sat this potentate of letters.' Nicoll himself estimated that he collected between

25,000 and 30,000 books, and recorded that the lane 'through this maze of letters' was 'a length of 51 feet, but is narrow and is getting narrower'.

Nicoll began his writing career as a student in Aberdeen. In 1868, the year Hodder & Stoughton was founded, one of his poems appeared in a Dundee journal, and the following year, while he was still a teenager (he was born in 1851), he published his first full-length article – on the subject of the novelist Henry Fielding. Journalism kept him fed and watered while he studied for a second degree in theology, and by the time he had taken on the minister's duties in Kelso he was already showing the interest in talent-scouting that made him such a valuable asset to Hodder & Stoughton. At one of his Bible classes he noted the intelligence of a young woman called Jane Stoddart. When she showed him some of her poetry he encouraged her to send him some of her other work; 'I want to see what prose you write', he told her, 'would you send me something else in prose?' He would later recruit Jane Stoddart to the Hodder & Stoughton literary family, and she was to be an influential figure in the firm's development as a general publisher.

In the summer of 1885, six months after taking over as the editor of the *Expositor*, Nicoll contracted typhoid during a holiday in Norway. By the autumn he was back in the pulpit at Kelso, but pleurisy came hard on the heels of typhoid, and he was forced to abandon preaching altogether. Under his doctor's instructions he came south, resting first in the Devon town of Dawlish and then moving near the Stoughton home in Norwood. 'I have always preferred this suburb,' he wrote to a friend back in Scotland, 'it is so high, with so much open country and such splendid views, and the air is the purest and most bracing in London.' He added, 'I have had so much encouragement from Hodder and Stoughton. They were anxious that I should undertake additional editorial work', and in the same letter he expressed his ambition to edit 'a paper which will serve the cause of the

Free Churches in this country – the said cause being, I believe more than ever, the cause of Christ.'

A year and a half after writing that letter he had fulfilled his ambition. The first edition of the *British Weekly* appeared on 5 November 1886. It would continue as part of the Hodder & Stoughton stable until after the Second World War, and was one of the triumphant successes of the firm's early years. The first edition proclaimed a bold editorial manifesto: 'We are believers in Progress because we are believers in the advancing reign of Christ. To His appearing, and to the work He planned and did, we trace all that marks the superiority of the new world to the old, and all that is pregnant with growth and improvement yet to come.' This was to be a 'A Journal of Social and Christian Progress'.

It sold for a penny and was twenty pages long. The publishers calculated that a circulation of 20,000 was needed if it was to survive, and Nicoll wrote to a friend that 'If the paper fails we must emigrate. Hodder thinks the Lofoten Islands [a Norwegian archipelago in the Arctic Circle], from which he has come lately, would do – as being cheap, healthy and free from humiliating reminders in the shape of books and papers.' He need not have worried: by the end of the 1890s, the *British Weekly* was heading for a thumping circulation of 100,000.

The first edition recorded that a quarter of London's population of four million had attended a church service on the last Sunday of October that year, and that on the same day 10,000 people were drawn to the Metropolitan Tabernacle at Elephant and Castle to hear Charles Spurgeon, the so-called Prince of Preachers. The popular appetite for religion was as keen as ever, and Nicoll's new paper was designed to satisfy it. One of his early successes was a series of investigations on the theme that so excited Matthew Hodder's brother Edwin in the novella outlined in the first chapter; *Tempted London* described 'the snares which beset young men and women in the crowded city', and, according to T. H. Darlow, 'These articles were the result of personal investigations and thoroughly trustworthy. They soon aroused deep and widespread interest, and the circulation increased so largely that there was no more doubt as to the future of the paper.'

There was a religious leader column – of a devotional character – on the front page of every issue; for the first three years every single leader was written by Nicoll himself, and for the next twenty years he usually wrote four out of five of them. He declared later that 'I had always thought that religious papers did not give enough direct religious instruction, and that the leading articles should be mainly devoted to this, not to ecclesiastical matters or politics or literature chiefly, but to religion.' It was sometimes strong meat, and the draughts of that wintry Wee Free childhood blow through the prose. Nicoll would have regarded the ecumenism of today's Christianity as – to use one of his favourite expressions – 'namby pamby'.

In one edition he wrote openly about his love of religious controversy: 'The enthusiasm of many good men for amalgamating all our denominations – Methodists, Baptists, Presbyterians, Episcopalians and the rest puzzles me. The day will come when a truly catholic [note the small 'c'– Roman Catholicism does not even qualify for a mention] creed, and then will the true unity of life be achieved. But if convictions are laid aside for the sake of union, we have not unity of the Church but the unity of the churchyard ... how many a living thing would die were these controversies to cease.' T. H. Darlow believed Nicoll's love of an intellectual scrap was one of the reasons the paper did so well: 'The British Weekly succeeded, not because it was amiable and colourless, but because its editor had definite convictions, and could use trenchant weapons in controversy, and never shrank from taking a courageous line', he wrote.

The paper's politics were equally polemical; though it proclaimed its political independence it was firmly aligned with the Liberal Party, and Gladstonian Liberalism was as much of an animating spirit as the Church Militant. The *British Weekly* began life at a time of crisis in Liberalism; the party had just split over Gladstone's conversion to Home Rule for Ireland. Lord Salisbury, the Tory leader, formed an alliance with the breakaway Liberal Unionists and won power in the summer of 1886.

The *British Weekly*'s first edition in November that year declared, 'We are under a Tory government, the leading spirit of which has gained his position by means from which an honourable man would recoil; and what is far worse the Liberal Party is rent in twain by an angry feud which ranges on opposite sides those who but yesterday were the truest comrades.' Nicoll called for the party to renew itself, and he affirmed his belief in the fundamentally moral character of public life, writing of 'The earnestness of the mind of England'. He declared that 'The ancient preference for cakes and ale have not prevailed over love for the moralities in the minds of the people . . . the movements of temperance and chastity are not temporary crazes, but great uprisings, which any statesman will treat with contempt at his peril.'

For all this high-mindedness, Nicoll had a good head for business, and the commercial character of the enterprise is very evident; on one front page an article lamenting the godlessness of the working man sits immediately above an advertisement for Page Woodcocks Wind Pills, which are described as 'The Finest Remedy on Earth'. Another regular front-page feature was the 'Publishers' Column', listing new books that had been brought to market that week, and the fiction section of the *British Weekly* allowed Nicoll to exercise his flair for talent-spotting.

In 1887 he admired an anonymous piece in the *Edinburgh Review*, and asked the paper's editor to help him contact the author. J. M. Barrie − for it was he − was a little younger than Nicoll, but his background was very similar. Barrie was born into a family of weavers in the town of Kirriemuir at the foot of the

Angus glens, so he too had a snowy Scottish childhood. Like Nicoll's father, Barrie's parents were adherents of the Free Church, which had split away in 'The Disruption', and their lives, as Barrie's biographer Lisa Chaney puts it, bore witness to 'Fear of God, great diligence and a reverence for education'. Barrie and Nicoll formed a life-long professional relationship and friendship, and it later brought lustre to Hodder & Stoughton as the house that 'discovered' the creator of *Peter Pan*.

Nicoll wanted Barrie to write on the Scottish Church, and Barrie's first piece for the *British Weekly* was about Alexander Whyte, a fellow son of Kirriemuir and another star in the Free Church firmament. But his next article – appearing under the pseudonymous byline Gavin Ogilvie – was entirely devoted to the rather less weighty topic of a houseboat he had hired on the Thames with the journalist T. H. Gilmour, and his writing took off in an altogether lighter and sometimes decidedly quirky direction. One of these early articles bore the nonsense title *Ndintpile Pont*, and consisted entirely of a *jeu d'esprit* on the conceit that he could not read his editor's handwriting, and did not dare ask the formidable Nicoll what he was supposed to be writing about. Nicoll joined in the joke with an indignant note defending his penmanship at the end of the piece, and seems to have been unfazed by the unexpected literary direction his protégé was taking.

When Barrie began work on a novel the following year Nicoll arranged for Hodder & Stoughton to publish it; *Auld Licht Idylls* was based on a collection of columns Barrie had written for another London-based magazine, and consisted of a series of sketches about the Auld Lichts of the title, a splitting Christian sect of now impenetrable obscurity and severity. The book was followed a year later by *A Window in Thrums* – Thrums being his pseudonym for Kirriemuir – and these gentle satires on rural Scottish life sold well and secured good notices. J. M. Barrie's literary career was well and truly launched.

I managed to find an early Hodder & Stoughton edition of *Auld Licht Idylls* while researching this book; the stories have not weathered the changing tastes of the past century and a half very well, but the book is a wonderful artefact; the paper is so thick and rich that reading it is like eating clotted cream.

4

Christadelphians, Perfectionists, Anglo-Israelites and others

Nicoll's upbringing might have inclined him to narrowness of thought, but he seems to have meant what he said about the cause of progress in that first edition of the *British Weekly*. He showed a real streak of social liberalism in his pursuit of talent, and the other two Scots who played a central role in the life of the magazine were women.

He had stayed in touch with Jane Stoddart, whose facility with words he had marked during his Bible classes in Kelso, and encouraged her ambitions, warning her, as she recalled, against wasting 'my best years in poorly paid work as a governess'. With his approval, Jane spent a year in Hanover studying German, and on her return Nicoll began to commission translation work from her. In early 1887 he asked her to come to London to help with one of his many religious projects (the 'preparation and editing' of a series of 'homiletic volumes').

Her first pieces for the *British Weekly* took her up another of those religious byways that seem so obscure today but made such popular copy then; in 1890 she was commissioned to write 'a series of unsigned articles on "Life Among the Close Brethren"' – the closed or 'Exclusive' Brethren being an extreme wing of the extreme sect known as the Plymouth Brethren. The project led to her first visit to Paternoster Row, and she later sketched an attractive picture of Matthew Hodder 'sat at a massive desk facing his partner, Mr T. Wilberforce Stoughton'. She recalled that 'His manner was kind, but very prompt and businesslike. No one would have ventured to waste his time with talk extraneous to the matter in hand, yet every word he spoke gave confidence to the beginner.' He had, she noted, a 'wide acquaintance with the fascinating story of Plymouth Brethrenism', and was able to give her a reading list of books and pamphlets for her research. The articles paid well enough to allow her a walking holiday in the Black Forest, and not long after her return she was offered a full-time job on the *British Weekly*. She was to remain at the paper until 1937, writing books of her own (and publishing them with Hodder & Stoughton) in her spare time.

Jane Stoddart describes the working rhythm of the paper's week in her autobiography, *My Harvest of the Years*. She spent Fridays and Saturdays researching her articles, usually in the Reading Room of the British Museum (like Karl Marx a few years earlier); she would generally produce a piece about a literary or public figure who suited the magazine's ethos (as examples she cites Thomas Hardy and the women's rights campaigner Annie Besant), and her series on the Close Brethren was followed by studies of even more weird and wonderful religious groups – 'Christadelphians, Perfectionists, Anglo-Israelites and others', she writes. Nicoll had by this stage moved from Norwood to Bay Tree Lodge, a large house in Hampstead (which still stands today), and the editorial team convened in his study there on Monday mornings to discuss the week's edition.

Nicoll wrote much of the copy himself, and liked to work in bed, surrounded by letters, manuscripts and cats. On Tuesdays the operation moved down to Paternoster Row, and after a day's work on the copy the editor and his assistant adjourned to the Hatton Garden offices of Hodder & Stoughton's printers, Hazell, Watson and Viney, for an evening of copy-editing. The paper was 'put to bed' on Wednesday mornings, and Nicoll was then free for 'luncheon with some of his cronies at the Devonshire Club in St James Street or the Reform Club in Pall Mall'. Success opened the door to the smart literary and political life of the capital, and Nicoll seems to have relaxed some of the standards of that grim Scottish childhood; George Doran, who often attended these Wednesday lunches when he was in London, recalled that the great man enjoyed high-class gossip (he would beg for copies of any 'fugitive book of note, distinction or scandal'), and that after the meal Nicoll would repair 'to the Bath Club for his weekly Turkish Bath, his hearty dinner and his bottle of wine'.

The final member of the literary clan at the heart of the *British Weekly* was the prolific romantic novelist Annie Swan, little read now but, in her day, immensely popular among women readers, especially those from her own middle-class, religiously minded background. Annie grew up in Edinburgh and the Midlothian countryside south of the Scottish capital, and, like so many of Nicoll's circle, she too had had a childhood dominated by a militantly Christian parent; her father, Edward Swan, 'read the Bible to his family from cover-to-cover, and believed every word in it to be inspired. He saw the hand of God in every fortune and misfortune in his career; when it was misfortune, he made no complaint. In this sturdy faith Annie Swan was reared . . .'

She began writing as a teenager – spinning her yarns for the entertainment of her Midlothian neighbours' children. Her aforementioned father, a merchant and farmer, was persuaded to finance the publication of her first novel, *Aldersyde – A Border Story*, and the book received a good review in the London journal *The Athenaeum*. Annie Swan had heard the Liberal leader, William Gladstone, give one of the great speeches of his Midlothian campaign, which led to the Liberal election victory of 1880, and, on impulse, she sent a copy of *Aldersyde* to Downing Street; the prime minister thanked her personally and wrote, 'I think it beautiful as a work of art, and it must be the fault of a reader if he not profit by its perusal.' In 1883 Annie married an aspiring doctor called James Burdett-Smith, and supported him through his medical training by her writing. By the time the young couple moved to London her reputation was already established.

In 1887 Nicoll serialised one of Annie Swan's stories in the *British Weekly*, and she proved so popular that he was moved to propose a new venture based on her brand: *Woman at Home,* with the subtitle *Annie S. Swan's Magazine*, was launched in 1893. Jane Stoddart was made editor (acting under Nicoll's guidance), and Annie Swan provided the stardust. In its subject matter and tone *Woman at Home* was very different from the high-minded evangelising of the *British Weekly*, and it is a mark of Nicoll's publishing genius and breadth of imagination that he was willing to stray so far from his natural turf. The pioneering publisher Sir George Newnes had opened up the field of popular magazine journalism a decade earlier with *Tit-Bits*, which presented easily digestible material for younger readers – the magazine eventually reached a circulation of 700,000, and both the *Daily Mail* and the *Daily Express* were created by *Tit-Bits* alumni. Nicoll spotted a similar gap in the market for women readers.

Many of the features are easily recognisable as the staples of women's magazines a century later. A 'Lady Mary' offered 'The Glass of Fashion', and there were beauty tips for readers; Andrea was told that 'redness and roughness of the upper part of the arm is generally caused by insufficient drying after washing', Flossie was advised that 'the dark mark is probably the result of sunburn or exposure. Mix calcined magnesia with milk or cream to a stiff paste, and apply thickly', and Beatrice was reassured, 'Don't worry about the freckles, they are often becoming and sometimes a mark of good health.' A long piece on wrinkles declared that they were usually caused by 'over-anxiety'. 'Those who wish to avoid wrinkles must never on any account wear tight shoes', the piece declared, adding, intriguingly, 'Women who work with their brains should eat cream, apples and brown bread between meals – all of these, the latter in the form of biscuits, could be easily taken at odd times.' One cannot imagine that these subjects featured much in Nicoll's conversation during dinner at Bay Tree Lodge or lunch at the Reform Club.

The moral assumptions that informed the magazine, however, came straight from the pulpits at Lumsden and Kelso. The advice to young women whose letters provided the material for the agony aunt columns could be bracing. 'Wilmott finds herself in a sad pickle, having engaged herself to two men at the same time, for her own amusement', began a paragraph in a feature on 'Love Courtship and Marriage'. Wilmott is condemned as an 'atrocious flirt', and the author (possibly Annie Swan herself, although the piece is unsigned) continues, 'she writes to ask my advice, but not my opinion, which I should rather like to give. The best advice I can give her is to break with both of them, for it is quite evident that she is not worth any man's serious consideration.' Poor Gertie is told that 'If she has been walking out with the man a whole year I should think she knows him sufficiently well to become engaged to him. Her mother is right in forbidding further intimacy unless a distinct understanding is arrived at . . .', and in the same feature we read that 'Again and again in these columns have I and others warned young girls against carrying on a clandestine correspondence with men of whom their parents know nothing. Secrecy in such matters is a danger signal . . .'

Annie Swan was a genuine pioneer in the way she pushed back the boundaries of what women could achieve professionally (in 1906 she was elected President of the Society of Woman Journalists), but her views on family life were authentically Victorian: 'When a man is cursed with an extravagant and irresponsible wife, there is only one course open to him if he would save his home from shipwreck,' *Woman at Home* declared, 'and that is to keep the reins of domestic government entirely in his own hands. She must not have the handling of money, since she neither knows its value nor apparently its uses.'

Laughter was permitted in the paper's pages; indeed a column called 'Smiles' included some truly terrible jokes ('I wish you'd help me with this bread,' said the baker. 'I never promised to be your business assistant,' said his wife. 'You promised to stand by me in my hour of knead,' said the baker.) But some areas were out of bounds; a column on 'Mothers and Children' instructed that 'Jokes on Biblical words and subjects should be prohibited, for the sake of reverence, and because they impair the proper use of Scripture questions.' Annie's own byline appeared above 'Over the Teacups', a column of somewhat inconsequential readers' correspondence, and she contributed lashings of her ever-popular romances, with titles such as *A Woman of Character* and *The Lost Bracelet*.

Just before the new magazine was launched, Nicoll's wife wrote to a friend that 'he is terrible over-wrought with the new *Woman at Home* coming out in October. I think he has plenty to do without another magazine.' But Nicoll's appetite for work was prodigious. His magazine stable also included the *Bookman*, a literary monthly founded in 1891, and in 1895 he persuaded Matthew Hodder and Thomas Stoughton to back yet another new magazine called – ironically, as it turned out – *The Success*. The new journal was directly inspired by the huge sales *Tit-Bits* was then enjoying, but it flopped, and was sold within a year (the firm suffered a serious financial loss as a consequence, but Nicoll wrote later that the partners 'were excellent losers. Neither was ever heard to make any reference to any failures').

All of this magazine work was carried out while Nicoll was running one of Hodder & Stoughton's big-money religious projects, *The Expositor's Bible*, an examination of all the books of the Bible 'by the outstanding commentators of the day'. The fifty volumes were published in eight series between 1887 and 1896, and almost as soon as it was finished Nicoll began editing *The Expositor's Greek Testament*, published in five volumes and offered 'handsomely bound in buckram cloth'. Then came *The Clerical Library* (twelve volumes), *The Expositor's Dictionary of Texts* (two volumes) and *The Expositor's Treasury of Children's Sermons* (for the last two Nicoll recruited Jane Stoddart as a co-editor).

In 1886 Nicoll was appointed Hodder & Stoughton's literary adviser, with a brief to develop the fiction side of the business, and while wearing his multiple editorial hats he was ever on the spy for new talent. When the Scottish theologian the Rev John Watson came to stay at Bay Tree Lodge to discuss a series of articles for the *Expositor*, Nicoll was struck by the 'racy stories and character sketches' with which his guest regaled the company. While walking Watson to the station at the end of his stay, Nicoll persuaded him to write up some of his tales of Scottish life for the *British Weekly*.

After a couple of false starts Watson sent in the first four chapters of the book that became known as *Beside the Bonnie Briar Bush*, and Nicoll recalled that 'I knew on reading them that his popularity was assured.' *Beside the Bonnie Briar Bush* was published in 1894 under the pen name Ian Maclaren, and sold over a million copies worldwide. Nicoll was also responsible for persuading Ellen Thorneycroft Fowler, the daughter of a distinguished Liberal minister, to put pen to paper for the first time; noting that she was both a society figure and a keen Methodist, he encouraged her to 'write a novel dealing truthfully with Nonconformity'. *Concerning Isabel Carnaby*, which came out in 1898, was described by the *Spectator* as 'the novel of the season', and sold 40,000 copies in the first nine months.

Nicoll was such a big figure, and such a significant force in Hodder & Stoughton's development, that a degree of scratchiness in his relationship with the founding partners was probably inevitable. An exchange of letters from the mid 1890s survives in which he complains that he feels under-appreciated; it begins with his arch apology for taking a little time to answer an earlier letter from the partners; he had, he said, 'written some 15,000 words for the BW [*British Weekly*] that week' and had consequently found it difficult to spare the time. He suggests that the partners are not sufficiently committed to the development of a literary list and that he needs more power to make offers for new books.

He added, in the best tradition of such letters, a veiled threat that he might otherwise take up 'an offer from an American publisher'. In January 1897 he returned to the subject, and again pushed for a bigger role in developing the firm's list, writing formally to argue that Hodder & Stoughton needed 'a literary man with a tolerably free hand who will look out for writers, suggest subjects, conduct negotiations and do what he can to make the transaction straight between author and publisher'. Again there was the threat of resignation; Nicoll claimed that 'Since coming to London I have had at least seven offers from publishers to become their literary advisers.'

The job description he was proposing for himself sounds impossible, since it would have combined great publishing power with something very like the role of a literary agent (a job that had only recently been invented). Thomas Stoughton wrote him a polite but firm refusal, pointing out that Nicoll owed a great deal to that visit to Kelso the previous decade: 'but for our "discovering" you,' he wrote, 'your literary career in London might not have commenced when it did.' Stoughton expressed the firm's 'hearty appreciation' of Nicoll's achievements, but insisted that the partners should retain their 'independence to use their own judgement, experience and convictions'. He added that if Nicoll was unhappy with the position he was 'perfectly free to work for another publisher'.

Nicoll, who had just remarried (his first wife having died three years earlier), opted for security, and the matter was dropped. The couple kept two tortoises in the garden of the Hampstead house, and when Sir George Williams paid a call Nicoll pointed them out. 'You see those two tortoises,' he said to the YMCA founder, 'I call one Hodder and the other Stoughton.'

5

Two gold watches and *The Times*

Matthew Hodder was no tortoise in business matters – indeed Nicoll himself frequently remarked on his energy and love of speedy decision-making, writing that he 'detested dawdling and loitering'. This was one of the qualities, Nicoll argued, that made him such a suitable adventurer in the American market. 'He found that when he saw an American publisher face to face he could get a definite answer,' Nicoll observed. 'He had a marvellous skill in placing books, both in America and Canada, and was frequently described as the best merchant that came from London.'

Matthew made his first trip to the United States a year after his partnership with Thomas Stoughton was formed, and Thomas's son Cecil liked to claim that 'Hodder was the first English publisher to go to the United States.' In fact, Macmillan & Co sent over an agent to sell their books at about the same time – George Brett set up shop in Greenwich Village, and his son later established the American Macmillan Company as an independent partnership. And the venerable firm of Longmans, Green, which was founded in 1724 and had been active in the American market since colonial days, began publishing in the United States in the 1880s. But Matthew was certainly a pioneer. And he was venturing into the Wild West of the publishing world; nineteenth-century American publishers relied heavily on English authors, and piracy was commonplace. John Tebel, in his history of American publishing, *Between the Covers*, writes that even the great house of Harper's was guilty, pirating works like Dickens's *Martin Chuzzlewit,* and 'selling them on the streets through newsboy hawkers'.

Matthew arrived in New York on 22 June 1869, furnished with a stash of books from the Hodder & Stoughton list, and began his rounds immediately; his diary for 23 June records that he was 'most cordially received at Messrs. Scribner and Co., Randolph & Co., Willmer & Rogers, G. P. Putnam & Son, H. W. Dodds, and Nelson and Sons', so he was dealing with many of the big houses from the off. It was travelling salesman work; Hodder would turn up with his samples and hope to make a sale or two. That year's list included *The Mystery of Suffering* by the French Evangelical preacher Edmond de Pressensé, and *Adrift in a Boat*, a Napoleonic-era story of a group of young British boys who are kidnapped by French pirates – so Matthew was selling a characteristic Hodder mix of religion and adventure.

Within a week he was reporting success: 'Went to Scribner's by appointment at 10 o'clock to meet Drs Carlton and Lanahan – very successful interview, see business memo', he wrote in his diary on 29 June; 'Left parcel [of books] at Leypoldt & Holt. Called at Hurd and Houghton – to call again. My visit to Mr Dodd satisfactory, see mem.'

His diary entry for that day also provides an indication of his other great preoccupation during his American jaunts: 'Mr Dodge, President of YMCA, and an influential gentleman in the City, called in a carriage at my lodgings according to promise, at half-past four o'clock', he recorded, 'to take me to his country residence at Riverdale, on the Hudson River.' Matthew seems to have spent almost as much time on YMCA business as he did on the firm's during his trips to America, and his diary is packed with descriptions of prayer meetings, sermons and social calls on godly (and often influential) American luminaries of the Association. Serving God and Mammon simultaneously sometimes required heroic stamina; after camping out for two days at a revivalist meeting outside New York, he rose for 5 a.m. prayers, made a nine-hour train journey to Boston, attended the evening YMCA prayer meeting there when he arrived, rose for the Association's early prayers the following morning and followed that with a 'hard business day's work'.

He admired much that he found in the United States – the widespread passion for Evangelical religion and the vigorous growth of the YMCA movement, the early rising habits of the business people he dealt with and the 'naturalness' of Americans generally, which he put down to 'the absence of class distinctions'. He noted approvingly that there was 'Iced water at every meal, and no stimulants on the table of Christian families'. But he was shocked by some aspects of American society: 'It is only to look into the columns of the *New York Herald* to see the wickedness of married women', he noted, and, a little later, 'In Chicago, where no Christian principle regulates life, the spirit of freedom is too strong, which may possibly account for the tendency to disregard the sacredness of the married state. Unlegalized marriages are now being advocated – and by women, too, forsooth!'

In the course of this first trip he visited New York, Philadelphia, Boston, Detroit and Chicago, and then went north to Canada, doing business in Toronto and Montreal. Matthew was back in North America the following year, and the trips – which took him away from Paternoster Row for some three months at a time – became a regular feature of his life. In 1885, during a visit to Toronto, he came into contact with a young Canadian called George Doran, whose descriptions of Matthew Hodder and the firm I have quoted earlier. Doran was born the year after Hodder & Stoughton was founded, and he was greatly impressed by Matthew's patriarchal qualities, describing him as 'a fine and imposing figure notwithstanding his shortness of stature. He wore a great flowing snow-white beard and always reminded me of Moses.' Though Doran was so much younger, the two men had somewhat similar backgrounds, and Doran's story helps explain why they got on so well.

He left school at fourteen, and in *Chronicles of Barabbas*, his vividly told autobiography, he records that his publishing career began when he passed a sign outside a publishing house and book-seller that proclaimed 'Smart Boy Wanted'. He was employed immediately and assigned to the Willard Tract Depository, an evangelical branch of the Fleming H. Revell Company. 'We handled only religious books', Doran wrote; 'Novels were anathema, in fact everything that did not teach the necessity of repentance and the punishment of sin. We sold Christmas cards, New Year's cards, and birthday cards only if they had Scripture texts as messages. To our emporium of Faith came the zealots, fanatics, ascetics, the Plymouth Brethren with beards . . .'

The hours were punishing: Doran worked from eight in the morning till late in the evening from Monday to Saturday, and was paid $2.00 a week – an apprenticeship-style introduction to the trade not unlike Mathew Hodder's in St Paul's Churchyard thirty years earlier. Premillenarianism – the belief that Christ's Second Coming was imminent – was rife among the firm's customers, and Doran's tongue is very firmly in his cheek as he records that he and his fellow office boys were seduced by this faith in a 'new millennium of peace and sinlessness'; as they 'struggled wearily homeward . . .' they would, he wrote, 'fervently wish and hope for this promised early release from labour and strife. We were not especially spiritually minded – just exhausted and tired.'

While Doran was every bit as enthusiastic about religious publishing as his new friend Matthew Hodder, he took a more worldly view of the enterprise. Among the Hodder & Stoughton books that sold successfully through the Willard Tract Depository were early volumes of *The Expositor's Bible*, but Matthew Hodder was apparently greatly troubled by the conclusions of one of his scholars. Professor George Adam Smith of Aberdeen argued that the *Book of Isaiah* was the work of two separate authors, and insisted on producing a separate volume on each of them. This, Doran wrote, was 'rank heresy' to the 'Fundamentalist and evangelical minds and souls' of both Hodder and his own boss at Willard, 'But, after all, business was business, and they must accept the bitter with the sweet.' He continued: 'Curiously enough, this polemic of George Adam Smith's was among the "best sellers" of the day. Notwithstanding the fact that we kept the poisonous book under the counter and sold it only on request as one would sell a doubtful pornographic book in those days, the sale of this was easily six to one as compared to other volumes in the series. Reluctantly the copies were dispensed; avidly the proceeds were coffered for the benefit of the great work of evangelism.' Matthew later managed to sell all fifty volumes of *The Expositor's Bible* to the American firm A. C. Armstrong & Sons, an offshoot of Scribners – 'a monumental deal', as John Attenborough puts it in his company history, 'to thrill the heart of any salesman'.

The next development in Doran's career encouraged even greater cynicism about the religious book trade. He moved to Chicago to work directly for the parent firm's founder, Fleming Revell, who, like Messrs Hodder & Stoughton, had good evangelical connections – Revell's brother-in-law was the hugely popular preacher Dwight Moody, the Billy Graham of his day. John Tebel writes that 'Revell's twin talents were managing money and salesmanship.' He had set up the business in 1869 in response to a religious revival that swept through the United States in the aftermath of the American Civil War of 1861–5, and he was ruthless about exploiting religious sentiment. 'He could take a poor preacher's hard earned $500 or a $1,000 for the publication at the preacher's own expense of a volume of sermons or Bible studies without the slightest compunction,' Doran recalled, 'even though he knew that the same poor parson could not hope for any return . . . The operation was a painless one but many a poor patient suffered agonies afterward.'

Working with Revell, Doran discovered that 'one of the virtues of religious publishing was its imperviousness to depression'. According to John Tebel, the firm 'did record business in the panic year of 1893 [when a credit crunch and crop failure led to four years of economic depression in the United States] while secular publishers suffered'. A shared interest in religious publishing and a genuine affection for Matthew Hodder – and through him for the wider Hodder family – proved to be the basis for a long association, and in 1908 Doran established a new American house, George H. Doran and Company, in which Hodder & Stoughton held a one-third interest, and which became the partnership's North American branch.

Like Thomas Stoughton in Scotland, Matthew Hodder was scouting for new authors as well as selling the partnership's list, and his American adventures produced a publishing coup that illustrates what good luck and good judgement can achieve together. In 1881 he bought a biography of James Garfield, who had been elected President of the United States on the Republican ticket the previous November, called *From Log Cabin to the White House*. It was written by a clergyman, one William Thayer, and has been memorably described by John Attenborough as 'similar to many other stories which the firm was publishing at the time: the success story of a good man, well suited to Victorian taste and YMCA character building, and lacking all distinction'.

But in July 1881, just a few months after taking office, Garfield was assassinated (his killer was a disappointed office-seeker who had been denied the diplomatic post in Paris he felt he was owed). Garfield's misfortune proved a boon to Hodder & Stoughton; public curiosity about the murdered president turned *From Log Cabin to the White House* into a bestseller in Britain. The book sold nearly 80,000 copies within a year, and by the end of 1887 it had gone through twenty-seven editions and sold 161,000 copies.

According to Thomas Stoughton's son Cecil, one 'wealthy businessman in Glasgow so admired the book that he bought some thousands and presented all the bank clerks in Glasgow with a copy'. Cecil added that as a result of the Garfield triumph his father and Matthew Hodder 'decided to give each other a gold watch and also take in *The Times*, priced then at 6d. My father had it in the mornings and then handed it over to Hodder.' It seems a little unlikely that these publishing magnates had, until then, been unable to afford sixpence a day for a newspaper, but the gold watches ring true, and the anecdote suggests the partners still found the publishing game great fun. After bringing out forty editions of *From Log Cabin to the White House*, the partners finally flogged the book to Routledge in 1893.

6

Our tiny tribute to a man we loved

The breathless pace of those early years did not encourage caution, and the partners fell foul of a couple of the more dubious characters on the Victorian literary scene.

Three years after setting up shop, they were sued for libel by George Augustus Sala, a literary buccaneer who had been supported by Dickens and Thackeray, and became famous as a commentator and correspondent for the *Daily Telegraph*. Sala objected to the way he was described in *Modern Men of Letters Honestly Criticised*, a collection of essays by the literary critic James Hain Friswell. Friswell had in fact paid Sala something of a compliment simply by including him; the book also contained pieces on Dickens, Bulwer-Lytton, Tennyson, Ruskin and Disraeli. But Friswell's intemperate language ought to have set all sorts of alarm bells ringing in Paternoster Row. Here is a report of proceedings in the High Court:

> *The article about Mr Sala, which was read at length, advanced a number of insinuations of an offensive character, mixed up with much in laudation of his talents and capacity. It said he belonged to a class of Bohemian writers of a very bad school, who did very little good, but whose dribbling, tipsy, 'high-falutin' found great favour with the public and the proprietors of cheap newspapers . . . It was insinuated that the plaintiff could rarely be relied upon by the newspaper proprietors who employed him to furnish his work; that he was often drunk, always in debt, sometimes in prison and was totally disreputable. In*

winding up it was asserted that Mr Sala gained his money recklessly and spent it recklessly.

There was an enjoyably literary quality to the evidence. One of the barristers, a Mr Seymour, asked George Sala whether he objected to being described as a 'Goguenard'. The court report continued:

Mr Sala – *It is an idle, offensive word, but I do not particularly object to it.*

Mr Seymour – *Does it not mean jolly or rollicking?*

Mr Sala – *Yes. But if you refer to an old French dictionary you will find it also means 'goggle' and as I have an affection of the eye I have no doubt Mr Friswell thought by using the word he was inflicting additional pain; and it also shows the feeling with which the libel was written.*

Hodder & Stoughton argued that 'the plaintiff had not put a proper construction on the article in question, which at the outside could only be regarded as legitimate criticism of a public man'. The jury did not agree, and awarded George Sala £500 in damages. The journalist's later career suggests that Friswell's views were, on many points, well judged; Sala went on to write a notorious pornographic novel called *The Mysteries of Verbena House; or, Miss Bellasis Birched for Thieving*, (it is set in a girls' boarding school in Sussex, and involves a sadistic chaplain from Eton) and lost his money trying to set up a magazine called *Sala's Journal*, which flopped; he was forced to sell his library of 13,000 books and in 1895 died, a broken man, in Brighton.

The partners were also drawn onto dangerous ground by a rare lapse in judgement on the part of William Robertson Nicoll, who was among the many people fooled by the great literary forger Thomas Wise. Wise began buying rare books as a schoolboy and built up one of the greatest collections in the world, known as the Ashley Library. His eminence as a bibliographer was widely recognised; he was awarded an honorary degree from Oxford, and an honorary Fellowship at the same university's Worcester College, and was elected President of the Bibliographical Society. But when, after his death, his widow sold the Ashley Library to the British Library it was found to contain a significant amount of material that had been stolen from the British Library's own shelves. Wise was also involved in the sale of forged manuscripts that he had himself authenticated, and is now regarded as one of the great swindlers of the era.

Nicoll came into contact with Wise through a journalist friend from Fleet Street, and commissioned him to write pieces for the *Bookman*, describing him as 'the well-known collector and bibliographer'. Wilfred Partington, who wrote up his investigation of Wise in his book *Forging Ahead*, concluded that the articles were being used to 'boost the values of publications that were proved to be forgeries'.

Nicoll and Wise then began a collaboration on a series of books called *Literary Anecdotes of the Nineteenth Century*. Ten volumes were planned, but only two actually appeared, and years later it emerged that many of the stories were bogus. Nicoll also picked up a whisper that Wise knew the whereabouts of some unpublished Charlotte Brontë letters; he determined to buy the copyright and, as John Attenborough puts it, 'publish an edition of the Brontës which would really bring Hodder and Stoughton into the front line', but the deal collapsed. In *Forging Ahead*, Partington represents Nicoll and the partners as innocent dupes in all this; Attenborough believes that they may have been 'among the first to smell a rat'. Fortunately, all concerned were dead by the time the extent of Wise's trickery was exposed in the 1930s and 40s.

Matthew's natural cheerfulness seems to have remained undented by the firm's occasional reverses. One young newcomer, Ernest Roker (whom Matthew recruited, characteristically, after meeting him at a YMCA lecture), remembered the stoical manner in which the senior partner dealt with the fact that 'In the early days at Paternoster Row we had some pretty big failures in publishing, like everyone else in the trade.' Matthew Hodder asked him to check on the sales figures of a book (*Tropical Africa*, by Henry Drummond, yet another celebrated Scottish preacher), and when Roker produced the grim news the boss remarked, 'Well what a disaster, hardly any sales at all. I don't know why you or anyone wants to come into the publishing trade, for it is a greater gamble than horse-racing.' Roker expressed his surprise at this verdict on the profession to which the senior partner had devoted his life, to which Matthew replied, 'Well, my boy, the bookmaker and racing man generally has the pleasure of seeing his horse come down the course, but we often never see the books we back leave our premises.'

That was of course a great exaggeration; by the end of the century Hodder & Stoughton had gone from what we might today call a 'disruptive start-up' to being a solidly established player on the publishing scene. And Matthew Hodder had fulfilled his Dickensian destiny, winning both prosperity and high regard in the best tradition of a Dickens hero. One of the documents that has survived from the firm's early days is the text of what appears to be an encomium delivered in his honour at the celebration of his half-century in the publishing trade in 1894. It quotes 'St Paul's famous verse' – which featured in the book by Matthew's brother that I quoted in the first chapter – 'Not slothful in business, but fervent in spirit, serving the Lord.' That, the anonymous author declares, 'has ever been Mr Hodder's motto; and this has been exhibited in no vaunting, pharisaical manner, but quietly and unostentatiously'.

Matthew Henry Hodder, founding partner and patriarch, with Cuthbert Huckvale, commander of the counting-house, and Joseph Apted, 'one of the greatest and most daring production managers in London publishing'.

Thomas Wilberforce Stoughton, literary big game hunter of the Scottish Borders.

'June 11th 1869. Started by NWest express train at 2.45…' Matthew's American diaries burst with business energy and YMCA-style piety.

The heart of the book trade; Paternoster Row in the 1830s.

How it all began; rollicking adventure and reformed religion rub shoulders on the original list.

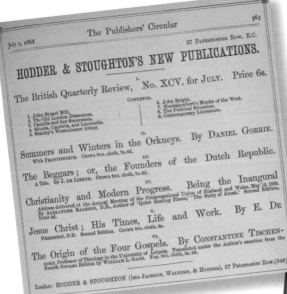

Jane Stoddart, who could 'turn out a paragraph, or a review, as quickly as she could write it down', was a pioneering woman in the publishing world and served half a century on *The British Weekly*.

Annie Swan's writing was admired by Gladstone. Her romantic novels were early Hodder & Stoughton bestsellers and her *Over the Teacups* column was a regular feature of *Woman at Home*.

Sir Ernest Hodder-Williams, 'a ten-talent man'.

Ernest's first wife Ethel with the family dog.

Caesar, one of Ernest's most successful authors and the pioneer of a new literary genre. His master, Edward VII, is pictured in 'those rough things he wears at Sandringham', which Caesar preferred to the suits and uniforms that showed up dog hairs.

In Edward's funeral procession Caesar walked a few steps behind the royal charger and ahead of nine kings. He does not appear to be wearing a lead.

In 1902, the year of his marriage to Ethel and his appointment as a partner, Ernest bought his first American bestseller. The story of *Mrs Wiggs of the Cabbage Patch* spawned a Broadway play and four films.

Peter Pan began life as a minor character in an early novel by JM Barrie and emerged as a literary superstar with the 1904 play *The Boy Who Wouldn't Grow Up*. Arthur Rackham's 1906 illustrations remain classics.

'Oh, plagued no more with Human or Divine,
        To-morrow's tangle to itself resign,
    And lose your fingers in the tresses of
    The Cypress-slender Minister of Wine'.

Matthew Hodder was shocked by Edward Fitzgerald's sensuous *Rubaiyat*, but Edmund Dulac's illustrations helped deliver a healthy profit.

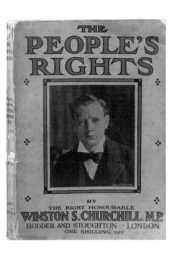

THE PEOPLE'S RIGHTS

BY
THE RIGHT HONOURABLE
WINSTON S. CHURCHILL, M.P.
HODDER AND STOUGHTON · LONDON
ONE SHILLING net

Ernest's list included some of the leading lights of the government which took Britain to war in 1914.

John Buchan was one of several Hodder & Stoughton authors who contributed to the government's secret propaganda campaigns.

GREENMANTLE
JOHN BUCHAN
AUTHOR OF
'THE THIRTY NINE STEPS'

THE DAY OF GLORY. By Sir Ernest Hodder Williams,

BRITISH WEEKLY
A Journal of Social and Christian Progress.

The manuscript of Ernest's *British Weekly* article on the Peace Parade in 1919 reflects the intensity of the day's emotions.

Sir Ernest Hodder-Williams and
Sir William Robertson Nicholl –
two literary knights in court dress.

Admiral 'Jackie' Fisher, 1st Baron Fisher.
His memoirs provided Ernest with
a 'lovely scoop'.

George Doran first met Ernest
as 'a gangling boy' and became
one of his closest collaborators,
but they were divided over
The Green Hat, which Doran
described as 'the first of
modern novels with a
nymphomaniac as a heroine'.

The piece continues, 'It is refreshing to find gentlemen like Mr Hodder and Mr Stoughton, men who would scorn to depart a hair's breadth from the strictest line of rectitude to gain any personal advantage . . . and whether many or few be his remaining years, they will, I am sure, be characterised by the same energy and integrity which have placed him in the front rank of London publishers, and by the same hearty enthusiasm for the spiritual welfare of his fellow-men which has made his private life so bright and worthy of imitation.'

Matthew Hodder still had seventeen 'remaining years', and grew comfortably into the role of patriarch. Ernest Roker, who did not join until 1904 (by which time Matthew had worked in publishing for sixty years), remembered his daily visits to the shop that the firm operated, in the traditional manner, from its premises in Paternoster Row. The London trade then involved a system of 'Collectors', who made daily rounds of all of the publishers, and 'called over a list of books they required, and in the case of odd copies took these away with them in their green baize bags, and paid cash for them over the shop counter'. Matthew still checked the cash accounts at 4.30 p.m. before going home. Roker also recalled that 'He had a wonderful camellia tree in his garden at Brockhampton, Bromley Common, and this had lovely white blossoms on it for a long time each year, and the old gentleman always came to business with one of these in his button-hole, and had it in a small cut glass on his desk during the day, but he always left it behind and never wore it on his journey home.'

George Doran's business relationship with Hodder & Stoughton ensured that he was a frequent visitor to Paternoster Row during Matthew Hodder's final years. There is a slight edge to the picture he paints: 'There was a definite system of pure paternalism in the firm of Hodder and Stoughton,' he wrote, 'Employees were drawn from Bromley and Norwood. Each Saturday morning alternately Mr Hodder and Mr Stoughton disbursed to the staff their earnings of the week. The employees one by one would pass in front of the desk where either Mr Hodder or Mr Stoughton was seated. As he handed a young man his wage Mr Hodder would smile and benignantly pat him on the back, telling him of his loyalty and his fidelity – this to be the equivalent of half a crown or five shillings which should really have been added to the wage of the worker; but the sunshine of the pleasure of the employer was more than silver and gold – for the moment of passing. Mr Stoughton was much more formal and stoical; he paid in the manner of a just steward. So each Saturday there was instilled into the minds of these co-workers in a great cause the fear of God and the fear of Matthew Hodder and Thomas W. Stoughton.'

Doran's knowing tone perhaps reflected his transatlantic background and the more competitive ways of the American market. There was a genuine innocence at the core of the Hodder & Stoughton spirit, and it is engagingly reflected in the tradition of the annual sports days, which were a feature of summer life in the firm for more than half a century.

In the early days, they took place in the countryside, not far from Matthew Hodder's childhood home of Staines, and they had the clean-living flavour of a YMCA event. One of those who took part in 1904, T. G. Davy, was moved to poetry by the experience, and his verses, though execrable, evoke something of the Edwardian charm of the day. We can only hope that Davy was not involved in copy-editing, as his poem is full of howlers. I have cleaned up some of the worst of them to make it easier to read.

A Few Verses on our Annual Outing
by T. G. Davy, July 16, 1904

Please give me your attention
And I will to you relate
How we spent our Annual Outing

Which is always up to date.
By the Firm's kind invitation
We travelled down by train
To that pretty little village
Of Egham known to fame.
As we travelled swiftly onward
Through the country so sweet
The orchards and the green fields
All looked so very neat.
We arrived quite safely
At our destination
And made our way to Runneymeade
Without any hesitation.
Nature was dressed all in her best
Our Old Friend Sun came out to see
And gave us a warm reception
That we might happy be.
Arriving on the Mead
We very quickly found
A bell tent which we soon erected
Upon the running ground ...

The events laid on included a hundred-yard flat race for the under-seventeens (a reminder of how much earlier many people began work then), an open three-legged race over the same distance and a tug of war between married and single members of staff. The card for the day also listed something called a fifty-yard 'Thread the Needle Race', although it does not provide any clue what this involved. Thomas Stoughton's son Cecil entered the long jump but could manage only seventh place, so there was clearly no nepotism on the field of play. Both Cecil and Matthew's grandson Ernest took part in the mile, but they came in second and third last in what was, according to the versifier Davy, a close field.

The sports soon began in earnest
All ready for the fray
Each one bent on winning
The first mile race of the day.
Our starter was delighted
When he saw a very tight race
Each one doing his best
To increase his worn-out pace …

Gold, silver and bronze in the mile went to H. M. Wookey, A. Cutler and F. Dale, but they were rewarded – not unnaturally – with books rather than medals; as prizes they were given, respectively, *A Hermit's Wild Friends*, *Daughters of Nijo* and *Nurse Charlotte*. *Daughters of Nijo* is subtitled *A Romance of Japan*, and the evangelical flavour of that first Hodder & Stoughton list in 1868 is quite absent from the tally of books given out as sports day prizes three and a half decades later. The books awarded to the winners in the three-legged race, for example, all sound enticing: the winning pairs were given *The Wild Marquis*, *The Phantom Torpedo Boat*, *A Crime of the Under Seas*, *The Money Hunger*, *White Heather* and *Three Feathers*. But some evangelical disciplines remained in force: there is no mention of wine or beer at lunch and, however jolly, the occasion appears to have been teetotal. Davy continues:

When the signal was given
For that appetising dish
Then in duty to our maker
The grace for meat was given
Then all sat and did duty
To a splendid bill of Fare.
There was cold Roast Beef and Mutton
Of quality I am sure
Potatoes hot and salad
And pickles in galore.

Blanc Mange Jellies and pies
And cheese without question
In case after you had eaten so much you might get indigestion.

Lunch was followed by a team photograph and a boating trip 'up the river for a spin', followed by tea with strawberries. Davy's poem ended with a flourish of company loyalty:

> *Now I hope I have pleased you all*
> *Which has been my intention,*
> *But there is one thing I've forgot*
> *The Firm's name to mention.*
> *Then Health, Peace and Prosperity*
> *To the Firm for their kindness today*
> *And may God's blessing fall*
> *On the heads of you all*
> *To crown our most delightful holiday.*

The competitors listed in the firm's official record of the 1904 Annual Excursion include one W. Smart – he was part of the third-placed team in the open fifty-yard wheelbarrow race. William Smart was one of the promising young men Thomas Stoughton had recruited from Norwood, and he would go on to have a long and successful career at Hodder. He has left a touching account of the senior partner's last day at Paternoster Row.

Smart was tidying up his office at the end of an afternoon in 1911 when the eighty-one-year-old Matthew Hodder put his head round the door. 'I look at the drawn face and I know there is some serious trouble,' he remembered. 'After a moment a sob breaks out. He says "I have come to say goodbye." Naturally I ask if there is anything in this world I can do to ease the pain. The reply is "I shall be unable to come back. Tomorrow morning go and take the chair I have been sitting in, bring it down to your office and use it as long as you are at Hodders."

'Since I have great affection for this gentleman, who had been a real Father in business to me and to many others on the staff, I am disturbed and unhappy. I know that Mr Hodder is not well, but I also know that business is more than his life. I walk over to Holborn Station and put him in the train. Since he is known to the clerks on these trains. I tell this particular conductor that Mr Hodder is not well, will he see him into the hands of his friends when he arrives at Bromley even if he has to hold up the train for a few moments. His reply was "It's good as done". Before I say goodbye to my dear Chief, he says he will not live long, [adding] "I want you and Fred Austin [another Norwood recruit] to attend my funeral."'

Matthew Hodder died on 18 October 1911. Thomas Stoughton became the firm's senior partner and lived for another six years, but by the time of Matthew's death he was already suffering from rheumatoid arthritis – an especially cruel curse for an addict of the outdoor life – and played little part in the business. If I was writing this history with a biblical plan – which both men would surely have approved – the Book of Genesis would end here.

And William Smart provided an appropriately biblical coda. He and Fred Austin were – as instructed – among the 700 or so people who crowded into St Luke's Church in Bromley for Matthew's funeral, and they both bought a new set of clothes for the occasion. 'Fred looks like a very graceful person, I look like a farm labourer with his Sunday clothes on,' Smart recalled. 'We sadly attend the funeral and come back to Warwick Square. Most everybody is gone because it is an unhappy day. There is a furnace in the basement; we strip off all our new duds, and get into our ordinary working clothes. Fred says, "Bill, we will never use these again, we are too fond of the Old Chief. We put the whole lot into the furnace. That was our tiny tribute to a man we loved."'

7

A pretty hard road, but worth the journey

King Edward VII died on 6 May 1910, a year and a half before Matthew Hodder, and the monarch's passing inspired a publishing coup that must surely have brought pleasure to the senior partner's final days. His grandson, Ernest Hodder-Williams, brought out a bestselling dog book.

In size, *Where's Master? By Caesar, the King's Dog* scarcely qualifies as a book; it is fifty-three pages of very simple sentences – as befits the doggy style of its supposed author – in huge type. Ernest's genius lay not so much in writing it as in the idea itself. Edward was described by J. B. Priestley as 'the most popular king England had known since the 1660s', and some 400,000 people processed past his coffin as it lay in state in Westminster Hall. Ernest wrote the book in just a couple of days, and caught the popular tide of national mourning in the flood.

The dog-loving example of Edward's mother, Victoria, had encouraged the British to be sentimental about their pets, and Edward himself personified the love of country pleasures that many of his subjects liked to claim as part of the national character. *Where's Master?* begins with Caesar (a Wire Fox Terrier) wandering around Buckingham Palace asking the question of the title; 'I want Master,' he declares sadly, 'he knows just how to rub my hair up the wrong way, just how I like my ears twisted; I want to feel his warm hand catch hold of my nose and waggle my head slowly to and fro . . . he knows just how to find the little ticklish place under my chin.' As he sniffs his way around the palace corridors he reminisces about their life together, recalling their walks in the grounds at Sandringham. 'I went back and just rubbed my nose gently against his trousers,' he writes of one outing, 'I love those rough things he wears at Sandringham – they don't show my hairs as his uniforms and black suits do.' There is even a memory of a trip to Biarritz, which allows Caesar to play with national stereotypes. He growls when he meets a French poodle ('an over-dressed thing, all tied up with ribbons') on the beach, and the King admonishes him: 'What a typical Englishman you are, Caesar,' said Master, 'you can't meet a foreigner without beginning to growl and strut about as if the whole world had been created just for you.'

Historians look back on Edward's funeral as one of the final flowerings of the world order that would soon disappear in the carnage of the Great War. It has been described as 'the greatest assemblage of royalty and rank ever gathered in one place and, of its kind, the last'. No fewer than nine kings came to see Bertie, as he was affectionately known, laid to rest, and Caesar – this is historical fact, not Ernest's imagination – walked ahead of them in the procession along Whitehall and the Mall. 'I'm marching in front of the Kings', Caesar writes in *Where's Master?*, 'I've no history, I've no pedigree, I'm not high-born. But I loved him, and I was faithful to him, and he didn't care how lowly or humble man or beast might be as long as they did their best and were faithful.'

The book ends with a sentimental flourish: 'We've come to the end of the journey,' Caesar reflects. 'They say I can't follow Master any further. They say there are no little dogs where Master has gone, but I know better.' It was published in June 1910, just over a month after the King's death; the sales topped a 100,000 within a few weeks, and by the beginning of December it was in its fifteenth edition.

An unpublished collection of reminiscences about Ernest in the Hodder archive claims that Edward's widow, Queen

Alexandra, initially refused to endorse the publication, and gave Ernest a grilling about his sources. Ernest published the book anonymously, but sent Alexandra a copy; 'The author's presence was commanded', according to the archive reminiscences, 'and he was desired to inform Royalty how he had obtained the information for the book. A certain man was suspected, then a certain gardener at Sandringham, but the author declared that he had had no informant.'

There are, however, letters in the archive that suggest a rather friendlier relationship between the author and the Royal Family; four months after the King's death, the Honourable Elizabeth Charlotte Knollys, Queen Alexandra's private secretary (the first woman to hold such a post), wrote to Ernest to say 'how touching and pathetic and true everyone thought your description of poor Caesar's grief at the loss of his beloved Master', and she revealed that when the dog first returned to Sandringham after the funeral 'he ran straight up to <u>his</u> room and then into every corner of the house looking for him'. She followed this up with a letter to 'obey Queen Alexandra's command to thank you most sincerely for these special copies of your book which you have been so good as to send'.

The correspondence blossomed into doggy gossip. The Queen later sent Ernest a signed photograph, and in the accompanying letter Miss Knollys observed that Edward's widow 'is absolutely devoted to all animals, and naturally more especially so to one who so loved, and was so loved by, our late lamented King'. This was followed by reassuring news about the new star of the Hodder & Stoughton list: 'I am sure you will like to hear that Caesar is now quite contented . . .', the royal secretary wrote, although, she added, 'he has never attached himself "exclusively" to any individual as he did to his beloved Master.'

And in September 1912, when the Hodder-Williams household suffered a dog bereavement of its own, Charlotte Knollys sent Ernest a letter of condolence from aboard the Royal Yacht, which was then moored in Copenhagen: 'Queen Alexandra has read your letter and commands me to condole with you most seriously on the death of your beloved little dog', she wrote. Ernest Hodder-Williams, the grandson of one Victorian apprentice and great-nephew of another, had parlayed his clever little book into connections at court.

Biographers routinely search the childhoods of exceptional men and women for signs of destiny, and almost everything written about Ernest Hodder-Williams is coloured by the idea that he was marked out from an early age. In his official company history, John Attenborough welcomed him to the Hodder & Stoughton story with the full Bethlehem Star treatment: 'Nobody in the family ever doubted that he was born to greatness', he wrote, and that judgement seems to have been widely shared among Ernest's friends and, eventually, obituarists.

He was born in the autumn of 1876, the eldest of seven children. His parents, Matthew Hodder's only child Mary, and George Williams' nephew John, lived next door to the Hodders in Bromley. Confusingly, he went through several names in the course of his life; he was christened John Ernest Hodder Williams (Mary expressed her dynastic ambitions by including her maiden name among the forenames of all four of her sons), and was often referred to by his initials, J. E. H. W. He formally changed his surname to Hodder-Williams in 1919, and dropped the 'John' when he was knighted. For clarity's sake, I have used Ernest Hodder-Williams throughout.

Matthew introduced Ernest to the publishing trade early, and took him on one of his American trips in 1887. George Doran remembered 'a tall, gangling boy, his spindly legs accentuated by his knickerbocker suit with the legs of the pants drawn up after the manner of present-day plus-fours [he was writing in the 1930s] but stopping just below the knees. He had an overwise head, a thin, pointed face, with spectacles so thick that his eyes assumed undue prominence.' He was only eleven years old, but it appears that he had already acquired his reputation for working too hard; Doran adds that 'the spectacles were the result of too close application and study'.

Ernest was educated at City of London school, leaving at sixteen to spend a year in Paris and Berlin, from which he returned with good French and German. William Robertson Nicoll persuaded Matthew Hodder that he would also benefit from higher education, and the family patriarch paid for Ernest to spend another year at University College London, before he joined the firm.

Even then he was a compulsive reader; in a speech he gave on publishing much later he said, 'I am often asked how you can learn publishing. There is only one way, and that is to travel books yourself. It is a pretty hard road, but it is worth the journey . . . you have to eat, drink, sleep and dream books.' As an undergraduate he devoured them, making copious notes on their contents, and listing any vocabulary that was new to him at the end of his reviews. He kept up the habit of reviewing for himself after leaving University College London, and his judgements were made with the sometimes cruel confidence of youth; George du Maurier was dismissed as 'Twaddle, and irreverent nasty twaddle at that', while Thomas Hardy's *Jude the Obscure* was 'Intensely boring'.

But his tendency towards censoriousness was tempered by a sense of humour. John Attenborough quotes the response Ernest gave to the Williams family nurse when she inquired about the holiday packing she had done for him: 'Very good, Jane,' Ernest told her, 'But next time please don't pack the Enos in my shirt. I fizzed every time I played tennis.'

Like Nicoll, Ernest seems to have been on the scout for talent from a very early age. During his time as an undergraduate he became friends with G. K. Chesterton, who was, somewhat fitfully, studying art at the Slade School, which is part of University College London. Chesterton began attending English lectures with Ernest, and states in his autobiography that the relationship was responsible for the beginning of his writing career. 'Hodder-Williams and I often talked about literature, following these lectures', he remembered, 'and he conceived a fixed notion that I could write . . . In consequence of this, and in connection with my art studies, he gave me some books on art to review for the *Bookman*, the famous organ of his firm and family. I need not say that, having entirely failed to learn how to draw and paint, I tossed off easily enough some criticisms of the weaker points of Rubens or the misdirected talents of Tintoretto.' The future author of the *Father Brown* stories added, 'I had discovered the easiest of all professions; which I have pursued ever since.'

Much later (in an article on 'Authors I have Met') Ernest Hodder-Williams reflected that one of his proudest possessions was a copy of Chesterton's first volume of poetry (*Greybeard at Play*, which was published in 1900), inscribed by the author with the words 'To J. E. Williams, who made me write, the only unwise thing he did in his life.' And his seriousness about Chesterton as a publishing prospect is attested by an 1894 letter in which Ernest writes, 'I have every confidence in your literary ability and pray you earnestly to let me see your first book – as a matter of business.'

1894 was the year that Ernest joined the firm, and in his letter to Chesterton he described his feelings on fulfilling the destiny for which he had been prepared. Despite the showy flourishes you might expect from a clever young intellectual, the letter reflects a seriousness of purpose about the publishing calling: '*Oh, mon ami, je suis maintenant un homme d'affaires* [Oh, my friend, I am now a man of business]', he wrote, 'I am working at my grandfather's place in Paternoster Row . . . I like the work very much: indeed, I think I was cut out to be a business man, and so much the better for me since I have got to make every penny myself – *vous comprenez, n'est-ce pas?* [you understand, don't you?]'

His first job appears to have been in the advertising

department of the periodicals, which then included the *British Weekly*, the *Bookman*, *Woman at Home*, the *Expositor* and the *Clergyman's Magazine*. The position meant he was working closely with William Robertson Nicoll, who quickly began to delegate editorial duties to him. 'If Jane Stoddart could unofficially edit *Woman at Home*,' writes John Attenborough, 'Ernest could surely do the same for the *Bookman*.' Ernest began writing *Bookman* reviews and securing contributors, and before long he was coming up with ideas of his own; he edited *The Bookman Directory of Booksellers, Publishers and Authors*, and launched a series of *Bookman* booklets, writing the first, on Thomas Carlyle, in collaboration with G. K. Chesterton.

Ernest and Nicoll formed an extremely close relationship during this period. Both men had a great talent for friendship, but Nicoll's biographer, T. H. Darlow, suggests this went deeper: 'The relations between the older man and the younger ripened into deep affection and regard', he wrote, 'and there grew between them a sympathy which became almost paternal on one side and filial on the other.' In some of their letters they communicate as families do – without bothering to fill in facts that are taken as read. There is, for example, a brief undated note from Nicoll to Ernest from 'The Grand Pump Room Hotel, Bath', which simply reads, 'What characters these novelist women are. Never marry one of them! No man is really safe except with a girl who plays the organ or sings in the choir!'

When, in 1902, Ernest was forced to take time off to recover from overwork, Nicoll wrote him a fatherly letter of advice. 'I was very much vexed to receive your long letter, which shows that you are exciting yourself very much on matters of business,' he began, 'the only chance of recovery is to put all those things out of your mind until you come back. Read good novels, and talk to people, and keep your mind easy, or you will never get well.' He urged Ernest to emulate the equanimity of the firm's founding fathers; 'You must borrow a leaf out of the book of

Messrs Hodder and Stoughton, whose admirable composure I have often admired . . . I am most anxious that your health should be re-established, and I am sure that what is putting it wrong is those two things – first, doing too much; and next, taking things too hard.'

The Ernest–Nicoll double act was pivotal to the next phase of Hodder & Stoughton's development; they broadened the firm's range and, without leaving its religious roots behind, they transformed it into a general publisher. They also drew Hodder & Stoughton close to what today we might call the Establishment.

Ernest was still in his mid-twenties as the Victorian era drew to a close, but he was ready for bigger things, and in 1901 he for the first time replaced his grandfather on one of those regular trips to the United States. Thomas Stoughton's two sons, John and Cecil, had joined the firm in 1895, and Ernest's younger brother Robert Percy Hodder-Williams arrived straight from school the following year, but Ernest was clearly the head of the family pack. In 1902 he was made a full partner in the firm.

That same year he married Ethel Oddy, who came from a suitably Nonconformist background, and was emphatically not one of those 'novelist women' Nicoll had warned his young protégé against. The couple settled in the tribal homeland of Bromley, moving into Gothic Lodge, Matthew's original house there. Ernest stood on the threshold of the new century full of energy, talent, ambition and social aspiration. His tailor's bills suggest an elegant Edwardian gent; a 1902 invoice from a firm in Gresham Street, not far from Paternoster Row, shows that he bought four suits, one frock, one Norfolk, one dress and one flannel, plus what was known as a 'Raglan', a style of overcoat said to have been favoured by Lord Raglan after he lost an arm at the Battle of Waterloo. In October he added badminton gloves and skating garters to his wardrobe.

Nicoll had, of course, already begun to develop the firm's fiction list, but Ernest's freedom to choose new novels was constrained by the firm's publishing ethic. Thomas Stoughton addressed the issue in a long letter to the new partner underlining his view that 'We should be jealous of our reputation.' Citing Nicoll's worries about the direction of modern novel-writing, Stoughton expressed support for the idea that 'our firm's name ought to be a guarantee that novels published by us might be safely read aloud in families', adding, 'in short I would rather forgo profit than be identified with objectionable novels. I have reason to believe that we shall never have reason to regret our being particular in this way.'

This was not just a moral stand; it was in Hodder & Stoughton's commercial interests to publish the kind of books that would appeal to its evangelical base – in fact it could be argued that the real risk of 'forgoing profits' lay in alienating the religiously minded readers who had made the imprint such a success story. It is difficult today to imagine ourselves back into a world where religious and moral questions played quite such a role in publishing decisions, but there is a note in the Hodder & Stoughton archives that gives a sense of the climate of the day; it is an 1899 letter to Ernest from a Protestant magazine, *The Rock*, accepting his proposal for a column of literary criticism, and it includes the proviso that Ernest should not endorse any work 'no matter how high its literary value, which is in any degree of immoral tendency, or subversive of Protestant and religious teaching'.

The American market offered Ernest one avenue to books that were morally sound and commercially successful. On his first American trip he bought the rights to Alice Hegan Rice's book *Mrs Wiggs of the Cabbage Patch*, a suitably uplifting story of a Southern widow and her large family struggling with poverty. It was published in Britain in the year he became a partner, and in his energetic way Ernest promoted it by travelling to Kentucky, where it was set, to meet the author and 'visit the Cabbage Patch myself'.

In his subsequent article he reported that 'The Cabbage Patch really exists. Anyone in Louisville will direct you to Mrs Wiggs' home, for the Cabbage Patch has become a shrine of literary pilgrimage.' The book was conceived when the author was engaged in charity work in a poor area of her city, 'this queer neighbourhood where ramshackle cottages played hop-scotch over the railway tracks', and Ernest praises her for writing 'from life, the life that lay at her door, describing the scenes she had witnessed when on charity bent'. He ended the piece by quoting the couplet the author used to establish the book's hopeful tone: 'In the mud and scum of things,/Something always, always sings.' It certainly sang for Alice Hegan Rice and Ernest Hodder-Williams. The book was an immediate bestseller in Britain as well as the United States, it was staged as a Broadway play three years after its publication in book form and four film versions were produced, the last in 1942.

Another purchase he made in the United States came to him with the enormous publicity bonus of a place on the *Index Librorum Prohibitorum*, the list of books Catholics were forbidden to read because of their heretical or lascivious content. The first decade of the twentieth century was a period of boneheaded resistance to the modern world in the Vatican; the Pope of the day, Pius X, required every priest to swear that, among many other things, 'dogma may [not] be tailored according to what seems better and more suited to the culture of each age; rather, that the absolute and immutable truth preached by the apostles from the beginning may never be believed to be different, may never be understood in any other way . . .' And a Monsignor in Pius's Curia, the Vatican civil service, established a network of snoopers called the 'Fellowship of Pius' to inform on priests and bishops suspected of liberal opinions.

Il Santo, The Saint – no obvious relation to the Simon Templar character later played on television by Roger Moore and Pierce Brosnan – is the last book in a trilogy by Antonio Fogazzaro, a distinguished Catholic Italian novelist and Christian Democrat senator, and is very clearly framed as an attack on the way Pius was running the church. The hero 'finds God' after fleeing from an inappropriate love affair (his wife is in a lunatic asylum, but he is still married, and his paramour is separated from her husband) and becomes a wandering holy man under the name Benedetto. He eventually finds his way into the presence of the Pope himself, and appeals to the Holy Father to purge the Church of its errors, which sounds remarkably similar to Pius's efforts to close down free thought and modern ideas. In Fogazzaro's story the Pope is not the true villain; the real baddies are, it turns out – in a literary and journalistic trope that is still familiar today – the 'crafty, able, remorseless cabal of cardinals who surround him, dog him with eavesdroppers, edit his briefs, check his benign impulses, and effectually prevent the truth from penetrating to his lonely study.'

At one point Benedetto is confronted by a government official with the words: 'They tell me you are a Liberal Catholic. That simply means you are not a Catholic.' Given the climate in the Vatican at the time, it is unsurprising that the book was put on the *Index*, and for a section of Hodder & Stoughton readers both the story it told and the ban on reading it would have confirmed their views on the Vatican.

Ernest bought the rights to the English translation from G. P. Putnam's Sons of New York. He does not appear to have been especially anti-Catholic himself (he remained Chesterton's friend after the latter's conversion, after all) but the opportunity was too good to miss: 'Time was when it was the avowed enemies of the Church – of some mocking Voltaire, some learned Renan, some impassioned Michelet – which they thrust on the *Index*', declares the introduction to the Hodder edition, 'now they pillory the Catholic layman with the largest following in Italy, one who never wavered in his devotion to the Church. Whatever the political result of their action may be, they have made the fortune of the book they hope to suppress, and this is good, for *The Saint* is a real addition to literature.' The firm shifted 20,000 copies.

The Saint was published in 1906 – which, even by the breathless standards of Ernest's first decade as a partner, was something of an *annus mirabilis* for the firm. Hodder & Stoughton made the short move from Paternoster Square to St Paul's House in Warwick Square – still close to the cathedral, but a roomier berth for the growing company. Ernest negotiated a joint venture with Oxford University Press that took the firm into children's books and textbooks, and was later followed by another venture into educational publishing with the University of London Press. And there was a publishing landmark in the shape of J. M. Barrie's *Peter Pan in Kensington Gardens*, which came out with illustrations by Arthur Rackham.

Barrie's best-known character has an unusual publishing history. Peter first appeared – very briefly – in *Tommy and Grizel*, a novel that Barrie published in 1900; the Tommy of the title describes 'a reverie about a little boy who was lost. His parents find him singing joyfully to himself because he thinks he can now be a boy forever, and he fears that if they catch him they will compel him to grow into a man, so he runs farther from them into the wood and is running still and singing to himself because he is always to be a boy . . .'

Peter emerges as a more fully formed figure in *The Little White Bird*, which Hodder & Stoughton published two years later. This peculiar novel – it involves time travel, fantasy and social satire – revolves around the relationship between a retired army officer, Captain W, and a little boy called David, and parts of the book make extremely uncomfortable reading today; the description of the 'adventure' they share when the 'lonely old bachelor' and the young boy spend the night together, for example, is suggestive in ways that no mainstream publisher could possibly allow now.

The captain tells David that 'all children in our part of London were once birds in Kensington Gardens; and that the reason there are bars on nursery windows and a tall fender by the fire is because very little people sometimes forget they no longer have wings, and try to fly away through the window or up the chimney'. Peter Pan is introduced in the course of a description of Kensington Gardens and the Serpentine lake in Hyde Park: 'A small part of the Serpentine is in the Gardens,' Barrie wrote, 'for soon it passes beneath a bridge to far away where the island is on which all the birds are born that become baby boys and girls. No one who is human, except Peter Pan (and he is only half human) can land on the island . . .' Peter's doings in Kensington Gardens fill around a hundred pages of the book.

But the cult status Peter Pan now enjoys did not really emerge until the first production of Barrie's play *The Boy Who Wouldn't Grow Up*. From the opening night, 27 December 1904, the drama proved an overwhelming success, and immediately established itself as a regular feature of the Christmas season. Hodder & Stoughton capitalised on its success with the firm's 1906 edition of *Peter Pan in Kensington Gardens*, reprinting the six Peter Pan chapters from *The Little White Bird*, and adding the Arthur Rackham pictures that so brilliantly capture the fantastic character of the story. Four years later, Barrie produced a full novel on the basis of the play – *Peter and Wendy* was also published by Hodder & Stoughton, and took its hero on yet another stage of his journey from novel to drama and back again.

The Reverend John Watson, known to his readers as Ian Maclaren and one of Hodder's most popular authors, died in 1907, and his bestselling *Beside the Bonnie Briar Bush* had by then given its name to a whole literary movement. The book's title is taken from some lines by Robert Burns: 'There grows a bonnie brier bush in our kail-yard,/There grows a bonnie brier bush in our kail-yard;/And below the bonnie brier bush there's a lassie and a lad,/And they're busy busy courting in our kail-yard.' A kail-yard was a kitchen garden or cabbage patch, and the term 'Kailyardism' was coined to cover Scottish literature of the genre.

The *Oxford Companion to English Literature* defines it as 'a term applied to writers of a class of romantic fiction affecting to describe, with much use of the vernacular, common life in Scotland'. Other definitions insist that only authors who were members of the Free Church qualified for the school, and the list of recognised members reads like a roll call of Hodder's finest; as well as Ian Maclaren, it included J. M. Barrie, Annie Swan and the hugely successful S. R. Crockett.

Critics of Kailyardism claimed that their works presented a sugary and unrealistic picture of Scottish life, and around the turn of the century an anti-Kailyard movement took shape. The most notable novel it produced was *The House with Green Shutters* by George Douglas Brown, which tells the tale of a struggling 'carrier' (the job of transporting people and goods) who is persecuted by the busybodies of his Ayrshire village – malicious versions, in fact, of the kind of folk who were so gently and affectionately portrayed in Barrie's *Auld Licht Idylls*. Hodder & Stoughton had laid themselves open to the terrible literary charge of sentimentality.

But they could afford to ignore the literary sniping, because their Kailyard books remained hugely popular. Ernest made a trip to the United States with John Watson and Ian Maclaren just before the latter's death, and reported the pop-star-like reception he was given. 'As we watched the reporters around him in New York, and caught sight of the friends waiting for him on the dock,' Ernest wrote, 'there could be no doubt as to the enthusiasm of his welcome.' When Watson preached in New York, Ernest turned up to listen. 'I had literally to fight and beseech and fight again before I could gain entrance to the Fifth Avenue Church on the morning he preached there', he wrote. 'People were fainting in the porch so great was the rush.'

Ernest's affectionate account of the trip pays tribute to the author's brilliance as a storyteller. Maclaren, he wrote, 'kept us laughing through two mid-winter gales' with his shipboard anecdotes about an earlier lecture tour of the United States, and 'in the evening, when every man's heart was a little lightened in view of another day snatched from the Atlantic storms, he would indulge in the broadest Scottish dialect. Then he was happiest of all. For although he would laugh at certain traits in the northern character, he loved everything Scottish with a deep and fervent devotion.'

The ability to spin a good yarn was precisely the quality that had appealed to William Robertson Nicoll when he first met Dr Watson. Ernest was a close reader of books, but he was not a literary snob, and good storytelling became the real hallmark of the Hodder & Stoughton list. There is no reason to doubt the sincerity of Ernest's valedictory reflection on John Watson: 'never were relations between author and publisher more cordial than those which existed for so many years between Dr Watson and the firm that was privileged to put its imprint on his writings.'

As well as taking the company into new areas of publishing, Ernest also showed great imagination in playing with the form of books. He can, among many other achievements, claim to be one of the fathers of the kind of lavishly illustrated volume that today we might call a 'coffee table book'. Hodder & Stoughton published a series of expensively produced classics – popular Shakespeare plays, for example, and Dickens's *The Pickwick Papers* – illustrated by artists like Arthur Rackham and W. Heath Robinson. Immense care was taken over their production – correspondence in the Hodder archive bears witness to detailed debates about the quality of paper needed – and today early editions fetch huge sums on the rare books market.

Several of these books showcase the work of the French-born artist Edmund Dulac, who settled in London after a commission from another publisher, J. M. Dent, to illustrate *Jane Eyre*. And the high point of Ernest's experiments in the field was an edition of Edward FitzGerald's *The Rubaiyat of Omar Khayyam* with Dulac illustrations, which was published in 1909. *The Rubaiyat*, a fairly free translation of a selection of verses attributed to a twelfth-century Persian mathematician and astronomer, was popular with artists of the day because of its exotic sensuality, and Dulac's pictures remain among the best known of the genre. 'A Book of Verses underneath the Bough,/A Jug of Wine, a Loaf of Bread—and Thou/Beside me singing in the Wilderness—/Oh, Wilderness were Paradise enow!' the poet declares, and there is a good deal more in similar vein. Both the text and Dulac's pictures belong to a very different world from all those sermons and biblical commentaries which featured so prominently on earlier Hodder lists.

The Dulac book did extremely well, but its success again brought into sharp relief the challenges Ernest faced in broadening the firm's range. Matthew Hodder, who, though nearing the end of his life by the time the book came out, still took a close interest in the business, looked it over during a weekend. Doran recorded a characteristically enjoyable account of his reaction. 'On that Monday morning,' he writes, 'fresh from the exhausting exhilaration of an evangelically active Sabbath, he thrust himself into the office and presence of J. E. H. W. In his shaking hand he held a copy of Dulac's work. This is the scene and conversation as related to me by J. E. H. W. himself:

Mr Hodder. Ernest, what is this pagan book you have dared to publish over my imprint?

J. E. H. W. : Why, Granddad, that is one of the great classics of all time.

Mr Hodder. Classic or no classic, I will not tolerate the publication of such heathen rubbish.

J. E. H. W. : Granddad, it is beautifully illustrated by one of the very greatest artists of our day – it is a proud production.

Mr Hodder. The artist only abets the author, whoever he is, in the presentation of a purely pagan and disgusting book. I will have none of it.

Ernest was eventually forced to appeal to his grandfather's commercial instincts, and pointed out that the book had made the firm £800 during the previous twelve months, a healthy return by the standards of the day. 'Gradually a peaceful expression came over the old man's face,' writes Doran, 'back came the benign and disarming smile. Patting his grandson gently on the shoulder, he admonished him, "You will be careful, Ernest my boy, won't you?" The incident was closed.'

Doran published the Dulac *Rubaiyat* for the American market – and it was one of the first successes of the new house he established with support from Hodder & Stoughton in 1908. Doran loved a good anecdote, and some of those in his autobiography are so well told that one cannot help suspecting they have been polished a little. One of the most enjoyable claims he makes is that, in the year the new company was founded, his wife 'discovered' Arnold Bennett.

Mrs Doran had been told to rest by the doctors – after suffering an attack of vertigo – and asked her husband for some books to read. One of those he had to hand was Bennett's *The Old Wives' Tale*, which Hodder had just brought out as a reprint (it was first published by Chapman and Hall without attracting much attention), and he gave his wife a copy. 'This was early morning,' he remembered. 'Towards evening she called me on the telephone and said, "I have been reading the most marvellous book I have read for twenty years. It is *The Old Wives' Tale* by Arnold Bennett. Do cable at once and see if you can secure the American rights."'

On the strength of this he ordered 1,000 copies, and they arrived with a copy of a review from William Robertson Nicoll in the *British Weekly,* which began: 'I contend against all comers that *The Old Wives' Tale* by Arnold Bennett is the best English novel of the past twenty-five years.' The book moved slowly at first, but took off in spectacular fashion when a bookseller in Boston started to recommend it to his 'quite remarkable clientele'. It did so well in the United States that its fame echoed back across the Atlantic, generating healthy sales for Hodder & Stoughton too, and established the author's reputation. Bennett himself described it as a 'divine accident'.

8

Still harder struggles in still better causes

'The years from 1908 to 1914 were happy, peaceful, and progressive', George Doran remembered, 'G H D Co [George H. Doran Company] was prosperous. It had yielded handsome profits to Hodder and Stoughton in addition to placing them in a position to assure authors worldwide publication.' He visited London every six months, Ernest made the trip to New York every other year. When Doran arrived at the Savoy for one of his regular visits in 1914 he found a note from Ernest waiting:

My Dear G. H. D.

Welcome, Old Man. Things are a bit down here. I do not know whether to be more concerned over the Irish situation or the crisis in Serbia. At all events I have taken some Lloyd's insurance against the possibilities of war. Let us meet very soon.

Yours ever,

J. E. H. W.

The date was 27 July – almost exactly a month after the assassination of the Archduke Ferdinand in Sarajevo. The following day, the 28th, Austria-Hungary declared war on Serbia, and just over a week later Britain declared war on Germany. William Robertson Nicoll's biographer T. H. Darlow describes what it was like to live through those tumultuous days: 'Through the spring and early summer of 1914, people in London were concerned mostly with strikes and militant suffragettes and Irish rebels', he wrote. 'We went about our business and our pleasure in placid fashion – as men did before the Flood. Then suddenly the sky darkened and thundered, and earth rocked under our feet, the day of judgement had begun. For each of us the War became the supreme test: it searched his character and proved what stuff he was made of. By his bearing in the great ordeal every man betrayed what he had in his heart. Never did Nicoll play his own part more worthily than during those grim years of peril. The proud Highland blood in his veins leaped up to meet the German menace.' The edition of the *British Weekly* published on 6 August, two days after the declaration of war, carried a leader under the bold headline 'United We Stand', and set the tone for Nicoll's campaigning journalism throughout the conflict.

By 1914 Nicoll had established contacts at the heart of the Liberal Party, which had governed the country since 1905; he was on close terms with the then Chancellor, David Lloyd George, and Sir William, as he had become in 1909, enjoyed entertaining Lady Robertson Nicoll with gossip about cabinet meetings. The list of Hodder authors by now included several other big beasts of the Liberal Party. Edward Grey, the Foreign Secretary who negotiated for Britain during the tense days leading up to the war, was one (as a writer he is probably best known for his books on fly fishing and birds), as was Richard Haldane, who had served as Secretary for War and was a close ally of the prime minister, H. H. Asquith. Winston Churchill, who was a Liberal at this stage of his career and First Lord of the Admiralty at the outbreak of war, had published *My African Journey* with Hodder in 1908 and *Liberalism and the Social Problem* the following year. His note (on Admiralty stationery) thanking Ernest for the 'beautiful books' he received at Christmas in 1914 suggests the First Lord saw Ernest as a political ally as well as a publisher. It was Churchill's support for free trade that had forced his move from the Conservative to Liberal benches ten years earlier, and he wrote to Ernest that 'I shall always value them [the books] as a mark of your good will and our friendship, which began in the strenuous days of the free trade campaign – now eclipsed by still harder struggles in still better causes.'

Ernest was in his late thirties when the First World War began, and his poor eyesight meant he was unsuited to soldiering. But he threw himself wholeheartedly into the war effort, and the outbreak of war added a new dimension to his relationship with Nicoll.

The editor of the *British Weekly* went ahead with his annual August pilgrimage to Lumsden, his childhood home, but soon returned to London. 'We met for lunch, as was our custom every Wednesday, week in week out for over twenty years, in a little room at the printers' office where he had just passed the *British Weekly* for press,' Ernest remembered. '. . . We sat silent for a time, those pale mystic eyes of his, now clear, now cloudy, first questioning me almost fiercely across the table, then looking through me, past me, out beyond into the frowning future. I knew he saw terrible things, for he had fewer illusions about the war than most of us, and far more understanding. He stretched out his hand, that very sensitive hand, and gripped mine. We stood up, and then he told me of his faith, of his determination to see it through – "you and I together", as we had seen through many fights together in the past. "Never fear, we shall win – win in the end. But we shall pass through deep waters."'

At this point Ernest's account of his lunch with his mentor slips close to melodrama: 'There came into his voice the gentle, crooning note that came only when he was greatly moved. "I have no fear," he crooned, "Naked came I out of my mother's womb and naked I shall return." Then – with one of those sudden changes that never cease to startle those who know him best – in a voice like naked steel: "I have no fear. The blood of my forebears watered the fields of Culloden."' It was perhaps a surprising piece of history to evoke as a battle cry for a great

British campaign, but with that ringing declaration the two men sat down to 'the urgent business of carrying on and defining the policy of the paper during the Great War'. Nicoll had been intending to resign from the editorship of the *British Weekly* to spend more time with his books, but all such thoughts were now put aside. Ernest added, 'We saw through the war together as we had foretold. I know what I and mine owe to his glorious faith and courage during those years. I cannot measure what the Empire owes: it is a heavy debt.'

Ernest's claims sound like hyperbole, but William Robertson Nicoll's immediate backing for the war was in fact extremely valuable to his friends in the Liberal government. Many readers of the *British Weekly* would have been sceptical about their European policy. 'The majority of Liberal opinion was utterly opposed . . . to Britain going to war,' writes Cate Haste in *Keep the Home Fires Burning*, her account of First World War propaganda. 'They clamoured for neutrality, echoed by the Neutrality League and the Neutrality Committee, both set up specifically to disseminate arguments against Britain's participation in this Continental quarrel.' Nicoll's Nonconformist readers were also likely to be sympathetic to the anti-war message: 'Among Free Churchmen multitudes were by tradition and temperament averse from fighting', writes T. H. Darlow, Nicoll's biographer, 'and he laboured incessantly to bring home to them their sacred duty.'

His favourite woman novelist was straight into the field; the YMCA sponsored Annie Swan on a lecture tour to France. She was based in Le Havre, and worked in the nearby training camp at Honfleur; 'I started in to work at once,' she wrote, 'speaking in the huts every night. It was a message of gratitude and encouragement from the women at home I was charged with, as well as the burden of deeper things, and how joyfully they received it!' The full horror of the trenches had yet to become apparent, and she found that 'these young recruits were all Crusaders still, eager and undismayed, because convinced of the righteousness of their cause.'

She agreed to address a 'concentration camp' without knowing what it was, and on the way there the YMCA Superintendent explained that it held 'over a thousand men and lads . . . segregated from their comrades, having contracted venereal disease'. She confessed that this 'shook me a little' and wrote that it was 'a poignant moment when I, a woman, alone, faced them on that sunny hillside to offer them my message'. In her autobiography she added that 'It was my first introduction to one of the minor horrors of war.'

The First World War was the first conflict in which propaganda played a real role, and that made writers and journalists part of the war effort for the first time. 'War ceased to be the prerogative solely of military leaders', Cate Haste argues in *Keep the Home Fires Burning*, 'and came to involve the civilians of the belligerent countries on a scale never known before. For the first time the barometer of public morale needed as much careful attention as the efficiency of the troops in the front line, and this revolutionised attitudes to propaganda.' The government established its first propaganda agency – the Secret War Propaganda Bureau – as early as September 1914.

It was known as 'Wellington House' – after its offices in Buckingham Gate – and one of its functions was to commission pamphlets from well-known authors. The Liberal politician C. F. G. Masterman, who had served in the cabinet just before the war, was appointed to run the Bureau, and immediately convened a meeting of prominent writers, several of whom – including J. M. Barrie and A. E. W. Mason – were associated with Hodder & Stoughton.

The exact nature of the firm's relationship with the agency is not clear – the Bureau was, after all, 'Secret' – but it seems that Ernest was an enthusiastic supporter of the enterprise; records at the Imperial War Museum show that in the course of the war

Hodder & Stoughton published no fewer than 134 of the Wellington House pamphlets – more than any other publisher. Hodder also published books by the historian Arnold Toynbee, who was working for the Political Intelligence Department at the Foreign Office, and wrote extensively about German atrocities in Belgium and France.

Alexander Watt, the senior son of the second generation in the world's oldest literary agency, A. P. Watt, served as the 'business adviser' to Wellington House. A. P. Watt represented many of Hodder's authors, and the two firms were old sparring partners; there is a 1901 letter in the Hodder archive in which William Robertson Nicoll tells Ernest – with some relish – that he has caught the agency trying to push up the advance for one of its clients by falsely claiming she had been offered a fat fee to defect to Heinemann. It was, as the historian Sadia McEvoy writes in her study of propaganda during World War One, 'a small, incestuous world'. In 1917 Wellington House was absorbed into the first publicly acknowledged propaganda department – the Department for Information – and John Buchan was recruited to lead the new organisation. Buchan had by then become – with the publication of *Greenmantle* in 1916 – one of Ernest's authors.

Ernest's royal connections also played an important part in Hodder's wartime publishing. In 1914 the firm brought out *Princess Mary's Gift Book*, a collection of children's stories by popular authors including Rudyard Kipling, Sir Arthur Conan Doyle and J. M. Barrie, with illustrations by, among other favourites of the day, Arthur Rackham. The book sold 600,000 copies in two years, and the proceeds went to the Queen's Work for Women Fund, which promoted women's war work. Its success prompted Mary's mother, the Queen (also, of course, called Mary), to request the publication of *A Queen's Gift Book*, which came out in 1916, with proceeds going to, as the title page had it, 'Queen Mary's Auxiliary Convalescent Hospitals for soldiers and sailors who have lost their limbs.'

And Ernest himself joined this orgy of benevolent literary creativity by writing *The Way of the Red Cross* in collaboration with a journalist from *The Times*, Charles Vivian. He asked for some introductory words from Queen Alexandra, and in January 1915 his doggy friend Charlotte Knollys wrote to say that 'I am very happy to be able to forward the enclosed which Queen Alexandra has consented to have published as the Preface to *The Way of the Red Cross*.' Ernest was even willing to put some of the firm's money behind the war effort; during Red Cross Week in 1916, Hodder donated threepence in every shilling they made in book sales to the charity.

The Hodder fiction list that year was dominated by the kind of patriotic tales of derring-do that might lift British spirits. John Buchan's *Greenmantle* was immensely popular, and includes very clear propaganda messages. The villain, Colonel von Stumm, is, as Sadia McEvoy puts it, an 'archetypal German Hun', and when the hero, Richard Hannay, is recruited as a spy his minder at the Foreign Office tells him that the conflict with Germany is 'a wonderful war for youth and brains'. Another star of the list was *Men, Women and Guns* by Sapper (a pen name for H. C. McNeile, MC, who, as a serving soldier, was forbidden from publishing under his own name). The one – intriguing – exception to all this martial enthusiasm was Rose Macaulay's anti-war novel *Non-Combatants and Others*.

Rose Macaulay had moved to Hodder from John Murray after winning a Hodder writing competition; her entry, *The Lee Shore*, was published in 1912. *Non-Combatants and Others* appeared on the 1916 list alongside *Greenmantle*, but in tone and message it was a very far cry from the swashbuckling adventures of Buchan's hero Richard Hannay. The book was inspired by the author's experiences as a nurse treating soldiers sent home from France, and, in the words of Macaulay's biographer, Sarah Lefanu, 'picks apart and satirises a society that prefers not to listen to the testament of the soldiers sacrificing lives on its behalf'.

Ernest the propagandist – my word, but one he would probably have accepted – and Ernest the publisher must surely have wrestled about whether the book should see the light of day; the publisher won and Hodder remained loyal to their author, but the book was marketed as a romance; a newspaper advertisement explained, rather limply, that 'The story deals especially with the point of view of a girl, and different ways she tries taking the war, and the different attitudes of the people around her, and her relations with a man who is fighting.'

Ernest's own view of the war was developing. *One Young Man*, his best-known war book, appeared in 1917; though it is emphatically not an 'anti-war' book, it is very far from being a gung-ho call to arms. The country's mood had changed by then – not least because of the terrible carnage of the Battle of the Somme in 1916 – and the war had come close to home. Ernest's wife Ethel had turned The Orchard, their house in Bickley (an area of east Bromley), into a club for wounded soldiers, who, like Rose Macaulay's charges, no doubt brought their war stories with them. And Ernest's brother Ralph, who had been working as an academic in Toronto, joined Princess Patricia's Canadian Light Infantry as a lieutenant, and was wounded on the Somme. He was awarded a Military Cross for his actions, and the citation explains that 'Although wounded, he continued to lead his men in the attack, and after being wounded again he continued to command his men until the position was made good.'

One Young Man is not really Ernest's book at all; it is built around the letters and trench diaries of one Reginald Davis, a clerk at Hodder who joined up and fought on the Western Front. He survived terrible wounds at the Somme, and went on to become Hodder & Stoughton's Company Secretary in the 1920s, serving no less than fifty-six years with the firm. His identity is concealed in the book by the pseudonym Sydney Baxter, and his writings have been skilfully packaged by Ernest, who was clearly a brilliant editor. But the way Ernest orders the story and the interjections he makes as it unfolds reveal a great deal about himself. In a foreword for a commemorative edition published after the war his brother Percy wrote that the book 'tells the story of one young man in the Great War, but, in fact, it reveals no less the personality of the writer who knitted the young man's story together . . . My brother is revealed here . . .'

Ernest's description of his hero reads a little like a self-portrait. Sydney Baxter is presented as something of a swot – in his office he was nicknamed 'Gig-lamps' because of his specs. He comes from a religious family, but Ernest is at pains to point out that he was not, in a now old-fashioned piece of slang, 'pi', but had a lively sense of humour. He was also a great enthusiast for the YMCA; Ernest quotes extensively from Baxter's diary tributes to the 'YM', as he calls it, both as a source of companionship and clean fun in civilian life and as a source of comfort and support in the field, and the book is dedicated to 'The Greatly Beloved Memory of One Young Man who founded the Y.M.C.A., my uncle, Sir George Williams'.

Sydney Baxter joined up in October 1914; he was not one of those jingoistic enthusiasts who rushed to the colours, rather he was a reluctant volunteer who felt he must do his duty. And Ernest makes him a symbol of the spirit in which Britain went to war. 'He and the thousands like him, outnumbered and out gunned, fought the Prussian Guard, the most finished product of the German military machine, and halted them, held them, beat them', he wrote. 'In equal fight they thrashed them. Think of it in the light of history. The greatest and most wonderfully equipped and trained army the world has ever known beaten in fair fight by an army of clerks, schoolmasters, stockbrokers, University men, street waifs, shop-keepers, labourers, counter-jumpers, most of whom did not know one end of a rifle from the other when war was declared.'

But there is no attempt to sentimentalise the reality of war. Sydney Baxter was caught up in the notoriously bloody Battle of

Hill 60 in the spring of 1915. He was moving ammunition up a communications trench to the front line when British troops went 'over the top' to face the German guns. 'And then a stream of wounded poured down this communication trench,' he recorded in his diary. 'The wounds were terrible, mostly bayonet. None dressed; there had been no time, they were just as they had been received. Many a poor chap succumbed to his injuries as he staggered along our trench. To keep the gangway clear we had to lift these dead bodies out and put them on the parapets. It was ghastly, but you get accustomed to ghastly things out here. You realise that fifty dead bodies are not equal to one living. And these poor fellows, who only a few minutes before had been alive and full of vigour, were now just blocking the trench. And we simply lifted the bodies out and cast them over the top.'

Later in the battle Sydney's 'chum' George was hit by a German sniper. 'All he could do was point to his chin,' the 'young man' recorded. 'A dum-dum or explosive bullet had caught his jaw-bone and blown the left lower jaw and part of the neck away.' Sydney 'risked all chance of court martial and stayed with my wounded friend . . . He did not last many minutes, and I knelt there with my arm round his shoulders, hoping against hope that something could be done. He was called to pay the supreme sacrifice of all. And with just one gasp he died.' Sydney Baxter asked for permission to join the burial party, and worried about the shallowness of the grave. Ernest ended this extract with a vivid illustration of the power of the old literary adage that 'less is more'; 'to this written by Sydney Baxter, I add nothing. Not to me has it come to dig a shallow, shell-swept grave for my chum. What words, then, have I?' This was the real war behind that restrained citation for Ralph's MC, the one Rose Macaulay had come to understand in her work as a nurse.

One Young Man was followed by *Jack Cornwell: the story of John Travers Cornwell VC 'Boy – First Class'*, which described the experiences of a working-class lad from the East End who gave up his job as a delivery boy to enlist in the Royal Navy. At the Battle of Jutland in May 1916 he was acting as a sight-setter when shellfire killed everyone else in his gun crew; at the end of the engagement he was found standing at his post despite dreadful injuries, and died two days later. He was only sixteen, and the rank recorded on his citation for Britain's highest award for bravery gave Ernest's title its punch of pathos; he was described as 'Boy (First Class) John Travers Cornwell'.

These two books celebrated British bravery, and they can be called 'propaganda' in the sense that they were designed to influence the national mood. But they looked beyond the war to the challenge of mourning the dead and accepting the war's veterans. Towards the end of *One Young Man*, Ernest quotes Sydney Baxter's diary description of the wounds he suffered on the first day of the Battle of the Somme, and then adds, 'Thus far Sydney Baxter tells his own story of the great day of his life. I leave it as it stands, though I could add so much to it if I would. Will you picture to yourself this sightless young man, with torn head and shattered hand piteously struggling from these shambles. Will you look at him – afterwards? It is worth while trying to do so. You and I have *got* to see the war before we can do justice to the warrior.'

George Doran – who, though based in New York, was of course Canadian by birth – was every bit as enthusiastic about supporting the war effort as his British friend and colleague. 'When Wellington House began publishing material directly in America,' writes Sadia McEvoy, 'they frequently used Doran.' And Doran published for the American market some of the Hodder books – Arnold Toynbee's among them – that had influenced public opinion in Britain. Sir Newman Flower, another great publisher-writer of Ernest's generation, even credited Doran with ensuring America's entry into the war. 'Deluged from end to end by the welter of propaganda bearing the Doran imprint,' he wrote, 'America began to think more closely about a war which had hitherto seemed so remote, so much some other person's quarrel . . . It was the youthful house of Doran that helped America into the war.' The United States declared war on Germany in the spring of 1917, and the final outcome of the Great War became inevitable.

Any pleasure Ernest took in Britain's improved war prospects was tempered by a tragedy in his private life; his wife Ethel was diagnosed with incurable cancer, and she died in June 1918, just as her husband's firm approached its fiftieth birthday.

She was in some ways the opposite pole he needed: 'She was all verve and vivacity,' Ernest's brother Percy wrote in her obituary, 'but she was not a restless woman. Her ambition was to rest people. And this she did.' She was also a book-lover who shared his ambitions and interests, and her 'perfect passion for dogs, both big and small' no doubt helped Ernest to give Caesar such an authentic voice in *Where's Master?* In the obituary Percy added, 'There was not a shadow in his life she did not lighten. He once said that when he was very weary, the sound of her voice – "Now let's talk" – smoothed at once all the wrinkles from his life.' After her death Ernest sold the contents of their home and moved to a flat in Westminster, putting Bromley behind him forever.

In May 1919 Ernest was knighted. The dandy we glimpsed in his tailor's bills had, it seems, survived both war and grief; his secretary Sophie Hines recorded his fastidious care over his court uniform. 'He took a tremendous interest in clothes (both his and other people's)', she wrote, and 'the purchase of the silk stockings and other accessories of the Court uniform were all attended to personally.'

The following month he attended the Victory Parade along the Mall, and his account of this bittersweet moment of British history was published on the front page of the *British Weekly*. The manuscript copy in the Hodder archives is a maze of amendments, redrafts and crossings-out, which suggests he took great care over the text. It is a small emotional masterpiece.

'Before the procession reached us,' he wrote, 'there fell upon that vast mass of people an eerie hush. I could hear the leaves rustling . . . It was like the stillness before a burst of thunder.' Then came the 'massed standards of the British Army', followed by 'a little company not chosen, as most had been, for smartness and uniform height, a remnant that looked like a remnant. Men who could not be picked, just because there were so few to pick from. This was the Army of 1914, officers and men together, so representative in its pitiful inequality of all that was left of them . . .'

In the days before broadcasting most of the population would, of course, have relied on the written press for an account of great national occasions like this. Ernest does full justice to the climax of the parade: 'Our ears ached to the rumbling of the guns, to the endless tramping of the men and women marching, marching on. Our eyes grew dim as the steady ranks of khaki and of blue swayed and rippled before them until at length they rested gratefully on the pure white of Army nurses marked with the Red Cross. On my left, my friend was sitting, staring at the ground. On the other side one stood rigid and did not know that the soldiers were still marching by. I understood that both were very lonely. And then I, too, was quite alone. Each of us was in his own hallowed field among the many crosses. For each of us there is one cross.'

9

The best novel I've ever written ...

While strolling in a Sussex garden with his publisher friend Walter Newman Flower (of Cassell and Co) Ernest fell to musing on their trade. 'Talk about navigators and explorers,' he said, 'we publishers get more adventure out of life than they ever did. The books we pledge our hopes to that never come off; the other books with only a fighting chance for which we strive that become big best-sellers! There's joy in the game, and it's the biggest game in the world.'

His sense of the 'joy in the game' never seems to have left him, even amidst the powerful emotions generated by the war and the great grief he evidently felt for his wife. He saw everything from a publisher's perspective, and the end of the war offered opportunities; there were new national heroes with memoirs to write, there would soon be more paper to print them on (shortages had been a real problem during the war) and the reading public was eager for the pleasures of peace.

In the autumn of 1919 Ernest secured what he called a 'lovely scoop', in the shape of the autobiography of Admiral Lord Fisher, one of the most colourful characters in public life. Fisher's long naval career had begun in the days of wooden ships and muzzle-loading cannon, and lasted until the modern era of submarines and aircraft carriers. He served as First Sea Lord from 1904 to 1910, and was responsible for many of the innovations that prepared the Navy for war. He was called out of retirement to serve in the same position in 1914, but fell out with Churchill over the Gallipoli campaign and resigned six months later. He had a short fuse and could forget himself; in one of the enjoyable anecdotes in his book he relates that the King once asked him to stop shaking his fist in his face as he made a point.

The deal was signed at the beginning of September, and was news in itself; *The Times* ran the story, and also announced that the paper would be publishing extracts. Fisher promised to deliver the manuscript by 22 September, and insisted that publication should be less than a month later, on Trafalgar Day, 21 October. It was a formidable challenge, but after a conference with his production manager, Joseph Apted, Ernest concluded it would be possible – just.

His secretary, Sophie Hines, describes the period that followed as 'Fisher Fever'. 'Probably no book has ever caused more excitement and thrills in the quiet and orderly routine of St Paul's House than the publication of Lord Fisher's *Memories*', she wrote, adding, 'It seemed as if the fiery temperament of the author had been in some way responsible for this state of affairs.' Ernest and the admiral had never met, and Lord Fisher decided to write up his life while a guest of the Duchess of Hamilton at her family seat in Scotland. 'Telegrams and express letters seemed to arrive almost every hour' from Strathaven, Sophie Hines remembered. Ernest estimated that 'over a thousand words of instructions, exhortations, protestations, and, I am pleased to remember, congratulations reached this office within the space of a few weeks.'

The book had to be carefully read for libel, and Ernest worked hard to make it publishable, cutting some of the stories and cleaning up the language. 'Any . . . fool can be a general, but it takes a . . . genius to be admiral' was one of the sentences that went. 'I shall probably get a most blasphemous letter from Lord Fisher when he sees what we've cut,' Ernest remarked. When it became apparent that there was too much material for one book, Fisher declared he wanted what remained to be used for a second volume, which he insisted should be published in early December, on the anniversary of the defeat of the *Graf Spee* in the Falklands, thus imposing another tight deadline on the team at St Paul's House.

Ernest was as enthusiastic about marketing as he was about the editorial side of the business, and just before publication day he sent a note out to the firm's customers urging them to 'order boldly, for Lord Fisher's *Memories* is going to sell BIG.' He was, he wrote 'too old a hand in publishing to prophesy as a rule, but in this case I have no hesitation in saying that our only difficulty will be in supplying demand. For Lord Fisher's *Memories* is going to be talked about and discussed from one end of the country to the other within a few hours of its publication. "Oh, did you see that perfectly priceless story about King Edward in Lord Fisher's *Memories*?" – "What did you think of Lord Fisher on Winston Churchill?" – that is the kind of question that will be asked at a thousand dinner tables next week. You know what publicity like that means for a book.'

And he showed some style in the way he handled his irascible author; Ernest had the first copies sent to Scotland by 'aeroplane post' – a novel service at the time – and arranged with the Duchess of Hamilton that one of them should be placed on the admiral's bedside table before he awoke on Trafalgar Day. The book was of course recommended to readers of the *British Weekly*; William Robertson Nicoll described its author as 'the very incarnation of force'.

Lord Fisher was suitably impressed, and when he finally met Ernest – for lunch at the duchess's London home in St James's Square – he presented him with a bunch of red roses. Ernest had the blooms pressed and preserved in an envelope at St Paul's House, and remarked after the lunch that Fisher was 'a little difficult, especially after champagne, but he did not swear once'. The episode formed the basis of an unlikely friendship. Fisher later sent Ernest a card that he had 'washed over with paint, apparently from some playroom paint box', with a message to say that it was the colour of his favourite rose, the beautiful deep-pink climber Zephirine Drouhin. He offered to send Ernest a dozen plants for his garden.

In the midst of 'Fisher Fever' the country was paralysed by a strike by the National Union of Railwaymen. Ernest reacted as if he were fighting a military campaign. He laid in supplies of Burgundy and brandy at St Paul's House – which must have made his teetotal Hodder and Williams forebears turn in their graves – and organised fleets of cars to bring staff into the office. He was determined that the *British Weekly* should be published as usual, so he hired a 'chara-banc' to take copies to Manchester, and flew a set of proofs to Edinburgh – again using the new 'aeroplane post' – so that a Scottish edition could be printed and distributed.

Throughout this period, he was suffering chronic toothache, which meant that he had to visit the dentist almost every day. And somehow or other he found time to court a new wife; he married Lilian Pakeman, the daughter of a City friend, in 1920. In the Hodder archive the marriage is marked by another glimpse of Ernest the dandy; it was said that Robert Sare, a senior member of staff who had worked for the company since Matthew Hodder's days, was asked by Ernest on the day of his wedding 'to go round to Hope Bros in the Old Bailey and buy him two sets of the best silk underwear he could get'. Ernest and Lilian made their London home in Cadogan Place, in Chelsea, and bought a farmhouse near Crowborough.

Given the pace of his life, it is unsurprising that some of Ernest's decisions seem to have been made almost in the spirit of a gambler. In 1920, Robert Sare (of the silk underwear incident) suggested that Ernest should consider buying the business of Wakely and Son (1912) Ltd, which published the medical journal the *Lancet*. Ernest immediately agreed – with the proviso that Sare himself should run the operation – and the paper remained part of the Hodder stable for more than seventy years.

The same year the firm published the first of Sapper's Bulldog Drummond adventures. The eponymous hero is sometimes compared to James Bond, and it is true that, like Bond, he had a gentleman's tastes, with bachelor rooms in Mayfair's Half Moon Street, a servant called James and a '30 h.p. two-seater [that] made short work of the run to Godalming'. But put aside thoughts of a well-groomed Roger Moore in a white dinner jacket; Bulldog Drummond was, as his name suggests, a rather more straightforward and sometimes brutal fellow. Proudly boneheaded and determinedly anti-intellectual, he had unconventional skills honed in night forays from the trenches in France, where he served with the brilliantly named 'Royal Loamshire Regiment'; he could 'move over ground without a single blade of grass rustling' and 'kill a man with his bare hands in a second'.

Drummond was not overly fond of foreigners, and reading the early stories today is not always a comfortable experience. But he had a long and productive life, selling nearly 400,000 books between 1920 and 1939. McNeile (Sapper) made him the hero of ten novels, four short stories and four stage plays before his death in 1937. The irrepressible Drummond survived his creator, and the last Bulldog novel, *Some Girls Do*, by Henry Reymond, came out in 1969.

In 1921 the literary agency A. P. Watt brought Ernest one of his most profitable authors. Alexander Watt had discovered that the prolific Edgar Wallace – he had already written nearly thirty novels by this stage – had been selling his books outright for £70 or £80 apiece. Alexander and Ernest already had a strong business relationship, and the two men had been part of that close-knit circle involved in the Wellington House propaganda operation during the Great War. They very quickly agreed a six-book contract, which would pay Wallace a royalty advance of £250 on delivery of each book.

The deal transformed Wallace's fortunes, as the writer himself readily admitted. Wallace's biographer, Margaret Lane, credits

Ernest with a 'prophetic instinct which told him that this none too successful man, already nearing his fifties, had the makings of one of the great popular entertainers of all time'. Ernest's strategy, she wrote, was to push for 'quantity rather than quality, quantity that would flood the reading market and penetrate to levels which had not been reached before to bring entertainment, excitement and pleasure within the grasp of a vast public of which publishers had never dreamed'.

Ernest believed Wallace worked best at 'white heat'. The writer had a taste for good living and especially for gambling, and he was chronically haunted by debt. He could also work at incredible speed, dictating his stories onto wax cylinders and having them typed up by secretaries. He would sometimes work flat out for seventy-two hours, and it was said that he could finish a book in two or three days. A popular story had it that callers who telephoned his home would offer to hold if they were told he was 'engaged, writing a new serial'.

All this made him highly susceptible to the lure of the advance. John Attenborough has a good anecdote about one of the Hodder-Williams brothers trying to draw up his list; he 'asked Ernest if he knew anything about the new Wallace. "No," replied Ernest, "but it's the St Leger meeting at Doncaster this week so you are bound to receive something after the weekend." True to form, Edgar entered St Paul's House the following Tuesday, slapped his new typescript onto Ernest's desk and, fitting a cigarette into the famous cigarette-holder, made his invariable speech: "And that, Hodder-Williams, is the best novel I have ever written."'

The arrival of royalty cheques was a constant source of pleasure to Wallace; 'Until I came to you I had never seen a royalty cheque', he wrote to Ernest, and, in another letter, 'I am living on bread and raw apples until my royalty cheques come in.' Ernest managed to extract forty-six books in ten years from Edgar Wallace, and the worldwide sales ran into the millions. At home

Ernest sent placards out to bookshops bearing the bold legend: 'MAKE THIS YEAR AN EDGAR WALLACE YEAR'.

Both Sapper and Edgar Wallace made many of their sales in the firm's famous Yellow Jackets. Ernest's younger brother Percy was responsible for much of the design work on the series, but the inspiration behind it was Ernest's own. These cheap, mass-produced books, with low-quality paper and small print, were the antithesis of sumptuous pre-war volumes like the Dulac *Omar Khayyam*, and it is another mark of Ernest's flair that one publishing mind could have pioneered such very different formats.

The use of yellow to define the brand was an inspiration with a long cultural pedigree. According to Thomas Abraham, a Hodder employee who has amassed a significant collection of Yellow Jackets, 'French publishers wrapped "sensational" books in yellow wrappers to single out their sensational and/or lascivious content – a clear and in-your-face commercial and mass market statement.' In Victorian Britain the colour was similarly associated with the 'penny dreadful', and thrillers like Wilkie Collins' *The Woman in White* were printed with yellow wrappers. In the 1890s *The Yellow Book* quarterly came to be associated with figures like Oscar Wilde and Aubrey Beardsley (the magazine's first art editor) and their reputation for decadence, and the period was sometimes referred to as the 'Yellow Decade' because of the influence of wicked Parisian culture.

Ernest's Yellow Jackets foreshadowed the Penguin paperback revolution. There were two series; the first ran from 1923 until it was interrupted by the outbreak of war in 1939, and the brand was reintroduced in 1949, surviving, in a very different publishing environment, until 1957. Romances, westerns and thrillers were the staple, and many of the authors published in the format have faded into that sad literary Hades reserved for last year's best beach books. But some of them have survived – Conan Doyle, Baroness Orczy (of *Scarlet Pimpernel* fame) and Rider Haggard all had their books published in the series.

The Yellow Jackets were so successful that they qualify as a cultural phenomenon; John Attenborough, who belonged to the generation of readers who grew up with them, looked back at the Yellow Jacket years with nostalgia; 'what memories they conjure up for those who first met them in the days of their youth', he wrote in his history of Hodder & Stoughton, 'when the cinema was one colour only, when there were no "talkies", no technicolor, no television! What pleasure they gave to their generation! And – let a publisher-author make the point – how loyal they [the authors] were to those who sponsored their work in Warwick Square and "out on the road".'

Thomas Abraham believes Hodder & Stoughton was the first house to 'institutionalise' the use of yellow in this way, and he notes that the Italian imprint Mondadori soon followed Hodder's example, publishing 'adventure thrillers and crime fiction' in a series that became known as '*i libri gialli*', or 'the yellow books'. The phrase, he writes, later became synonymous in Italy with mass-market, popular literature.

Sharp-eyed readers will have noticed that we have heard nothing about the Stoughton part of the partnership for a while. John Stoughton, Thomas's elder son, never settled into the firm and left to pursue a career as a country solicitor before the First World War. Cecil, the founding partner's second son, was said to be 'handsome and easy of address . . . to the manner born'. But he left in 1923, and there is a sad piece of social history behind his departure: Cecil was almost certainly gay.

John Attenborough, writing in the 1970s, could only hint at this apparently troubling information. 'As a bookman wealthy enough to "do his own thing", he [Cecil] preferred the leisure of the dilettante to the hectic activity of the publisher's life,' he wrote in *A Living Memory*. 'At the end of 1923 he retired to Downlands, Guildford, where he lived with his friend C. A. Williamson of George Bell and Sons [a now defunct publishing house] for the next forty years.'

The Hodder archives contain a franker interview with a member of a later generation of the Stoughton family, a Dr Raymond Stoughton, who said that 'Cecil's very strict parents disapproved of his relationship with Williamson, to whom he left everything in his will', adding that 'this was probably of a homosexual nature and may have been the reason for Cecil's retirement in 1923.' Dr Stoughton insisted that he 'never heard Cecil say anything but good about the firm, of which he was very proud; he spoke with great admiration of Sir Ernest . . .' But Ernest's secretary, writing of her boss in the early 1920s, described him as a 'genuine and rigid puritan', which suggests that the relationship may not have been entirely easy. In his retirement Cecil hired a herald from the College of Arms to study his family tree, and his researches 'established beyond doubt that the STOAT pronunciation of his surname is correct'. That legacy was the last Stoughton contribution to the life of the firm.

In a letter to his younger brother Ralph, who had returned to academic life in Canada after the Great War, Ernest mentioned that 'Cecil Stoughton is not very robust', and, clearly sensing that the last Stoughton partner might soon leave, urged Ralph to 'come back and enter the family business'. Ralph was well established in his new home; at thirty-three he was married with a young daughter, and had built a successful career at the University of Toronto, where he was an Associate Professor of History. But Ernest persuaded him that his future lay at St Paul's House, and in August 1923 he and his family settled in London.

1923 was a watershed year; it also saw the death of Ernest's old friend and mentor William Robertson Nicoll. Nicoll ended his life loaded with honours and recognition; he became a Companion of Honour for Services to Literature in 1921, and the guest list for his seventieth birthday party that year was glittering; Lloyd George proposed a toast to 'one of his oldest and most valued friends', and a heady mixture of cabinet ministers, writers (John Buchan, Arthur Conan Doyle and J. M. Barrie among them) and aristocrats (including the Duchess of Hamilton, who had proved such an important Hodder ally during 'Fisher Fever') gathered in the Hyde Park Hotel for the reception. Nicoll fell ill in the spring of 1923; he continued to work, and in March began one of the 'Claudius Clear' columns on literary matters that he had been writing since the early days of the *British Weekly*. But he could not finish it, and the work had to be taken over by Jane Stoddart. He died on 4 May.

By the time of William Robertson Nicoll's death Ernest had been working in publishing for nearly thirty years, most of them at the top of the profession. He was still an innovator in the 1920s, and eagerly embraced new technology. Hodder experimented with 'Bubble books', which were sold with a gramophone record, and Ernest recruited John Reith, head of the newly founded BBC, to the Hodder list. The *British Weekly* published an article on 'The Church and the Wireless', ruminating on the opportunities for evangelism offered by the new medium of radio.

But Ernest's literary judgement had been formed by the Victorian world in which he had grown up, and the evangelical spirit of departed patriarchs – Matthew Hodder, the YMCA founder George Williams and, now, William Robertson Nicoll – ran deep within his soul. As jazz, flappers and the Charleston invaded British life this 'genuine and rigid puritan' found his tastes increasingly at odds with the age.

His secretary, Sophie Hines, reported that after reading *Penny Plain* by Anna Buchan (John's sister, and a writer Ernest published and usually admired) he commented, 'It may be old-fashioned and sentimental, but the more I read of this modern stuff, the more old-fashioned and sentimental I become.' And when laying out his ideas about his profession to an audience of publishers he conceded that 'You cannot expect the public to view matters of sex, for instance, as they did before the war', but insisted 'there are healthy as well as unhealthy books which treat matters of sex.

You know which are which: so do I.' Britain had been profoundly changed by the great struggle of 1914–18, and Ernest suddenly found himself on the front line of what today we would call a 'culture war'.

His defining battle was fought over a novel called *The Green Hat*. The book, by Michael Arlen, contains nothing that could remotely be described as explicit sex, but its central character would have been very shocking indeed to the *milieu* in which Ernest now moved. The aristocratic Iris March – who first turns up late at night in the then louche London area of Shepherd's Market, wearing the eponymous hat – is a class traitor and a femme fatale. She has a fast car, and an even faster reputation – she is widely suspected of stealing husbands and ruining men.

We get to know her in a set-piece scene when she settles into the narrator's drawing room for a literary conversation. Her views are iconoclastic, and she takes a swipe at the alleged anti-Semitism of G. K. Chesterton: 'Jews', she declares, 'are the last towers of chivalry. Mr Chesterton goes running after them shouting about beer and the Pope, but if you are going to leave chivalry to beer drinkers and the Pope, God help enchantment.' This occurs early in the book, and we can imagine Ernest's reaction to this casual swatting of his old friend.

The denouement occurs in the library of a country house, to which Iris is summoned by a group of stuffed-shirted men who are made – none too subtly – to stand for the pre-war Establishment. They are determined to frustrate her latest romantic adventure, which they believe to be immoral. But in a dramatic narrative twist it emerges that she has, in fact, behaved with heroic decency all along, and is the book's true moral heart. The pre-war morality of her self-appointed judges is shown up as empty hypocrisy.

Since it is unlikely that many of today's readers will struggle through the now-dated prose to reach this point, I shall risk a spoiler; having demonstrated her generosity of spirit, Iris removes herself from the scene by deliberately driving her car into a large tree where she played as a child with her true love. In a most enjoyable period detail, the tree had been nicknamed 'Harrods' by the young lovers. *The Green Hat* is one of those books that succeeded because it captured the mood of a moment, not because of its merits as a novel. It was published in Britain by Collins in 1924.

George Doran, who described the book as 'the first of modern novels with a nymphomaniac as a heroine', had already begun publishing Arlen's novels and was delighted by the controversy that greeted *The Green Hat*. 'The banning of *The Green Hat* by the libraries gave it a much greater sale and circulation than otherwise it might have achieved', he wrote. 'The repercussions of all this reached America, and . . . prepared the way for a really sensational sale of *The Green Hat*.' The book became a craze in the United States, inspiring 'Iris March hats, green of course, Iris March gowns, and Iris March this's and that's, all of which worked no damage to the sale of the book, which, after all, was merely a clever *tour de force* and never for a moment presented Arlen at his best.' Even better, Doran reported, 'it got me into the newspapers and trouble – not too much trouble, but enough. *The Green Hat* easily sold 250,000 copies in America alone.'

By an unfortunate coincidence, Doran was also pushing sales of one of the heavy-hitters on the Hodder religious list, the *Translation of the New Testament into Modern English* by the distinguished Scottish scholar James Moffat, one of William Robertson Nicoll's recruits to the Hodder & Stoughton family. While doing business with a Canadian colleague Doran was challenged to say whether he thought *The Green Hat* 'a book suited to the Christian home', and he admitted that 'at times I feel the slightest shade of embarrassment in going forth with Michael Arlen's *The Green Hat* in one hand and Moffat's New Testament in the other'. He justified his position by comparing it to the servants of the British Crown 'going to China with the opium of India in one hand and the products of the British and Foreign Bible Society in the other'.

Hodder & Stoughton still owned a third of Doran's company, and Ernest did not find the position at all funny. Those over-bearing men who confronted Iris March over their bridge and whisky and soda at the climax of *The Green Hat* could have been his friends. At their next meeting the two men argued the toss for an hour, and although they seem to have parted as friends, it was clear their houses were heading in opposite directions. Doran bought the Hodder & Stoughton share in his firm, at a price that represented a 400% return on Hodder's original investment.

Sir Ernest Hodder-Williams died of a heart attack in April 1927; he was only fifty. George Doran called him a 'ten-talent man', who had lived 'more than a century of progress' in his relatively short span. Doran judged that 'more than any other publisher of his time, Sir Ernest left upon his chosen profession the imprint of a great and constructive personality'. Walter Newman Flower (later Sir Walter, and the chairman of Cassells) echoed that praise; 'Ernest Hodder-Williams was unquestionably a great publisher', he wrote in an obituary. 'He knew exactly what he wanted; he knew with more accuracy than most what the public wanted. He had his ideas and the courage of them.'

In his own writing Flower liked to tidy up the truth a bit; he edited the journals of Arnold Bennett, and was criticised for what another writer called his 'prudish timidity' in the way he did it. Both Flower and Ernest belonged to a generation for whom publishing – though it could be fun – must have a moral and, as Ernest clearly felt during the Great War, patriotic core. Hodder & Stoughton stands out in the publishing world because of the way, for good or ill, that ethos endured; as we shall see, Ernest's influence was felt right up to the Chatterley trial and beyond, and the late-Victorian ideas that formed him were still a living memory in the 1960s.

Flower's obituary for Ernest continued: 'He would not publish questionable books even if he knew – as he must have known many times, and often when such books were offered to him – that certain works would make big money for him. He kept his publishing business *clean*, and made it a great business by sheer business cleverness without smirch. He has left the escutcheon of Hodder and Stoughton high in honour.'

10

Not the done thing

The year of Ernest's death was also the first year the firm's annual sports day was run by the new Hodder & Stoughton Sports Club in Bickley. Ernest's brothers Percy and Ralph were the patrons, and they contributed a suitably uplifting introduction to the day's race card: 'We cannot isolate ourselves: we must be friendly;' it reads, 'we have to remember that happiness is a duty we owe to others as well as ourselves. The Club affords the proof that we can play together just as well as we can work together and it is going to give us many more opportunities of demonstrating the fact that the greatest happiness is the ability to make others happy.'

The sports day programme was larger and more formal than it had been in the days when Matthew Hodder presided over these outings in Egham. It included tennis and cricket, and there was more for female members of staff, including a ladies fireman's lift – which sounds almost risqué – and a ladies egg-and-spoon race. The book prizes had been replaced by rewards that reflected changing tastes: handbags and manicure sets for the ladies, tobacco pouches, cigar trays and cigarette lighters for the gents.

But the sense of continuity with the past is strong. The Sports Club was based in the area of Bromley where Ernest made his first married home, and the evening's dinner dance was held at the St Luke's Institute, attached to the parish church where Matthew Hodder's funeral was held on Bromley Common. The fare was still wholesome – 'Rolls and Butter, Fruit Salad, Jellies, Cream, Fancy Pastries' – and the teetotal tradition seems to have survived.

Even the facetious humour had endured; there was space at the back of the day's programme for 'Recording heroic athletic successes, and also for chronicling the grouses, excuses and general misery of competitors, who through misfortune, slow motion, anno domini, avoir du pois or what not, did not scurry past the other fellows.' And some wag had contributed a ditty for the dinner menu cards in the form of a quiz:

Did You Know?

Is Warwick Square?
Why did Paternoster Row?
Why was Ludgate (H)ill?
Who wore Bartholomew's Close?
When Farringdon Road why did Birdcage Walk?

The fortieth-anniversary edition of the *British Weekly*, which came out the previous year, conveys a similar sense of continuity. The front page quoted the editorial manifesto of the very first edition – beginning: 'We are believers in Progress because we are believers in the advancing reign of Christ' – and declared, 'After forty years we stand by the same Belief and the same Hope of Progress.' The contents page includes many names that would have been familiar to the magazine's regular subscribers, including J. M. Barrie and Jane Stoddart, who was still serving faithfully as deputy editor.

David Lloyd George penned a piece on the need for the Liberal Party to renew itself – just as William Robertson Nicoll had dilated on the same subject in the first issue of the magazine four decades earlier. Annie Swan was there too, writing on 'The New Drift in Fiction', which she heartily deplored. 'During the last five years the drift in modern fiction has become very pronounced,' she declared, 'and not in a direction likely either to improve taste or steady the morals of this generation.' She condemned popular novels as 'Pernicious stuff taking the bloom off youth and thrusting into undue prominence that which has its proper place in the scheme of things and should be rigidly assigned to it.'

The paper still reported stories such as the 'Autumnal Meetings of the London Congregational Union'. The *Table Talk* section relayed holiday correspondence from distinguished churchmen on their travels through Europe, and the successes of the bazaar to raise funds for Paddington Chapel. Advertisers who had been taking space continuously in the magazine since its foundation were rewarded with a star next to their copy; the Shaftesbury Society, soliciting donations for 'London's Poorest Children', and McVitie and Price's, plugging 'Genuine Scotch Shortbread', were among those so honoured.

Percy and Ralph Hodder-Williams, 'The Brothers', as they became known, were comfortable in the past. Percy had already put in thirty years with the firm by the time of Ernest's death, and John Attenborough represents him as the ideal second-in-command, 'quietly rejecting Ernest's bad ideas and setting the good ones in motion, the perfect interpreter of genius'. He became chairman, and moved into the office where Matthew Hodder and Thomas Stoughton had once sat across their desks from one another. From here, he and Ralph ruled as a diarchy; Percy would announce his decisions with the phrase 'My brother and I have decided . . .'

Their routine would have sat comfortably in the Victorian world of the original partners. The morning was spent opening correspondence – Percy wearing gloves – and, with the assistance of a group of loyal secretaries, sorting it into baskets that were distributed by 'boys' to the relevant departments. It was, John Attenborough recorded, a 'woefully slow process', but one which ensured that 'the brothers were remarkably well informed about every facet of the business'.

After this ritual, by Attenborough's account, 'Percy expatiated on the state of the family, the business and the nation while Ralph urged him to get a move on. Out in the corridor printers' representatives waited hopefully for their orders.' At 11.30 a.m. the two men dictated their own letters 'in a sort of harmonious duet to a battery of secretaries'. Lunch, at which they were some-times joined by the editor of the *British Weekly* or, if he was visiting London, the biblical scholar James Moffat, was teetotal, and was followed by conversation over pipes and coffee. It gener-ally lasted from just before one until half past three. It sounds very much like the leisurely working life of Mr Jackson, whose habits the impatient Matthew Hodder had so chafed at more than half a century earlier.

But the world beyond the precincts of St Paul's had changed, and even that triumphant fortieth-anniversary edition of the *British Weekly* reflected how different it was. David Lloyd George was still a big name, but he had left office in 1922, his reputation irredeemably tarnished by his sale of honours. The Liberal Party was hopelessly split, and would never recover the pre-eminence it enjoyed in the great days of William Robertson Nicoll's editor-ship of the magazine. No Liberal leader would hold cabinet office again until Nick Clegg became David Cameron's deputy prime minister in 2010.

Nonconformism was running out of steam too. Its decline had in fact begun in the late nineteenth century, but at first it was largely masked by a growing population and the vigour of public figures like William Robertson Nicoll. Around the middle years of the first decade of the twentieth century it accelerated, and, according to Jeffrey Cox in *The English Churches in a Secular Society*, in 1906, 1907 and 1908, 'every single Nonconformist church suffered a decline'. By 1926, the year before Ernest Hodder-Williams' death, the church historian Dr Albert Peel could write that, 'It is probably true to say that the Free Churches have less political influence than at any moment during the past century, that never since the Reform Bill of 1832 [which began the process of modernising and cleaning up Britain's electoral system] has the "Nonconformist conscience" counted for so little in the counsels of the country.'

The foundations of the political and religious order that nurtured Hodder & Stoughton's early successes had been shaken by the great cataclysm of war, and by the late 1920s they had all but disappeared. Percy and Ralph's world may have looked secure from the chairman's office, but it was built on shifting sand.

The journals suffered most from the changes in taste and intellectual fashion. The biblical scholar James Moffat tried to keep Nicoll's the *Expositor* alive, but it proved too much alongside his other work, and this venerable relic of Victorian religious enthusiasm was eventually allowed to expire. A bright young literary journalist from the *Yorkshire Post*, Hugh Ross Williamson, took over the editorship of the *Bookman* in 1930, but the sales kept falling, and the magazine was sold in 1935. The *British Weekly*, with its high proportion of topical content, was especially vulnerable to the strikes that plagued the 1920s. To add to the paper's woes J. M. E. Ross, Nicoll's successor, died in 1926, just three years after taking over the editor's chair.

Jane Stoddart soldiered on as deputy editor until 1937 – notching up an astonishing half-century with the magazine – but the journal's voice was reaching a diminishing circle. Charlotte Reid, who joined the paper as a secretary in the mid-1930s, remembered it as something close to an exercise in vanity publishing, kept going largely by announcements about the doings of individual churches: 'These tiny items were our local life-blood,' she wrote, 'the paper could not have survived if churchgoers had not bought it to see the name of their church in print in our pages.' Miss Reid also wrote admiringly of Jane Stoddart's ability to 'turn out a paragraph, or a review, as quickly as she could write it down' and to 'chart theological minefields without a false step', but she described her as 'a product of a world now gone'.

There was one robust exception to the attrition of Hodder & Stoughton's standing as a publisher of journals: Ernest's gamble on the *Lancet* paid handsome dividends. Under the management of Robert Sare – whom we met briefly as the provider of Ernest's wedding-day underwear – the medical journal's sales increased steadily, and in the summer of 1929 it was able to buy its London home, a magnificent house near the Strand built by Robert Adam. The *Lancet* would remain a prized part of the Hodder & Stoughton group for another six decades.

The book publishing side of the business also remained robust in the immediate aftermath of Ernest's death; most of the authors he had signed up stayed loyal to Hodder & Stoughton, and he left a very strong stable. The firm's reputation continued to attract new authors, and at the end of the 1920s the agent Raymond Savage brought in the young Leslie Charteris.

Born Leslie Bowyer Yin – his father was a Chinese doctor and the family lived in Singapore – Charteris changed his name in 1926, after abandoning Cambridge for a writing career. The character known as the Saint, his most enduring creation, first appeared in a 1928 novel called *Meet the Tiger,* which was published by the now defunct house of Ward Lock. He said later that 'from the day he decided to be a novelist, he wanted to be one of the company of Wallace and Sapper and the yellow-jacket headliners'. His first novel with Hodder, *Meet the Saint,* came out in 1930, and in later years he sometimes identified this book rather than *Meet the Tiger* as the true beginning of the Saint series.

Simon Templar – his initials supplied his soubriquet – was a literary descendant of Bulldog Drummond and, like Drummond, a literary ancestor of James Bond. He is an English gent, a 'buccaneer in the suits of Savile Row, amused, cool, debonair, with hell-for-leather blue eyes and a saintly smile'. He operates just the wrong side of the law, but his victims are, in the best Robin Hood tradition, all villains, and their villainy changed to suit the times – international criminal masterminds and white slave traders in the 1930s gave way to Nazis in the 1940s. He had a slightly naughty Edwardian catchphrase – 'as the actress said to the bishop' – and he had, daringly for the day, a live-in girlfriend. But in every other way he was a quintessential Hodder hero.

And, like Bulldog Drummond, he had a heroically long publishing life. His creator featured him in fourteen novels, thirty-four novellas and ninety-five short stories. Charteris himself stopped writing Saint books in the 1960s and died in 1993, but his hero was kept alive by a number of other writers, and in the early 1990s one of them, Burl Barer, published a history of the character's many incarnations in books, on radio and television and in films. The *Saintly Bible* website lists Hodder & Stoughton as the first-edition British publisher of all Saint books published between 1930 and 1983, and the firm republished the original books in a new edition in 2013.

But even the miraculously popular Saint could not altogether insulate the firm from the impact of the Great Depression, the worldwide economic crisis that began after the American stock market crash in the autumn of 1929. Britain began to feel the full impact in 1931. Unemployment in the United Kingdom hit twenty per cent that year, and exports fell by half. In 1933 thirty per cent of Glaswegians were unemployed, and in some areas of the north-east of England the figure was as high as seventy per cent.

The book trade was not hit anything like as hard as heavy industry, but that backdrop makes it unsurprising that people were spending less on reading. The value of Hodder's trade book sales fell from £637,770 in 1928 to £552,330 in 1935. By 1935 the firm's turnover was £381,477, and at the outbreak of war in 1939 it had sunk to £289,375, less than half what it had been ten years earlier.

Percy Hodder-Williams managed to find one silver lining in the storm clouds of the Depression – the general fall in property prices allowed him to buy the freehold on the firm's premises at

St Paul's House and Little St Paul's House. But John Attenborough, in his official company history, lays some of the blame for the company's woes at the door of Percy and his brother Ralph. 'The innate shyness of the two brothers conspired to leave them out of touch with the trends of literary and popular taste', he wrote, adding that 'They disliked literary parties in London and were both conspicuous by their absence.' Ernest, by contrast, had been anything but shy and was completely confident in his ability to shape and lead literary trends. Attenborough quotes Ernest's publishing principles – 'Hard work; publish what interests the public; study the newspapers; "travel" books yourself' – and judges that the brothers 'most faithfully observed the first of these principles, but at the expense of the other three'.

The regular visits to the United States and Canada, which had been such a feature of the way both Matthew Hodder and Ernest ran the business, simply stopped – even though Ralph Hodder-Williams had connections in North America through his wife's family and from his years as an academic there. Neither brother visited the new Hodder operations that Ernest had established in South Africa, New Zealand and Australia, and – an especially damning piece of evidence from John Attenborough, this – 'neither brother was ever known to talk with a bookseller inside his shop'.

And the Grim Reaper was thinning Ernest's magnificent list of authors. Edgar Wallace died in 1932 after a characteristically flamboyant final flourish. In the British General Election the previous year he had stood as an Independent Liberal, lost heavily and headed for Hollywood in the hope of paying off yet another set of debts. In December he began work on the movie classic *King Kong*, creating the storyline with the American film-maker Merian C. Cooper and contributing the famous Empire State Building scene, but he was diagnosed with diabetes in January 1932, caught double pneumonia and expired in February. Sapper died of cancer in 1937 – just short of his fiftieth birthday

– while working on a Bulldog Drummond play. John Buchan lived until 1940, but in 1935 he was created Lord Tweedsmuir and disappeared to serve as governor general of Canada.

Some of the stalwarts of the very early days were also disappearing from the scene. Cuthbert Huckvale, the king of the counting house, who joined in 1873, died in 1927. In an obituary in the *British Weekly*, Percy Hodder-Williams praised him in terms that Matthew Hodder and Thomas Stoughton would have appreciated: Huckvale was, he wrote, 'a good man and a straight guide. All his life he tramped the high path of duty and surely that was his reward in death – "for duty is the great mountain road to God."'

Joseph Apted, who joined the same year as Huckvale and had shown his mettle as a production manager so impressively during 'Fisher Fever', lasted five years longer, dying in 1932. Percy reminisced that 'When I first met him, as a boy, he was a confidential clerk in a little glass corridor behind a pigeon hole through which Mr Hodder and Mr Stoughton issued their instructions. When I last saw him in town (59 years later) . . . he was sitting beside his two directors (one of whom – and his chairman at that – he had trained as a boy) opening the morning mail.' Robert Sare went in 1929; he was only fifty, Ernest's age at the time of his death two years earlier, and Attenborough reports speculation that 'he died of a broken heart, for he had truly been Sir Ernest's shadow towards the end'.

But Percy and Ralph could still count on a deep well of loyalty to the firm's founding family, and Ernest's protégés continued to deliver the kind of results it needed to survive the 1930s. William Smart, who as a young man left such a touching account of Matthew Hodder's last days, had been sent to Australia by Ernest in 1921, and became a legendary figure on the Australian market. He spent six months of the year travelling across Australia and New Zealand accompanied by a vast 'sample room' of books, which was moved from one town or city to the next in ten great hampers on wheels. 'Everybody knew him,' writes Attenborough, 'a tough little man with twinkling eyes, dressed in a brown suit and waistcoat (however hot the day), smoking continuously, completely teetotal, every bookseller's friend.'

Pre-war Australia was even more dependent on British writers for its entertainment and education than the United States had been in the nineteenth century; eighty per cent of books in Australia came from the United Kingdom, and some two million were shipped out each year. During the 1930s and 40s Australia was, according to Valerie Holman in her study of wartime publishing, *Print for Victory,* 'by far the largest overseas market for British newspapers, periodicals and books, accounting for 25 percent of total exports'. In 1935 the United Kingdom exported £882,366 worth of books to Australia, more than twice the figure for the next largest market, the United States.

And the 'fantastic physical feat' of Smart's annual sales odysseys made Hodder pre-eminent 'down under'. Most Australian readers wanted cheap fiction, and the 'Yellow Jacket' list, with its adventure stories, mysteries and thrillers, was well placed to meet the demand. Hodder's prominence in Australia was reflected in traffic coming the other way too: in the 1920s the firm established itself as the leading publisher of Australian novels in London.

The tradition of recruiting from religious organisations continued to supply the firm with fresh talent. In 1922 R. J. Davis (the hero of *One Young Man*) and the religious adviser, Arthur Hird, hired an eighteen-year-old called Leonard Cutts, whom they had come to know through the Brotherhood movement, an early-twentieth-century organisation dedicated to applying Christian principles to society. When Hird died Cutts took over responsibility for the – still important – religious list, and by the mid-1930s he was part of the Brothers' inner circle. Michael Attenborough, a member of the Hodder tribe (he was John's son) and, many years later, managing director of the firm, described Cutts to me as 'the family's faithful Labrador', and he has a prominent place in company folklore.

Like most Labradors, Cutts had, as Attenborough readily acknowledged, a good nose, and he was responsible for one of the few real publishing coups of the 1930s. In 1933 he bought *Goodbye Mr Chips* from his friend James Hilton for the Christmas edition of the *British Weekly*. The story – a sentimental account of the life of a schoolmaster at a minor British public school – is more of a novella than a full-length novel, and it was reprinted in the American magazine the *Atlantic Monthly*. It proved popular, and that prompted the American firm Little, Brown and Company to bring it out in book form that summer. The initial run was small, but the book sold so quickly that Little, Brown soon found themselves issuing two reprints a month.

Only then did Hodder follow their lead; the British edition came out in October 1934, and sold 15,000 copies on the first day it went on sale. The review in *Punch* must have raised a cheer in Warwick Square: 'One lays down the book with the satisfaction that comes from contemplation of works supremely well-done,' the magazine declared. 'This is too good a book to be borrowed – it should be bought.'

However much Percy and Ralph Hodder-Williams may have valued employees like William Smart, R. J. Davis (who became company secretary in 1926) and Leonard Cutts, these men were not members of the family, and the Brothers saw Hodder & Stoughton as very much a family business. Ernest had left no children, and Percy's marriage was also childless until he and his wife adopted a son in 1925. Ralph, the youngest of the Ernest generation, had one son, but he was an infant at the time of Ernest's death. So in 1928 the Brothers turned to their nephews – as Matthew Hodder had done three decades earlier – as they planned for the company's future. Paul Hodder-Williams, the son of the one brother of Ernest's generation who had not joined the firm, was recruited along with John Attenborough, the son of one of Ernest's three sisters, and author of the official company history from which I have often quoted.

There is a personal edge to some of John Attenborough's criticisms of the way his uncles ran the business. As the evidence of Hitler's aggressive intentions increased in the mid-1930s, he picked up a tip that the *Daily Telegraph*'s Vienna correspondent, G. E. R. Gedye, wanted to write about what the Nazis were doing in Austria. Gedye had a good track record and had already brought out four books about Austria – so Attenborough rang him in Vienna, and commissioned a book over the telephone, a rather more glamorous way to conduct business in the 1930s than it would be today. The Watt agency, Hodder's long-standing partners, tied up the details.

The typescript was 'written at white heat' (the book is dedicated apologetically to 'Somebody's Summer Holiday and Somebody's Week-Ends . . . the ready sacrifice of which alone enabled me to write this book'), and it opens with a dramatic description of a Nazi rally in the aftermath of the *Anschluss*, the German annexation of Austria, in the spring of 1938. Describing the crowd chanting '*Sieg Heil*' to Hitler, Gedye writes, 'In these regimented shouts was all the soul of the Nazi movement – the militarisation of enthusiasm, the herd instinct, the mob spirit, the threatening, jubilant fanaticism of men who had surrendered gladly every iota of individuality to idolatrous worship of the man addressing them in terms of extravagant self-praise.' Gedye was, among other things, the only journalist to have succeeded in persuading the Nazi authorities to allow him visit the pre-war concentration camp at Dachau, and the way he mixes personal testimony and political analysis makes the book a fine piece of journalism. It was a prescient warning about Nazi ambitions.

The text was, however, extremely critical of Neville Chamberlain's policy of appeasement, and in particular of the prime minister's actions during the Munich crisis in the autumn of 1938, when Britain and France agreed that Hitler should be

Edgar Wallace worked best at 'white heat', dictating his stories onto wax cylinders.

' "Put your hands on the table – both of you," snapped Drummond'. Sapper's hero sold hundreds of thousands of books, made it into motion pictures and long outlived his creator.

Percy Hodder–Williams ruled with his brother Ralph after Ernest's early death.

Cecil, the last of the Stoughtons, who 'established beyond doubt the STOAT pronunciation of his surname'

Ralph in uniform; decorated during the Battle of the Somme in 1916, he rose to senior rank in the Home Guard during World War II.

The Yellow Jackets were a cultural phenomenon, treasured by a generation as their source of adventure and excitement in the days before television.

Leonard Cutts, a faithful servant of the family firm whose publishing nose brought Hodder *Goodbye Mr Chips.*

The classic novel of school life

JAMES HILTON

Goodbye Mr Chips

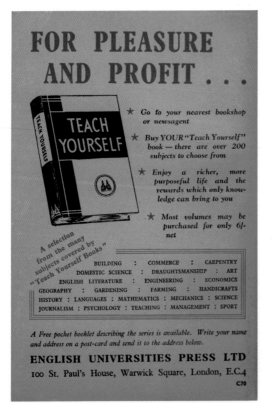

FOR PLEASURE
AND PROFIT . . .

TEACH YOURSELF

★ Go to your nearest bookshop or newsagent

★ Buy YOUR "Teach Yourself" book — there are over 200 subjects to choose from

★ Enjoy a richer, more purposeful life and the rewards which only knowledge can bring to you

★ Most volumes may be purchased for only 6/- net

A selection from the many subjects covered by "Teach Yourself Books"

BUILDING : COMMERCE : CARPENTRY
DOMESTIC SCIENCE : DRAUGHTSMANSHIP : ART
ENGLISH LITERATURE : ENGINEERING : ECONOMICS
GEOGRAPHY : GARDENING : FARMING : HANDICRAFTS
HISTORY : LANGUAGES : MATHEMATICS : MECHANICS : SCIENCE
JOURNALISM : PSYCHOLOGY : TEACHING : MANAGEMENT : SPORT

A Free pocket booklet describing the series is available. Write your name and address on a post-card and send it to the address below.

ENGLISH UNIVERSITIES PRESS LTD
100 St. Paul's House, Warwick Square, London, E.C.4
C70

Cutts was part of the team behind the *Teach Yourself* series – 'perspicacious and pertinacious impresarios', in the words of one *TY* author.

TEACH YOURSELF

TO FLY

SQUADRON LEADER
NIGEL TANGYE
R.A.F.O.

No subject, it seems, was beyond
TY's ambition.

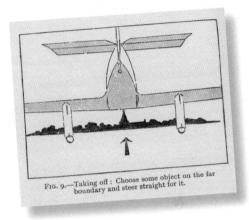

FIG. 9.—Taking off : Choose some object on the far boundary and steer straight for it.

Some of the squadron leader's 'clear
diagrams' might be misinterpreted.

Building instruction proved
popular after the Blitz.

TEACH YOURSELF BUILDING
GENERAL EDITOR· E.G.WARLAND

ROOFING

J.LEE

TEACH YOURSELF

**GOOD
MANNERS**

The classic
guide to
etiquette

W.S. NORMAN

A timeless classic – this TY title first
appeared in 1958 and was reissued
with this cover nearly sixty years later.

The spirit of George Williams' YMCA endured; the first Hodder sports day was held when Edward VII was on the throne, and the tradition continued until the year of the first manned space mission to orbit the moon.

Messrs. HODDER &
STOUGHTON'S
STAFF

Annual Excursion

SATURDAY
JULY 8, 1905
TO
EGHAM

All to meet at Waterloo Station
at 9.40 a.m.
On arrival at Egham, walk through
Town to a Marquee on Runnymede

Sports Programme

We have decided to pay everybody on the staff full wages this week. Your usual weekly wage is therefore enclosed.

If you are on active service, either in the Forces or on full-time Civil Defence, you will naturally come off our pay-roll for the time being, from now on.

We shall be glad, however, if you will kindly fill in the form attached, so that we may have all particulars before us as we wish to keep in touch.

While it is impossible to foresee the future, we shall most certainly give first consideration at the close of hostilities to all those who were, at the outbreak of the War, members of our staff.

May God defend the right.

R Percy Hodder Williams
Chairman

Sept. 1939
Outbreak of War

Hodder goes to war – and Percy rallies the home front.

The firm's first contribution to the war effort: 'In the first few months of our evacuation, our lives revolved round the QBRC' wrote a staff member.

FROM THE ORIGINAL BY EDMUND DULAC

"It is the evil things that we shall be fighting against"

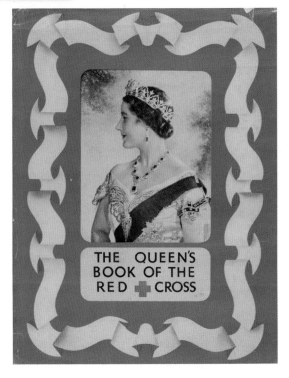

THE QUEEN'S BOOK OF THE RED ✚ CROSS

With contributions from a stellar list of authors and artists – this is by Edmund Dulac – it was a remarkable production achievement in wartime conditions.

St Paul's House was left standing when most of the publishing world was wiped out by German bombers in December 1940.

An emergency warehouse at the Old Bailey; paper shortages made it impossible to satisfy demand.

cross into swastika?

A Hodder & Stoughton pamphlet on the spiritual issues of the war

The government line looked less like propaganda when published under the Hodder banner.

allowed to occupy German-speaking areas of Czechoslovakia – known as the Sudetenland – in return for what turned out to be a short-lived 'peace in our time'. Gedye accused the prime minister of the 'complete betrayal of Czechoslovakia to Germany', and wrote that in Prague people told him, 'Chamberlain has just played a clever hand against us, with the unfriendliness towards our nation and the affection for Herr Hitler that in our hearts we had always expected.' The book, he wrote, expressed 'what the Austrians and Czechs sold to fascism felt and suffered, but under the thumb of Hitler, under the threat of the concentration camp could not say themselves.'

The one-time Hodder author Winston Churchill was making similar accusations against the government from the Tory backbenches, but the Brothers would not have it. They refused to publish the book because they believed it might annoy the government. *Fallen Bastions – The Central European Tragedy* went to the rising left-wing publisher Victor Gollancz, and proved an important influence on British public opinion in the run-up to war. It went through five editions in two months.

Attenborough also writes that more and more initiatives that might have lifted the firm out of the doldrums were deemed to be 'not the done thing'. In an effort to refresh the fiction list, he asked for permission to approach C. S. Forester, later famous as the author of the Hornblower novels, who was then publishing with The Bodley Head. Hornblower would surely have been a hero worthy of the Hodder stable, but Attenborough was forbidden to poach him because The Bodley Head was going through a rough patch. His attempt to woo the historian Arthur Bryant, who burst on the publishing scene with his bestselling biography of Charles II in 1931, was also ruled out of order on the grounds that Longman, Bryant's publisher, was a 'friendly neighbour'.

And three decades after Thomas Stoughton instructed Ernest Hodder-Williams that 'our firm's name ought to be a guarantee that novels published by us might be <u>safely</u> read aloud in families', the firm was, it seems, more willing than ever 'to forgo profit [rather] than be identified with objectionable novels'. In the early 30s Leslie Charteris – who was producing plenty of profit for the firm – wrote a Saint story called The Intemperate Reformer, which was banned by the Hodder directors.

The Intemperate Reformer begins with a magnificent sentence that immediately tells you the sort of world you are entering in the company of the Saint: 'Simon Templar watched with a remorselessly calculating eye the quantity of caviar that was being spooned onto his plate, with the eternal springing hope that this would intimidate the head waiter into serving a more than normally generous portion . . .' The wine waiter is next up to the table with his 'frosted bottle' of Romanov vodka, and over lunch Templar learns that one of his former servants who has opened a pub is being persecuted by a wicked temperance campaigner called Isaiah Thoat. It emerges that Thoat is, in addition to this particular crime, corrupting British tastes wholesale with the production of a disgusting non-alcoholic beverage called Sanitade.

Declaring himself a true believer in the freeborn Englishman's right to drink and railing against licensing hours ('I love this country; but the equating of morality with the precise hour at which someone wants a drink is one refinement where they've lost me') the Saint sets out to save his manservant and bring about the downfall of the odious Thoat. He of course succeeds (tricking Thoat into getting drunk and then having him arrested for receiving stolen goods) and the story is told with wonderful wit and just enough cleverness to carry you through. Did Charteris reflect when he was writing it that it might jar with the teetotal traditions of his publisher? He later said, 'The Hodders of that era lowered the boom. It was too much of an affront to the nonconformist conscience.' And he described those running the firm at the time as 'the boss men, never seen without the bank-manager-stock-broker uniform of black coat and striped trousers'. Looking back at this era, Leonard Cutts expressed the view that the Brothers' obsession with the moral tone of the books they published 'nearly pushed Hodder and Stoughton into unimportance'.

In 1961, the year after the collapse of the obscenity case over D. H. Lawrence's *Lady Chatterley's Lover*, Hodder & Stoughton finally published The Intemperate Reformer.

11

The oblique shepherding of public opinion

The story of the beginning of the *Teach Yourself* series is told at Hodder with the sort of reverence the YMCA reserves for its founding moment in George Williams' upper room at Hitchcock and Rodgers in 1844.

The occasion was a meeting called to discuss the future of the English Universities Press, a new Hodder imprint (with no connection to any real universities) that had been set up by John Attenborough on the instructions of Percy Hodder-Williams. Percy reminded those present about a project that had once been planned by Sir John Adams, a Scottish educationalist who became the first Principal of the Institute of Education in London. Adams was a friend of William Robertson Nicoll, and the two had worked on a series of books under the general title 'Self-Educator'. The project foundered when it was passed on to another editor, but there were still copies of some of the original books stowed away in the basement, and someone was sent to dig them out.

'The books were brought up and passed around to the general approval of those present', writes Trevor Barnes in *People with a Purpose*, his history of the *Teach Yourself* books. 'The content was judged to be pretty sound, although the format left something to be desired. If the original titles were updated, given an eye-catching cover, and marketed under a snappy new title, they could be in business.'

Percy Hodder-Williams, who took an especially close interest in book design, commissioned the Slade-educated artist Ethel

Pares to come up with a 'look' for the new series ('Bip' Pares, as she was universally known, was Percy's favourite designer and produced dozens of wrappers for Hodder crime books in the 1930s and 40s). But it was Leonard Cutts who had the brainwave of launching the books under the *Teach Yourself* title.

In their editorial manifesto, Hodder declared that 'These books . . . are designed for living, not to enable you to decorate yourself with a little snobbish "learning". The test of your culture is your ability to tackle any situation that life presents, and though you know the names of all the stars and can recite *Hamlet* backwards, if you are helplessly defeated before a cut finger or the taps on the gas stove you have very little claim to call yourself a cultured person.'

The first list, which came out in 1938, reflected that practical philosophy; readers were offered the opportunity to teach themselves *French, Mathematics, Embroidery, Good English, Latin* (of less obvious practical use, even then) and *Public Speaking*. 1938 also saw the publication of *Teach Yourself; The Household Doctor*. 'You want to keep well. You want to keep your family well', wrote the anonymous author (doctors were forbidden to advertise their services). 'But if there is an illness, if there is an accident, you want to know what to do promptly and without a fuss. Here is the book to help you. It is pleasantly written so that you can pick it up at odd moments and absorb its instruction. Then you will avert a great many crises and be ready for those that are bound to arrive.'

The more alarmingly titled *Teach Yourself Flying* was published at around the same time. It came complete with a drawing of a typical cockpit and a diagram explaining good and bad ways to 'loop the loop'. The author, Squadron Leader Nigel Tangye, noted nostalgically that 'Almost gone are those happy, carefree days when a new type of aeroplane would appear out of the sky and land on the aerodrome, and the owner would come over to you and say, "Like to try her?" There are, alas! too many gadgets about an aeroplane now for an owner to feel so confidently generous.' He added a caution: 'however confident the reader may feel when he reaches the last page, it will not be advisable for him to go to an aerodrome and jump into a waiting aeroplane in the belief he will be able to fly it.'

The Munich crisis in the autumn of that year forced Britain to wake up to the likelihood of another war – until then many people had, not unnaturally, taken refuge in an ostrich-like optimism. John Attenborough claimed that with the *Teach Yourself* concept his English Universities Press stood, on the eve of war, 'poised to develop a series which would take its place beside Allen Lane's Penguins and Victor Gollancz's Left Book Club as one of the great publishing ideas of the thirties'. That is quite a claim, but it has some merit.

The success of the Left Book Club, which had been set up by Victor Gollancz in 1936 and offered its members a monthly book choice together with a political newsletter, was driven by the huge appetite for political information as the war clouds gathered; its membership peaked at 57,000 in 1939. In a similar way, the *Teach Yourself* series chimed with the self-help ethos of the Home Front. Government ministries and the BBC were soon pouring out advice on cooking, health and growing vegetables in the front garden, and issuing instructions on the proper procedures for blacking out windows and wearing gas masks. The *Teach Yourself* series was there to help. There were eighteen *Teach Yourself* books in print in 1939, and the number had risen to forty-eight by the end of the war in 1945.

And the books secured some official recognition. In a wartime foreword for *Teach Yourself Flying* Squadron Leader Tangye wrote, 'When this book was published it had a happy compliment paid to it. It was recommended by the Air Ministry to prospective R.A.F. pilots as a suitable book for their study. Since then we have passed from peace to war, but I have kept the flying instruction right up to date and the aircraft on which it was based is of the type extensively used in the Service for elementary instruction.' The back cover declared, 'Your first solo Flight will be made a great deal sooner if you study this book, for you can master the theory before you even come into contact with the 'plane. You can save your instructor time and patience and that is A SERVICE TO YOUR COUNTRY.' *Teach Yourself Trigonometry* helped gunners find their targets, and *Teach Yourself Roofing* helped householders with immediate repairs during the Blitz.

Neville Chamberlain's declaration that 'this country is at war with Germany' was made in a radio broadcast from Downing Street on the morning of 3 September 1939, and in London it was immediately followed by the sirens sounding an air-raid warning. It was a false alarm, but it brought home the fact that all Britain's plans for war were premised on the assumption that the beginning of hostilities would be immediately followed by an overwhelming attack from the air.

The senior Tory (and three times prime minister) Stanley Baldwin had, in a famous speech, told the Commons that 'I think it is . . . well for the man in the street to realise that there is no power on earth that can prevent him being bombed. Whatever people may tell him, the bomber will always get through.' A 1938 report for the Ministry of Health argued that the number of psychiatric casualties of bombing would greatly outnumber those who were physically hurt, and that there were likely to be 'between three and four million cases of acute panic, hysteria and neurosis during the first six months of war'.

So like many firms and government departments based in London, Hodder & Stoughton had a dispersal policy. The day after Chamberlain's broadcast the firm's headquarters moved to St Hugh's, a prep school in Bickley (the boys were evacuated to Malvern for the duration). The 'Stock and Despatch' department was evacuated to Aylesbury. St Paul's House in Warwick

Square and the adjacent Little St Paul's House in Warwick Row (which had been acquired in 1933) were retained for London sales.

A fortnight later the following notice went up under Percy Hodder-Williams' signature: 'In a week or a fortnight's time we shall know much more clearly how many members of the peace-time staff we can employ in war-time. We are sending you this week's wages in full, as you have been standing by, awaiting instructions. We shall try to make use of you very shortly, but, as a precautionary measure, I am sure you will understand that, for the time being, you are formally under notice, which means, of course, that we shall not be able to go on paying you your full wages after this week unless we are able to make full use of your services.' This curt announcement – which, coming so hard on the heels of the news that the country was at war, must have been more than a little unsettling – was followed by the information that those staff who did stay with the firm would be expected to take a ten per cent cut in their wages. 'Owing to the difficulties of business and the great expense of transporting our activities from Warwick Square to Aylesbury,' Percy told them at the end of September, 'we have decided that we must ask <u>every</u> member of staff, whether on a monthly salary or a weekly wage, to accept a certain deduction in wages.' The ten per cent cut remained in place for six months, and thereafter pay was frozen for the duration of the war.

Nearly half of the staff decided to leave for active service – publishing was not one of those 'reserved occupations' which the government judged essential to the war effort. Percy gave them a somewhat half-hearted commitment as they went off to war: 'While it is impossible to forsee the future,' he announced, 'we shall certainly give first consideration at the close of hostilities to all those who were, at the outbreak of war, members of staff.' He signed beneath the rallying cry: 'May God defend the Right.'

There was, however, no difficulty in selling books. Immediately after declaring war the government banned most other forms of entertainment; the cinemas, music halls and theatres were all shut down. During the so-called 'Phoney War' – before Hitler's invasion of western Europe in May 1940 – the country was as bored as it was fearful. Troops idling with the British Expeditionary Force in France and civilians in the blackout on the Home Front devoured books, and in some places there were ugly scenes as evacuees from London brought their literary tastes to the countryside; at Bedford library, for example, 'the huge crowds, which packed the cramped Lending department and fell over themselves and the reading tables, turned the library into bedlam, especially on Saturdays'.

Hodder simply sold out all its pre-war stock, including all its remaining Yellow Jackets. The real challenge lay not in sales but in production. How could the firm keep up the supply of new reading material with a diminished staff and a paper ration that was set at 37.5% of pre-war usage? And given those constraints, where should they direct their energies? These questions faced all publishers, not just Hodder. As Valerie Holman puts it in *Print for Victory*, 'At a time when the usual law of supply and demand was reversed, and normal market conditions no longer applied, publishers worried not about how they could sell their books but how, with inadequate means, they could continue to produce them.'

Ralph and Percy's first instinct was to emulate Ernest's First World War example by publishing a royal charity book in aid of the Red Cross. Doris Fisher, one of that 'battery of secretaries' who took dictation of the Brothers' correspondence, remembered that 'In the first few months of our evacuation, our lives revolved round the Q.B.R.C [The Queen's Book of the Red Cross]. Letters were written to authors, artists, short-story writers, poets, suggesting they might contribute to this composite book, and the response was overwhelming. The royal approval was given. In less than three months the book was published – a prodigious feat by any standard!'

The book included colour prints of pictures by Rex Whistler and Edmund Dulac and a photograph of the Queen by Cecil Beaton. William Russell Flint provided a plate of figures representing 'Fortitude' and 'Faith' beneath the King's message: 'We can only do the right as we see the right and reverently commit our cause to God.' Daphne du Maurier sent a short story, as did two relative newcomers to the Hodder lists, Eric Ambler and Georgette Heyer. There was a play by A. A. Milne, and T. S. Eliot offered a couple of his animal poems. The Queen's preface ('All of you who buy this book, as well as the distinguished authors and artists who prepared it, are helping to forward the great work of mercy on the battlefield . . .') was handwritten and reproduced in facsimile. The book does not have quite the glossy luxuriance of the old Hodder art books, but it was a handsome enough production.

The firm's involvement with the government also seems to have been conducted on the lines laid down by Sir Ernest in the earlier conflict, although the Hodder & Stoughton name does not appear much in the early government planning documents for war propaganda – a reflection, perhaps, of the way Percy and Ralph had slipped out of the swim of London literary life.

By the end of the First World War, the Secret War Propaganda Bureau and the Department for Information run by John Buchan had both been superseded by a full-blown Ministry of Information under Lord Beaverbrook. It was not much loved – there was a widespread feeling in Parliament that propaganda was an un-British activity – and it was closed almost as soon as the war was over. The government revived it in 'shadow form' in the late 1930s, but Whitehall was nervous about the way the public might react to the idea of official propaganda, so the Ministry's formal existence was only announced once war had been declared. On the day of the German invasion of Poland the Ministry's Home Publicity Division held an intense discussion on the restorative value of tea during those apocalyptic air raids everyone was expecting, and the following week this many-headed hydra of a government department burst into busy-ness. The imposing Malet Street Senate House of the University of London was requisitioned as its headquarters.

From the first, the Ministry suffered from a fundamental confusion about its purpose; Lord Macmillan, a Scottish judge who served briefly as its first minister, told the house of Lords, 'I have had considerable difficulty in ascertaining what are its functions.' In theory its remit was vast; among many other things it was responsible for the BBC. It comprised fourteen divisions divided into four groups – censorship, news and press relations, publicity and administration – and it was responsible for these areas not just on the Home Front but across the Empire. But at the heart of the whole enterprise lay that British squeamishness about the idea of propaganda, and that fed through into administrative confusion and sometimes outright chaos.

In the early weeks of war the Ministry considered the establishment of an advisory committee of writers, publishers and agents – including A. S. Watt of the ubiquitous Watt agency, who is described in Ministry documents as 'the doyen of literary agents' – to 'help bring the whole force of British culture to the aid of the British government'. The list of proposed members ranged from T. S. Eliot to P. G. Wodehouse (who would later be caught by the German invasion of France, and got into trouble by broadcasting for the other side) and included C. S. Forester, the rising star whom John Attenborough had been prevented from pinching. But the committee idea was abandoned, partly on the advice of George Faber, who was running the Publishers' Association; he warned that writers were a jealous bunch and liable to cause trouble. So the Ministry's relationship with the literary world developed in a more ad hoc manner.

That did not stop it becoming something of a honeypot for writers and other creative types looking for a way to help the war effort, and many of them proved George Faber right by making the Ministry the target of waspish commentary. John Betjeman, who worked in the Film Unit, called it the Ministry of Aggravation, or Minnie, and Evelyn Waugh satirised it in *Put Out More Flags*, one of the funniest books to come out of the war. The art historian Kenneth Clark, who rose to the senior role of 'controller of home publicity' (and was used by Waugh for one of his characters), condemned it later as a 'perfectly useless body'. And George Orwell, who began broadcasting propaganda up the road at the BBC in 1941, famously made the Senate House building the model for his Ministry of Truth, or Minitrue, in *1984*.

Individual Ministry divisions trawled for good publishers, and poached where they could. Tom Burns, for example, who had been building up a famously successful list of Catholic authors for Longmans and was heavily involved in the Catholic weekly the *Tablet* (of which he later became editor), was called in by the Ministry's Religious Division to help generate favourable religious writing about the war. He found himself working there five or six hours on weekdays and much of the weekend, which must have seriously impinged on his contribution at Longmans. Hamish Hamilton joined the Ministry as the head of the American publicity division, and combined his duties there with the running of his own imprint, 'nimbly leading a double life between the Ministry in Malet Street and his own concern in Great Russell Street', which was a short walk away.

Hodder & Stoughton's relationship with the Ministry was even more informal. Valerie Holman writes in *Print for Victory* that 'Without being on the pay-roll of the MoI, a publisher might cement his relationship unofficially', and she cites the example of Leonard Cutts, who 'conducted his normal business of dealing with contracts, correspondence, and catalogues early in the day, then, "in the late afternoons he joined his friends at the Ministry of Information, where he gained much goodwill for the firm, making the Hodder and Stoughton imprint available for books of importance to the war effort. He returned to his home, railway permitting, at 10pm."'

A meeting at the Ministry in late January 1940 concluded that a 'definite programme for the production of pamphlets, the first and more urgent for practical issues and the second for spiritual issues, should be formulated without delay'. Hodder & Stoughton, with its strong tradition of religious publishing, was particularly well placed to meet the second of those requirements, and in 1940 the firm began a series of essays arguing a religious justification for fighting. They were cleanly and handsomely printed, and each was introduced – in bold red type on the title page – as 'A Hodder and Stoughton pamphlet on the spiritual issues of the war'.

The authors were very far from being government stooges. One of the first pamphlets was written by William Temple, then Archbishop of York (in 1942, on the retirement of Cosmo Lang, he would become Archbishop of Canterbury), who had been a member of the Labour Party after the First World War and had a growing reputation for social radicalism. His pamphlet was entitled 'A *Conditional* Justification of War' (my italics) and is premised on the assumption that pacifism is the natural Christian position: 'War is a monstrous evil;' Temple wrote, 'of that there can be no doubt. Its occurrence is a manifestation of the sin of men. If there were no sin there were would be no war. Then ought not any good man, still more any Christian man, to refuse to have any part in it?'

There is nothing Jingoist or Hun-hating about the terms in which Temple makes his case. 'The soldier who accepts the call of his duty and performs it with no hatred in his heart – still more, perhaps, the father or mother who sends a son to fight without allowing bitterness to spoil the sacrifice – is also showing the way to permeate the world itself with the Christian spirit', he writes. And the socialist leanings that would emerge so clearly in the archbishop's most famous book, *Christianity and the Social Order*, are apparent; he argued: 'Only if we are determined to see that our victory really does serve justice and freedom; only if we are determined in our own national life to promote justice and freedom where now they are imperfectly attained; only on these conditions dare we come forward as their champions in war.'

Another contribution to the series came from J. D. Jones, a former Chairman of the Congregational Union of England and Wales. As a Liberal and a friend of Lloyd George he stood squarely in the Hodder tradition, and his essay on *The Power to Endure* addressed the practical challenges the churches faced as a result of the war. 'This war is like no other war in history,' Jones wrote, 'and it has forced the State to take precautions which seriously interfere with Christian work. There is, to begin with, the "black-out", with its serious dislocation of worship hours. There is the compulsory evacuation of our schoolchildren, with its catastrophic effects upon our Sunday schools and its disintegration of family life. There is the haunting dread of air attack which has led so many of our more prosperous people to evacuate themselves to what are considered to be safer areas, with consequent denuding of our town congregations and the diminution of our financial resources. It has been desperately hard, under these circumstance, for the churches to keep going.' Like Temple's pamphlet, this was printed in 1940, when Britain was fighting alone, and it is a religious call to the Blitz spirit; Jones declares, 'If there is one thing Christian ministers and Christian churches need in these terrible and tragic days it is this grace to endure, to carry on.'

Other pamphlets in the series included an anthology of views from different denominations published under the title *The Voices of the Churches – representative leaders and the War*, and *Cross into*

Swastika, a collection of quotations from German documents designed to demonstrate the Nazi determination to destroy Christianity. The fact that this material was published under the Hodder imprint rather than appearing as official government publications of course helped with what one Ministry memorandum described as 'the oblique shepherding of public opinion which is so difficult and so delicate, and so mischievous if done unskilfully'.

Putting across a government-approved message could be good business too. *The Sky's the Limit*, a history of British airpower by J. M. Spaight, a retired civil servant at the Air Ministry, was first published in August 1940, at the height of the Battle of Britain. It was reprinted six times in short order, and the revised edition that came out in May 1941 proudly proclaimed that 50,000 copies had been sold in its first six months in the bookshops. The *News Chronicle* called it a 'fascinating book', and the *Observer*'s review praised it as a work 'of immense value'. The book's success coincided with the worst weeks of the Blitz, so many of its readers and reviewers would have had a very personal sense of connection with the subject matter.

In a handwritten note preserved in the Hodder & Stoughton archive Leonard Cutts recognised that 'our use by the MoI (Ministry of Information) as propagandists' was a significant factor in the firm's survival through the war years. The fact that it fell to Cutts, rather than a member of the Hodder-Williams family, to nurture the firm's wartime government relationship reflected the way the firm was now run. John Attenborough writes, 'the twin preoccupations of Percy and Ralph inevitably meant that the responsibility for running the business was to a large extent undertaken by R. J. Davis (the hero of *One Young Man*) and Leonard Cutts'.

Ralph's preoccupation was the Home Guard, which this decorated First World War veteran joined as soon as war broke out. During the anxious weeks after the evacuation of Dunkirk,

Britain was braced against the threat of a German invasion, and the Bickley area of Kent would have been a natural target for German landings from the air. Ralph moved permanently into the temporary offices at St Hugh's school, referring to his occasional visits to his family in Somerset as 'leave'. He was appointed a company commander and, eventually, lieutenant-colonel. He 'tramped round the area noting the lie of the land. He went on special courses. He kept his company commanders on their toes', Attenborough writes. Hodder published two books on the subject – the *Home Guard Book* and *Home Guard Drill and Service Book* – and the company's secretaries at St Hugh's spent a good deal of their time typing out orders for the 54th (Chislehurst) Battalion.

Percy's wartime 'preoccupations' are reflected in the series of weekly newsletters he sent out to members of the wider Hodder-Williams clan throughout the war. These were later collected, bound in vellum and presented to his wife, and although they are often concerned with people and family matters that are bound to be obscure to outsiders (Lilian, we read, is 'still as busy and indomitable as ever with canteen work in the heart of London and with hospital work in Sunningdale over the weekends', while 'Fuddle has been visiting all round the family. She looks very well and competition for her hand-knitted socks is still keen'), they are, as John Attenborough suggests, a rich insight into an 'a typical English family scattered by war'.

The newsletters are, however, oddly light on references to what was happening in the firm. John Attenborough himself is praised in one of them for 'two excellent business ideas he sent along', but it is impossible to read these documents without coming away with a strong sense that the Hodder-Williams family occupied a much higher place in Percy's scale of values than the Hodder & Stoughton firm.

His account of the night his immediate family were bombed out of their home in Bromley, for example, is telling. In October

1940 – around a month after the beginning of the Blitz – he began the weekly round-robin by declaring 'we provide the headline', and revealed that 'Loken is no more. It was hit by a heavy bomb last Thursday night last [sic] and the whole of the back was blown away and the rest is a ruin.' He, the rest of the family and their servants were in their bomb shelter at the time, and 'we did not any of us get so much as a scratch'; the maids, he added, were 'wonderfully calm'. The following day, it seems, the ever-diligent R. J. Davis organised a team of Hodder employees to help clear the place up, and Percy records: 'It is astonishing how much we have salvaged from the ruins and I should like here and now to say how impossible it is for me to give adequate thanks to Mr Davis and my wonderful staff for "jumping to it" with the speed, efficiency and loyalty which is second nature to the Hodder and Stoughton staff in relation with the Hodder-Williams family.'

Like Ralph's battalion orders, Percy's newsletters were typed up, duplicated and circulated by those loyal and efficient secretaries at St Hugh's. One of them, Ralph's own assistant Doris Fisher, later recalled trying working conditions. 'Many were the pinpricks', she wrote, 'and tribulations. Tempers were not always even. Rooms had to be shared by too many people. The telephone was totally inadequate.'

The bosses seem to have made few allowances for the unusual circumstances; there is a ferocious note from Percy in the archives reminding the staff that normal working hours run from 8.45 a.m. to 5.45 p.m., and complaining that: 'Some thoughtless members of staff are shortening these hours by arriving late and starting to pack up for the day at 5.15 p.m. in their eagerness to get away as soon after 5.30 p.m. as they can manage.' In terms that must have reminded everyone that they were working in a prep school rather than a proper office, he ordered: 'This practice will stop immediately', laid out a new set of instructions on clocking-off procedures and, declared, with a headmasterly final flourish, 'I expect these

<u>rules to be rigidly observed</u>'. At about the same time he was driven into another rage by the way staff were queuing for lunch early. 'I <u>will</u> not have this queuing up <u>before</u> one o'clock', read the new managerial broadside, 'and this is the last time I shall say so without dealing with the individual offender.'

12

Cheerio, and down with Doodlebugs

Two months after Percy and his family were bombed out of their home, the area round the Hodder offices in London was almost entirely wiped out in one of the worst nights of the Blitz. There was a lull in the bombing over Christmas 1940, but on the night of 29/30 December the Luftwaffe attacked the City. Thousands of incendiary devices and parachute mines came down on the Square Mile, and by early evening on the 29th, a Sunday, the blaze was already so intense that one London-based American correspondent telegraphed back to New York: 'The second Great Fire of London has begun.' Churchill ordered that everything should be done to protect St Paul's, and the night produced one of the most famous photographs of all time; the stunning image of the cathedral's dome amid the smoke was taken from the roof of the *Daily Mail* offices just off Fleet Street, and filled the paper's New Year's Eve front page under the headline 'St Paul's Survives'.

But the picture had to be cropped to conceal the utter devastation that surrounded the church. One of the firefighters on duty recalled that 'By the time we finished tackling the fires on the roof of the [Stock] Exchange, the sky, which was ebony black when we first got up there, was now changing to a yellow orange colour. It looked like there was an enormous circle of fire, including St Paul's churchyard.' The publishing world that had grown up around Paternoster Row over so many centuries simply disappeared; the premises of seventeen publishing companies were completely destroyed, and it was estimated that more than a million books were lost. 'Such stock as escaped the flames', wrote Valerie Holman in *Print for Victory*, 'succumbed to water damage as firefighters desperately sought to gain control over the huge conflagration which engulfed the traditional publishing quarter around St Paul's and permanently changed the geography of the book trade.'

Lovers of the trade turned up the next morning to find a scene that almost defied description. The *Bookseller*'s correspondent wrote: 'As I picked my way gingerly across from brick to brick, hot gouts of sulphurous fumes from buried fires seeped up between my feet; desultory flames played in the remains of a rafter here or a floor joist there, and on either side the smoking causeway fell sharply into cavernous glowing holes, once basements full of stock, now the crematories of the City's book world.'

A City bookseller called Hubert Wilson found 'a scene of destruction so complete, so utterly irretrievable that it held me spellbound. Nowhere were pavements or road surfaces to be seen. From Warwick Square in the West to Ivy Lane on the East, from the Row nearly to Newgate Street, there lies now an undulating sea of broken yellow bricks. I looked around Paternoster Square and recognised nothing but a pillar box, the top beneath my feet; there was nothing left to recognise . . .'

The Hodder offices were among the very few buildings that survived that terrible night. When R. J. Davis turned up the next morning he found that the premises rented by the firm's University of London Press in Warwick Lane had been flattened, but Little St Paul's House was intact and St Paul's House itself had been only partly damaged. After the war the firm moved back there, but most of the publishers who had been bombed out of their old homes left for good, many of them migrating to the West End. The world where Matthew Hodder, Thomas Stoughton and George Williams plotted and prayed was gone for good. The only reminder of that world today is a plaque on the modern office building that stands on the site of the draper's shop where the YMCA was founded: 'From its beginning in this place inspired of God the Association grew to encompass the world', it reads.

Percy and Ralph had, with some foresight, planted a new colony of the Hodder empire some way from the capital – beyond, so they hoped, the reach of the Luftwaffe. The Brockhampton Book Company, named (like one of the family's early homes in Bromley) for the Dorset farm where their father, John Williams, was born, was established in Leicester in 1938 under the management of E. Roker, one of the real 'old school' Hodder & Stoughton men who had been with the company since its time in Paternoster Row. Its – rather sad-sounding – purpose was to flog off surplus stocks of theological works that were not selling quite as briskly as they once did.

Roker had, since working with Ernest in his early days with the firm, been interested in developing a list for children, and in 1940 he was given permission to experiment with children's books from the Leicester offices. He was told he would not be allowed any of the rationed Hodder & Stoughton paper allocation for his new venture, and, in the best make-do-and-mend spirit of wartime Britain, he solved the paper problem by buying cheap offcuts from the printers of colour magazines.

His first recruit to his new list was inspired. 'The accolade for the most enterprising use of Enid Blyton's talents during the war must go to Brockhampton Press [as the Brockhampton Book Company had been re-christened when it became a proper publisher] and its managing editor, Mr E. A. Roker,' wrote Enid Blyton's biographer, Barbara Stoney. 'It was his brainwave to use previously scrapped off-cuts from the highly popular *Picture Post* magazine to produce child's handsize cartoon booklets, measuring about three by six inches, and he engaged Enid to write his first script. She suggested at their meeting in bomb-scarred

London that a mouse might provide a good central character and within a few days she had completed outline stories.'

The first of the Mary Mouse books went on the market in 1942. By the end of the year, 'Ten thousand copies of *Mary Mouse and the Doll's House*, printed in two colours and selling at a shilling each, were', Stoney records, 'on the market'. She adds, 'its very Lilliputian size endeared the book at once to young children and other titles soon followed'. Books in the series were soon being printed in editions of 200,000, and by the mid-1960s Mary Mouse had sold over a million copies.

Enid Blyton was already well established by the time she joined the list of Hodder authors. She began writing in earnest in the early 1920s, and by the outbreak of war she was so successful and so productive (in the course of her writing career she published more than 700 books) that she was routinely bringing out books with several different publishers in the same year. In 1940 she churned out no fewer than thirteen titles, eight of them under the George Newnes imprint (her first husband worked for the firm as an editor). But her long relationship with Hodder was to prove especially fruitful. She followed the *Mary Mouse* series with one featuring four children and a dog, and the first of the *Famous Five* stories appeared in the same year. Enid Blyton's popularity clearly impressed Percy, as the new books were brought out under the Hodder & Stoughton imprint, and were given a share of the firm's paper allocation.

Enid Blyton also acquired one of her most successful storytelling conceits from a Hodder man. Ewart Wharmby, who met her through the Brockhampton Press, told her that his children had just formed a secret society, and she quizzed his eldest son about the details – which included a password and the use of the garden shed as a headquarters. She sent the children some money by way of thanks for the research work (it was spent, appropriately, on 'jelly and chips') and used the Wharmby children as the inspiration for the *Secret Seven* series. Hodder became one of her main houses; she published her last book with the firm two years before her death, and Paul Hodder–Williams gave the address at her funeral.

1942 proved something of a bumper year for new talent; Roker also brought the firm Captain W. E. Johns, and his first Biggles book, *Biggles Sweeps the Desert*, was published then. The Brockhampton Press continued to recycle magazine offcuts for the rest of the war, and by 1945 was contributing nearly £63,000 to the Hodder & Stoughton turnover.

Some projects were considered sufficiently important to deserve an extra paper allocation from the government. Just before the war Hodder had begun marketing technical manuals produced by the Temple Press, and they included plane-spotters' guides that, with the coming of war, were studied by everyone from eager schoolchildren to air-raid wardens and anti-aircraft gunners. Sales of the books realised £45,000 in 1943.

The Hodder & Stoughton staff working at St Hugh's would themselves have been natural customers, as their temporary prep-school home was in one of the most vulnerable areas of the country. In the course of the war Bromley, Beckenham and Penge lost 11,000 homes to the bombs, and air raids killed more than 670 civilians in the area. In the aftermath of the D–Day landings it was also on the receiving end of 136 flying bombs, the V, or vengeance rockets, which were fired at Britain in the closing months of the war.

On 27 June 1944 a 'Doodlebug', as the V-1s were nicknamed in Britain, scored a direct hit on St Hugh's. This was a sufficiently dramatic development in the life of Hodder & Stoughton to earn the firm a mention in one of Percy's weekly newsletters to the family: 'the eminent firm has not escaped the attention of the Doodle-bug,' he announced, 'and will now have to find the patronage and protection of another saint.' His brother Ralph, who was widely referred to as Tim within the family, was at his Home Guard command post at the time, and Percy reported that

'Practically all that remains of its recent housing is Uncle Tim's Cabin, occupied to the last by the Colonel, who, after experiencing a mighty quake, walked out of it with great aplomb, dressed in a tin hat and gum boots, to survey the surrounding desolation. Miraculously no one suffered serious hurt.' He ended with the observation: 'Our letter this week must be short for we have no duplicator, and only the ever faithful and undaunted Miss Fisher and Miss Knight, with two typewriters, to do all our correspondence, but cheerio, and down with Doodlebugs – preferably in open fields.' The destruction of the prep-school buildings was complete, and the firm's headquarters moved into Percy's own home at Weald Place for the remaining ten months of the conflict.

In the same year Percy's adopted son Geoff, a sergeant in the RAF, was shot down and killed over France, and one of Percy's last wartime family letters includes a touching farewell: 'Goodbye, Geoff, for the present', Percy wrote. 'It's a pity for the world that you are not alive today. You promised so well and it is boys of your urgent kind who will keep it fresh and clean. It is sad we shall not be able to welcome you into Hodder and Stoughton, for you were already almost one of us at St Hugh's, and such a favourite with the staff. Is your lovely body broken, does it lie in a little village cemetery in a foreign land? It does not matter to you now. Not even death can defeat God's purpose for you. You have done your duty and you have won a crown, for heaven crowns the brave.'

But peace brought two representatives of the next generation of the family back to the firm. Both had spent the war in the armed services. Paul Hodder-Williams had risen to the rank of Lieutenant-Colonel, and John Attenborough, who joined the Honourable Artillery Company before the outbreak of war in 1939, had come through the desert campaigns of 1941–2 and the invasions of Sicily and Italy in 1943, and had served as a staff officer during the Normandy landings in 1944. Percy continued to refer to both of them – evidently to John Attenborough's irritation – as 'the boys'.

Paper rationing was not abolished until 1949; a 1946 catalogue of new books includes a plea for early orders from abroad because 'it is still impossible to print and bind enough books to satisfy the demands from all corners of the world', and notes: 'We must not yet be prodigal of paper for lists and catalogues.' This practical challenge continued to dictate company policy. In the immediate aftermath of the war Pan Books, which had been established as an independent paperback imprint in 1944 (its logo of the Greek god Pan was designed by Mervyn Peake), was taken over by a consortium of publishers made up of Macmillan, Collins, Heinemann and Hodder & Stoughton.

Hodder's involvement was driven by the recognition that, with paper rationing still in place, this was the only way the firm could fulfil a promise it had made to its pre-war authors that their backlist would be back on the bookshelves once the conflict was over. Leslie Charteris and Georgette Heyer duly became Pan authors.

The Pan venture nearly foundered on Percy's rigid insistence that Hodder & Stoughton should remain a traditional family firm. Leonards Cutts had been a driving force behind the new consortium, and Alan Bott, the original founder of the Pan imprint, wanted him to be the Hodder & Stoughton representative on the Pan board. He also expected Cutts to 'carry the full authority of a director of Hodder and Stoughton'. This was too much for Percy; only members of the clan could expect to rise so high. Cutts nearly resigned, but, as John Attenborough put it, 'somehow his loyalty to the firm and partners . . . saved the day'. Ralph Hodder-Williams took the seat on Pan's board instead.

Percy Hodder-Williams retired as chairman in the spring of 1947, and his farewell message to the staff was similarly coloured by his commitment to the idea that Hodder & Stoughton was, more than anything else, a family concern. 'I take my leave with a heart full of gratitude for all the smiles and the friendships I have met on my business way,' he told them, 'and especially for the never failing kindness shown to me by members, past and present, of a staff that must always be the pride and concern of this family business.'

Passing the baton to Ralph, who succeeded him as chairman, he added: 'I commend to you my dear brother Ralph as your new chief; he has supported me with unsurpassed loyalty and devotion through the 21 years of my Chairmanship. If I have succeeded at all it is because he has been beside me and I am certain that I and you could wish for no better successor; no one more interested in your welfare, and no one more fitted to lead you in these difficult and responsible days. He is, as you know, the youngest of the three brothers who have been linked together in this Firm. First the famous Sir Ernest, then myself, and now, just as we have together planned it, MR RALPH.'

Hodder & Stoughton thus embarked on its journey through the second half of the twentieth century with a management ethic that harked right back to the Victorian world of its founders; the Luftwaffe might have wiped out the physical world familiar to the company's patriarchs, but the spirit of the old days at Paternoster Row lived on. The habit of referring to family members with the prefix 'Mr' would endure until the 1970s.

13

Miss Herron's quite splendid assistance

In the autumn of 1947 the new chairman of Hodder & Stoughton issued the following edict: 'I must make clear that I cannot under any circumstances permit card-playing for money, or any other form of gambling, to take place in the Warehouse or on any other premises of the firm, either during the dinner hour or at any other time.' Anyone hoping for a more liberal regime with the passing of the chairman's baton from one brother to the other would clearly have to think again.

The challenges of the post-war world did force some changes – even if they were grudgingly conceded. Labour was in short supply, and in November 1949 the manager of the University of London Press sent a memo to R. J. Davis asking whether the firm still enforced the rule that women should leave their jobs as soon as they got married. He pointed out that 'The Civil Service and the Teaching Profession have abandoned the "marriage bar"' and argued that it made sense for Hodder & Stoughton to follow suit. Some of the women working for him who had become engaged were, he said, 'quite useful servants of the Press; efficient workers with a certain amount of knowledge and experience of our work which is valuable to us'.

The answer to this important policy question came back from the chairman himself. 'It remains the rule of Hodder & Stoughton and its Associated Companies that all ladies who are employed in the organisation will be expected to resign their employment on marriage,' Ralph declared. However, he conceded that 'If there is no suitable successor within the organisation . . . the board will give consideration to the <u>re-engagement after marriage</u> of a lady whose services are regarded by a manager as being very exceptional.'

Ralph does seem to have been more outward-looking than his brother Percy. He had graduated from Oxford and was the first Hodder-Williams head of the firm to have a university degree – a remarkable fact given the firm's involvement in higher education publishing. He was also a prominent figure in the Publishers Association, the industry's trade body, serving on its council and rising to be its president in the early 1950s. But most of the real successes of his era seem to have been the work of those 'boys', the next generation of family members who were now beginning to make their mark.

John Attenborough, in his company history *A Living Memory*, lays claim to several profitable projects that capitalised on pride in Britain's record in the Second World War. *Operation Victory* by General Sir Francis de Guingand, an insider's account of Montgomery's successful North Africa campaigns, was published as a result of contacts that Attenborough had made as a serving soldier, and sold 50,000 copies in its original edition. 'A chance meeting in Chislehurst' brought him into contact with Oliver Philpot, one of the British PoWs who famously escaped from the German prison Stalag Luft III by digging a tunnel beneath a wooden vaulting horse they claimed to be using to keep fit. Philpot's story was published under the title *Stolen Journey*, and the contact led to the publication of an even more famous escaper's tale by R. P. Reid, *The Colditz Story*. Airey Neave, the first British officer to escape successfully from Colditz Castle, published his classic escape memoir *They Have their Exits* with Hodder in 1953.

And 1953 has gone down in Hodder history as a red-letter year. It began with the publication of Richard Dimbleby's *Elizabeth our Queen*, a bestseller about the new monarch in the tradition of royal books established by Ernest. At about the same time Walt Disney brought out a cartoon film of *Peter Pan*. Ralph Hodder-Williams and Spencer Curtis Brown (the son of the founder of the Curtis Brown literary agency) acted as agents for Great Ormond Street Hospital for Children, to which J. M. Barrie had famously left the Peter Pan copyright.

Peter had of course moved happily between literary genres since his earliest days, and the film generated no fewer than four-teen books from Hodder & Stoughton and the children's division in Leicester, the Brockhampton Press. The Hodder cata-logue included such offerings as *Walt Disney's Story of Peter Pan, illustrated in Colour,* and several reworkings of the original by the poet and writer May Byron, who had been producing abridge-ments of Barrie's work (with his approval) since 1915.

But the year is remembered above all for the publication of *The Ascent of Everest* by Sir John Hunt, which was masterminded by the second of 'the boys', Paul Hodder-Williams. It was, according to Paul's obituary in the *Guardian,* 'Hodder & Stoughton's biggest-ever bestseller, a success so great that it trans-formed the firm'.

The contract for the book had to be negotiated with the Royal Geographical Society, which sponsored Hunt's Everest exped-ition. Competition was tough; Attenborough writes that 'there was hardly a publisher of importance who was not willing to make the running'. Hodder had a strong tradition of publishing explorers and adventurers, which, like so much else, went back to Ernest, who wrote an account of Captain Scott's last, tragic expedition to the South Pole called *Like English Gentlemen* (it was still bringing in royalties in the 1950s). The firm had also published books on a number of earlier attempts on Everest, including *Everest Reconnaissance* by Eric Shipton, an account of the exped-ition that identified the route that made the success of Hunt's team possible. How far that record counted in the final decision is not clear. There was, inevitably, plenty of speculation about how much the firm paid for the rights to the story, and 'a wag in the Garrick Club . . . was reported as saying that "it cost Hodders £10 a foot to get to the top of Everest" '.

Hunt's team arrived at Everest in mid–March and spent several weeks working their way up the mountain. The first of the two climbing teams he had selected for the final assault on the summit came within some 300 feet of their objective on 26 May, but they were forced to turn back by exhaustion and problems with their oxygen supply. Three days later, at 11.30 a.m. on 29 May, the New Zealander Edmund Hillary and Sherpa Tenzing Norgay finally made it to the top. *The Times'* correspondent, James (later Jan) Morris, heard the news at base camp and sent a coded message by runner to the remote Nepali village of Namche Bazaar. From there it was forwarded to the British embassy in Kathmandu by telegram, and the news broke in London on 2 June, the morning of Queen Elizabeth II's coronation. It was heralded as a symbol of national renewal after the austerity years of post-war Britain, and it is difficult to imagine a more propitious marketing climate for the Hodder project.

But getting the book into the shops in time to capitalise on the national mood presented an Everest-like publishing challenge. Paul Hodder–Williams was a former lieutenant-colonel, and Sir John Hunt – his knighthood was announced before he even got back to Kathmandu – was a serving officer in the British army; 'Paul and the expedition's leader', Attenborough writes, 'planned the publication of the book with the exactitude of an operation of war.'

For most of June and July the expedition members were busy being feted around the world, so it was not until the beginning of August that Hunt began to write. Hodder's secret weapon was a woman called Elsie Herron, who had begun her career with the firm as Leonard Cutts's secretary in 1938, and had shown a talent for 'ghosting' and editing work with non-professional writers during the production of some of the Second World War escapers' books. She was described by one of her colleagues as a 'fierce teetotal but chain-smoking lady ... with an Oxford degree in English, a deep suspicion of all men, a strong Newcastle accent and a love of books'. She was despatched to the Hunts's cottage in North Wales with instructions to provide whatever help was necessary.

One cannot help wondering about the dynamics of the relationship between the brilliant but alarming-sounding Miss Herron and the mountaineering soldier, but it seems to have worked. She found that Sir John, who was paid a fee of £5,000 (a considerable sum in those days) had, with military thoroughness, given himself a schedule of deadlines for completing each chapter. Her job was to tidy up the material – which included a considerable amount of technical information – and circulate it to readers for checking and proofreading. The book, Sir John concedes in the acknowledgements for the first edition, 'would never have been possible but for the quite splendid assistance given me by Miss Elsie Herron'.

'The demand to tell the story quickly has been urgent,' Sir John noted (in something of an understatement), 'and it was written within a month.' Even with Elsie Herron's help that was a remarkable achievement; the book is around 250 pages of clear prose, it is well organised (as you might expect from someone who had planned an expedition to conquer the world's highest mountain) and has a strong narrative drive.

By 20 August, thirteen of the eighteen chapters had reached the printers. The final chapter, Edmund Hillary's account of the ascent to the summit, arrived by plane (accompanied by its author) in mid-September. His colour transparencies were held up by customs at Heathrow for forty-eight hours, and then rushed to the warehouse at Aylesbury; some of them are reproduced in the edition of the book that Hodder published in 2001, and they are still thrilling, bringing the mountain to life with that slightly surreal brightness that made slides so popular in the 1950s.

The Duke of Edinburgh contributed a brief foreword, declaring that 'In human terms of physical effort and endurance alone it [the expedition] will live in history as a shining example to all mankind.'

Publication day was fixed for 12 November and booksellers were told that they would need to make firm orders by the end of September if they wanted a guaranteed delivery from the first printing. It was a production achievement to rank with Ernest's triumph with Lord Fisher's book three decades earlier.

And it really was, as Paul Hodder-Williams' obituary put it, 'the book everyone wanted to have, even at the then extravagant price of 42 shillings (£2.10)'. The first edition had been exhausted before publication day, and by the beginning of December the firm was forced to take out advertisements to reassure the reading public that 'Further editions are on the way. You can safely trust book-sellers to distribute their supplies as fairly as they can – on the only possible method of "first come first served."' 329,000 of the first edition were sold, and a further 310,000 copies came onto the market in the form of two Book Club editions. There was a paperback, and the Brockhampton Press published a children's edition.

Attenborough estimates that 'altogether, the British market alone absorbed over one million copies', and translation rights were sold in twenty-six countries. The firm had developed a mechanism for measuring its growth against the value of sales at the time of Sir Ernest Hodder-Williams' death and the 'halcyon year' of record performance that followed it; in 1953 Hodder & Stoughton sales exceeded that gold standard for the first time. The Royal Geographical Society also did very nicely out of the Everest book; its records show that it was paid royalties of over £65,000 (in 1950s money) in March 1954 and a further £10,000 in December that year.

The 1950s was a decade of expansion in the publishing industry generally. The number of new titles passed the 10,000 mark for the first time in 1950, rising to 17,000 ten years later. There was a new hunger for books in English on the world market, and exports were rocketing, both in absolute terms and as a proportion of overall British production. In 1949 exports accounted for 28.6% of all UK book sales – 9,798,838 books, according to figures from the Publishers Association. By 1959 that figure had risen to 25,393,960, nearly 38% of all UK book sales.

Those figures reflect one of the legacies of Empire – the spread of English across the globe as the pre-eminent international language. But the process of decolonisation that began with India's Independence in 1947 meant that British publishers faced new competition in markets they once took for granted. 'First in India, and then in many of Britain's African colonies as they gained their independence in the 1960s,' writes John Feather in *A History of British Publishing*, 'nationalist sentiment naturally preferred that there should be a substantial infusion of local ownership and local expertise' in the publishing business. He notes that 'The developing nations of the Third World provided a vast potential market, especially for school textbooks and English-language teaching material, but political pressures gradually began to eliminate British publishers from much of the market.'

Hodder & Stoughton, which had had such a strong tradition of foreign adventuring, should have been well equipped to fight the battle for export markets, but it was not; John Attenborough concedes that the firm had become 'dangerously complacent' in the export field. Hodder had no one in West, East or Central Africa – all areas that were natural markets for English educational books – and were equally absent from the Caribbean and South East Asia. Putting the firm back on a footing to compete in the export market absorbed management energy throughout the immediate post-war period.

Bill Smart, the legendary Hodder & Stoughton 'original' who had made such a mark in Australia, was nearing seventy by the end of the war, and appears to have become somewhat eccentric. In 1949 he and his wife flew to London at the invitation of Ralph Hodder-Williams to discuss the future. Smart was convinced that he had been called back to be sacked, and as soon as he arrived he made 'an emotional visit to Sir Ernest's grave'. John Attenborough believed that 'This loyalty to one man's memory had become obsessive during his thirty-five years' isolation from his home country, and twisted itself into jealousy of anybody who had enjoyed his late chief's favour.'

As a result, Smart would have nothing to do with the candidate the directors put forward as his assistant and, they hoped, eventual successor; James Sare was the son of Robert Sare, who had managed the *Lancet* so successfully, and he had married the secretary of Smart's old friend and colleague A. F. Austin, so he was a Hodder man through and through. But Smart refused point blank to have him, and Sare had to set up shop in New Zealand instead. It was a reminder that the emotional ties at the heart of an old-fashioned family business are not always benign.

When Smart was finally persuaded to retire – in 1960 – he insisted that he would only hand over to a member of the Hodder clan. Philip Attenborough, John's elder son and a recent recruit to the firm, was working as a trainee in Australia and New Zealand at the time, and was deputed to perform the awesome function of presiding over the end of Bill Smart's long career. An announcement released to the *Bookseller* and the Australian papers duly declared: 'On 1st July, when Mr W. S. Smart relinquishes his Hodder and Stoughton responsibilities in Sydney, he will hand them back to Mr Philip Attenborough, at present in Australia, who is the great-great-grandson of the original Matthew Hodder who gave Bill Smart his first job in Hodder and Stoughton sixty years ago.' Once the formal handover was complete James Sare was finally able to take over the firm's Australian operation.

John Attenborough himself was given the task of restoring Hodder & Stoughton's North American links, which had played such a prominent role in the early days of the firm; in 1952 he and his wife sailed on the *Queen Mary* 'to visit a publishing community which had not received an editor from Hodder and Stoughton for thirty years'.

But the most significant step towards building an export future was the appointment of an outsider, Leo Timmermans, as the head of a new department dedicated to overseas educational publishing. Timmermans had the zest for travel and the wide-ranging ambition of a Matthew Hodder or a Thomas Stoughton. Simply reading the schedule of his early journeys – made of course when flying could be a much more trying process – is exhausting:

1948	9 May–19 June	Nigeria and Gold Coast
	20 Oct–10 Dec	Kenya, Uganda, Tanganyika, Sudan and Egypt
1949	27 Feb–29 May	New York, Bermuda, Nassau, Jamaica, Trinidad, Barbados, St Lucia, Antigua, New York
1950	May–June	Nigeria, Gold Coast
1951	20 Feb–20 Apr	Egypt, Calcutta, Singapore, Kuala Lumpur, Penang, Ceylon
1952	29 Jan–21 Mar	South Africa, Bulawayo, Salisbury, Blantyre, Dar es Salaam, Nairobi
1953	26 Feb-20 Nov	Dakar, Gambia, Sierra Leone, Gold Coast, Nigeria.

From these journeys Timmermans returned 'with vast textbook orders and, more significantly, a sheaf of contracts for local authors and localised publications'.

Timmermans – who is described by Attenborough as 'Physically and morally tough, endowed with a passionate belief in this country's overseas responsibilities' and was blessed with 'dynamic energy' – clearly felt at home at Hodder & Stoughton, and his name appears in the first heat of the gentlemen's pillow fight championship in the programme for the 1959 sports day. A YMCA-style enthusiasm for the great outdoors seems to have returned to the firm with a vengeance after the war, and corporate sport loomed large in company life. 'Sports Day tradition is now very firmly established', declared Ralph in his introduction to the day's programme, 'and it is much more than appears on just this one day: its organisers are busy all year round, with dances, darts and table-tennis competitions, cricket and other matches, and anything else that takes their fancy.' The Chairman's Message continued: 'We use no Welfare Officer, no "First Floor" direction, for all this, for we have always liked to do things a little differently from other people. Each year I invite one senior member from among our different companies to "get on with it."'

Participation in sports day was, it seems, now open to the canteen staff, and the events in 1959 included a waitresses' race – there were a wooden tray and table mats for the winner, and jam dishes in a walnut stand for the runner-up, while the third-place prize was a jewel boa. The usual roster of sprints, obstacle races and the ever-popular egg-and-spoon events (for both sexes) were further enlivened by a 'Mixed Spearing the Spud' competition. Coca-Cola had made it onto the drinks menu, Scotch skittles and a coconut shy were offered as sideshows and the day was rounded off with 'Dancing to Johnny Spice and His Music at Chieseman's Restaurant in Lewisham'.

The 1959 sports day took place on 10 June. Just over two weeks later, on 26 June, the company's staff newsletter announced a revolution; 'the directors of Hodder & Stoughton will . . . be augmented as from July 1st by the appointment of Leonard Cutts to the board. Thus, the board of Hodder and Stoughton now reads:

Ralph Hodder-Williams (Chairman)
Paul Hodder-Williams (Vice-Chairman)
John Attenborough (Vice-Chairman)
Toby Hodder-Williams [Ralph's son]
Leonard Cutts.'

It added that Cutts's first job in his new role would be to 'make an editorial journey to New York in September, where he will be looking for new books from America to cover every side of Hodder & Stoughton's publishing activity'. So Leonard Cutts would be treading in the transatlantic footsteps of Matthew Hodder, Ernest Hodder-Williams and Philip Attenborough.

A little earlier that year Ralph had restructured the business by creating a parent company, and he invited R. J. Davis to join the board of Matthew Hodder Ltd, as it was known. At last these two long-serving Hodder men had seats at the top table.

Immediately below the announcement of Leonard Cutts's promotion the staff newsletter carried a paragraph under the headline 'GRANDPARENTS'. 'We rejoice with Mr and Mrs Paul in their new capacity as grandparents', it read, '. . . Another generation – great-great-great-grandchildren of Matthew Hodder – is here.' The first board-level appointments of non-family members did not alter the firm's essentially dynastic character. When Ralph stood down as chairman of Hodder & Stoughton the following year Paul Hodder-Williams took his place. Paul also took over as the chairman of the Matthew Hodder group, and John Attenborough was appointed as his deputy.

14

Has this script been read for MC?

In a short memoir written for this book, Maggie Body, who joined Hodder & Stoughton as a secretary in February 1961 (on an annual salary of £590), gives us a glimpse of life in the firm as it stood on the threshold of change. She was quickly promoted to work as an editorial assistant for Elsie Herron, the heroine of *The Ascent of Everest* episode, who had by then risen to be a fully fledged editor. 'Elsie's Girls' – three of them – 'inhabited a room on the third floor of the old building of Warwick Lane', she writes, while Elsie herself presided from 'a little cubbyhole full of smoke' off the main office. London still bore the scars of the Blitz: '. . . the building at that time was half the original structure because it had been bombed during the war', she remembered. 'Even in the early sixties there were still bombed sites around St Paul's where people used to feed the feral cats in the lunch hour. Hodders tended a little garden in their front half ruins until the building was restored in its entirety in smart red brick.'

Maggie Body reports that Elsie Herron 'was not found easy by the other staff but was always fiercely loyal to her Girls'. Miss Herron was clearly a person of great and recognised talent; when she was given the title of Chief Resident Editor in 1960 the announcement in the staff newsletter noted that she had 'already contributed in no uncertain way to many of Hodder and Stoughton's post war successes'. But, in the pre-feminist world of early 1960s London, her scope for taking decisions was evidently limited. 'Though Elsie was called the Editor,' Maggie Body writes, 'she was not the channel for acquiring books and certainly not a director. Scripts mostly arrived via John Attenborough, Mr John as we always addressed him.' She adds, 'this feudal form of address was practical in a family firm. The two surnames that mattered were Attenborough and Hodder-Williams.'

The *Teach Yourself* series was still going great guns, and Leonard Cutts was ever on the prowl for new subjects and new experts. He 'breezed into Elsie's Girls and asked if any of us spoke Anglo-Saxon,' Maggie Body remembers. 'I said cautiously that I had studied Old English for a year and that was how I found myself reading a proposed *TY Old English*.' Cutts's signature appeared at the front of every *Teach Yourself* book and looked like 'Len Zoots'. Letters used to come in addressed to Mr Zoots, so that became his nickname. 'Everybody liked Len Zoots,' Maggie Body remembers, 'because he was quirky and independent and encouraged the junior staff.'

When change came to this sepia-tinted world it was swift. Frank Mumby, in his history *Publishing and Bookselling in the Twentieth Century*, identifies Hodder & Stoughton as one of two 'imprints founded in the nineteenth century and which remained privately owned' that 'grew prodigiously' in the 1960s – the other being Macmillan. 'It could be said', he writes, 'that Hodder's waited to make sure they had understood in which direction books, literature and public opinion were evolving' before they decided to plunge into the future. 'The Hodder-Williamses and the Attenboroughs . . . then transformed themselves into modern publishing moguls with great alacrity,' Mumby continues. 'The facts were that Hodder and Stoughton, a company of solid achievement and many bestsellers in educational and general publishing, but with a marked bias towards the conventional, suddenly in 1962 tacked in a new direction, taking on the other large general publishers in the grab for leading authors.'

The catalyst was Robin Denniston, who joined Hodder & Stoughton on a full-time basis in the spring of 1961, just after

Maggie Body. Denniston had made a name for himself at Collins, another publisher with nineteenth-century religious roots (there was a definite edge of rivalry between the two firms), and had been running a High Anglican imprint called the Faith Press. It seems Leonard Cutts first introduced him to Paul Hodder-Williams with the firm's religious list in mind, and he was wooed over lunch at the Athenaeum, in those days still enjoying its reputation as a favourite episcopal watering hole.

Denniston's real interest, however, lay in broadening the Hodder & Stoughton range and giving the firm a higher profile. The announcement of his appointment stated – somewhat opaquely – that he would be 'in charge of editorial publicity, the oversight of sub-leases of book rights', and take 'more general editorial interest in books which require special promotional activities'. The job description did not really matter; he was above all an inspirational and sometimes eccentric publisher. 'Working for Robin was fun,' Maggie Body remembers. 'You never knew what might happen next.'

He had a creative's careless attitude in matters of dress – often turning up for work in odd socks and minus a collar stud. The literary agent George Greenfield wrote, 'he had that vague, slightly shambling air that concealed a sharp and incisive mind. Untidy, with the knot of his tie screwed round almost under one ear and, more often than not, a spot of blood on his collar where he had nicked himself while shaving, he did not resemble the prototype of the smart young executive.' At moments of crisis he would resort to playing hymns on an elderly harmonium he kept in his office.

In 1962 Denniston brought out the book that most clearly defined his vision of the future: Anthony Sampson's *The Anatomy of Britain* was quite unlike anything Hodder & Stoughton had published before. John Attenborough recognised it as 'an editorial as well as a promotional triumph for Denniston', and one of Sampson's obituarists described it as a 'stellar event'. It was an inspired publishing idea because it both chimed with the mood of the moment and opened the way for a string of updated editions.

Sampson had established his reputation as the editor of *Drum* magazine in South Africa, where he had become friendly with Nelson Mandela, advising the ANC leader at his trial. He joined the *Observer* on his return to London in 1955, and *The Anatomy of Britain* reflected the paper's broadly liberal editorial line. *The Anatomy* was premised on the left-wing 1960s view that Britain was run by interlocking centres of power and influence that together formed what we would now call the Establishment – although that term does not appear to have been coined until the end of the decade. This view of the world is reflected in the book's endpaper, a pattern of overlapping Venn diagrams suggesting the links between groups such as 'Diplomats', 'Armed Forces', 'Industry' and 'Trades Unions'. The first three chapters cover Aristocracy, Land and Palace – only then is Parliament considered as a power in the land, and the chapter on Westminster is followed by one on Clubs.

There was just enough of the reference book about *The Anatomy of Britain* to win it a place in the libraries of the nation's reading households alongside works like *Who's Who* and the *Encyclopaedia Britannica*, and it was bought by many readers who did not share its ideological assumptions. I have found several copies on our own shelves, among them a first edition that came to us from a distant relation inscribed with the name of her grand country house, and a humbler 1982 paperback that includes, tucked between the pages, a short note from Sampson to my late father-in-law, a civil servant, thanking him for a correction on the subject of civil service pensions. The book became an institution, and Sampson produced new editions to reflect the changing times. *The Anatomy of Britain* was followed by *Anatomy of Britain Today* (1965), *The New Anatomy of Britain* (1971), *Changing Anatomy of Britain* (1982), *The Essential Anatomy of Britain: Democracy in Crisis* (1992) and *Who Runs This Place? The Anatomy of Britain in the 21st Century* (2004). Sampson died of a heart attack not long after the publication of the last on that list.

The year after the first publication of *The Anatomy of Britain* saw completion of the refurbishment of the bomb-damaged Warwick Lane headquarters. It was celebrated by two parties, one for the great and good of the press and the broadcasting world and one, on 5 June 1963, for authors. Sir John Hunt, whose book had done so much to give the firm the lustre it was enjoying, opened the building, and was introduced by his partner in the *Ascent of Everest* project, Paul Hodder-Williams. Paul's speech included a publishing manifesto that recalls the spirit of his uncle Ernest. 'The basic truth of publishing', he said, 'is that we exist to serve the authors who entrust the children of their imagination to us. You, the authors, provide us with our life blood. We provide you with the bodies for the spirit of your imagination. So far as the general public is concerned, we are only good publishers when we publish good authors. And so far as authors are concerned, we are only good publishers if we finance, clothe and distribute their books well. Those are the facts of life.'

At the same time Hodder & Stoughton initiated a graduate trainee scheme, a further sign that the firm was catching up with the late twentieth century. The first trainee, however, was a member of the clan. Michael Attenborough read law at Oxford without, he told me in an interview for this book, any intention of becoming a lawyer, and then studied accountancy without much interest in becoming an accountant. As a young man his first passion was golf – during his twenties he represented Britain against the United States in the Walker Cup – but as a child he had also been inspired by listening to his father John talking about the publishing adventures of the day when he returned to the family home in Kent each evening.

Immediately after joining in 1962 Michael was despatched to the West Country to replace the local rep, who had been forced to stand down for health reasons. The experience of bashing around the seaside bookshops with a supply of titles in the back of his Austin Cambridge turned him into a champion of the paperback, and his paperback strategy was to play an important part in the firm's expansion later in the decade.

Another development reflecting the firm's self-confidence in the early 60s was the introduction of a new colophon, the somewhat archaic term publishers use to describe the emblem that appears at the bottom of the spine on most books. Sir Ernest Hodder-Williams was said to have observed that 'the only colophon to make sense to him was the weathervane, because a publisher changed his policy with every wind that blew, and he was sorry that Heinemann had thought of it first'. His flexible ideas about branding were reflected in the Yellow Jacket designs, many of which included colophons attached to particular authors. Perhaps the most famous was the haloed stick man who appeared on the cover of Saint books, and the series featuring John Creasy's blue-blooded sleuth The Toff carried a stylised image of a top hat, monocle and cigarette.

The more corporately minded Paul wanted something solid that would express the group's identity. A design company came up with the conceit of four chessmen – a king for Hodder & Stoughton itself, a bishop for the University of London Press, a castle for the English Universities Press and a knight for the children's books from the Brockhampton Press. In his introduction to the 1963 catalogue of new books Paul Hodder-Williams expressed his ambitions for the new insignia: 'We hope that these new colophons will in time come to be connected by those who love books, with every field of human enquiry', he wrote, 'from that of the baby learning to recognise the difference between a cow and a goat, through the post-graduate scientist working on the perimeter of human knowledge to the man at the end of his days, tasting life and still learning through books at his own fireside.'

That aspiration was enshrined in stone at St Paul's House, the firm's new headquarters. The sculptor Alan Collins, who in Britain is probably best known for his work on Guildford Cathedral, was commissioned to carve a huge frieze of a stylised chessboard above the main entrance. The frieze appeared on the cover of the 1964 catalogue, and for a while the chessmen were indeed established as the group's emblems. But they disappeared in the 1980s, and since the mid-1990s the Hodder & Stoughton logo has been a stylised 'H'. Collins's monumental sculpture still survives on the front of St Paul's House, but Hodder has never settled on a colophon as enduring as Penguin's penguin or Pan's pipe-playing god.

Paul Hodder-Williams laid out his publishing strategy in the introduction to the 1962 catalogue. 'We have been through a period of re-appraisal, appropriate to the start of a new gener-ation', he wrote, 'and, having come out the other side, have decided unanimously and with enthusiasm to embark on a new and progressive editorial and promotion policy. We want to see more young writers, both of novels and non-fiction, on our list.' The firm was, he declared, 'working hard on our policy of recruiting the young and untried without in any way diminish-ing our concern for, and interest in, the famous established writers whose names will shine out of the list for you'.

Robin Denniston began to bring in a new range of books, broadening the fiction list by including more upmarket writers like Nicholas Mosley (son and biographer of the Fascist leader Oswald) and Nicholas Wollaston. 'These gentlemen even some-times used the f-word – with an asterisk or two of course,' Maggie Body remembers. 'In those days the cry would occasionally go up, "Has this script been read for MC?"' MC stood for moral censorship, so that cry was a distant echo of Thomas Stoughton's stern letter to Ernest Hodder-Williams about the firm's reputation as a publisher of family reading. There had been an attempt to update Thomas Stoughton's publishing principles at a company conference in the grand Connaught Rooms near Covent Garden in 1961; 'The Hodder and Stoughton imprint stands for quality and a liberal sanity that is neither Puritan nor subservient to the fashionable "anything goes" policy of the publisher who stands for nothing in the public mind', read the doctrine that emerged. Maggie Body notes that 'the defence of MC was weakening in the early sixties'.

The fiction list was also growing nicely plump with more popular authors. Gavin Lyall published *The Wrong Side of the Sky,* his first novel with Hodder, in 1961 and followed through with *The Most Dangerous Game*, a Book Society Choice in 1964, and *Midnight Plus One*, which won the Golden Dagger Award in 1965. Len Deighton's first novel *The Ipcress File* was published by Hodder in 1962 and became a hugely successful – indeed classic – film starring Michael Caine. In 1964 there were two big-screen productions based on Hodder books, a Disney version of Sheila Burnford's *The Incredible Journey* and a Hitchcock of Winston Graham's *Marnie*. *Marnie* flopped as a film – surprisingly for a Hitchcock – and Hodder lost Winston Graham as an author as a result of the poor paperback sales that followed. But the big and small screens were, for the most part, overwhelmingly positive factors for the sales teams; both Leslie Charteris's Saint and John Creasey's Commander Gideon were starring in television series that year.

And Hodder & Stoughton's bestselling novelist Mary Stewart was really hitting her stride. Her initial print runs were around 65,000, and between 1961 and 1968 she produced no fewer than six of her romantic suspense novels. Maggie Body, who became her editor, describes them as 'intelligent romantic thrillers set in nice places'. She was 'good at children, animals and the country-side', Maggie Body wrote in her memoir. 'They were reliable holiday reading and she had her formula.' One of the books, *The*

Moon Spinners (about a jewel thief on the island of Crete), was made into a Disney movie, and *The Gabriel Hounds* (1967) was pushed with the kind of campaign that showed what modern marketing could do. Mary Stewart appeared everywhere – on television, in bookshops and in the press. In the 1970s she switched – with equal success – to Arthurian sagas.

Hodder would, it seemed, do anything to keep their star happy. 'Hodders nursed her zealously, as they should,' writes Maggie Body, 'but she was not the easiest lady to handle.' When Mary Stewart offered a collection of her poetry for publication Hodder immediately agreed, but the production department decided that it could only be made to work if one of the poems was cut. The job of 'imparting this fact and negotiating the excision' was handed to Mary Stewart's editor. 'I chose the one for the chop and went to have tea with Mary at Brown's Hotel, her London watering hole when she came down from Scotland,' Maggie Body remembers.

What followed was a masterclass in handling difficult authors. 'Fortunately by now I knew our Mary,' Maggie Body writes, 'so when she gazed at me sorrowfully and said that had been her favourite poem, I had my next line ready and asked whether she would like me to resign as her editor then or at the end of the month. At which point we both got the giggles and she persuaded me into ordering an exotic brand of tea (we *were* at Brown's) before saying housemaid's would do for her. So she still won on points but I got the text to fit.'

Hodder had once been ahead of the game in the field of mass production reprints, but the war and paper shortages had, despite the second run of the series from the late 1940s, killed off the Yellow Jackets for good. The decision to join the consortium behind the Pan imprint had been driven by expediency, but by the 1960s the disadvantages of the arrangement were becoming more and more apparent; all their best authors came out in paperback with Pan, leaving Hodder with the remnants to flog under their own paperback imprint. This problem was solved almost by accident; to finance the rebuilding of the St Paul's headquarters the firm sold its holding in Pan for £90,000. The happy consequence, Michael Attenborough told me, was that 'Our obligation to offer anyone who came in to Pan books disappeared.'

Attenborough's months as a travelling salesman working the holiday resorts of the south-west had taught him some tough lessons. Booksellers in holiday spots like Newquay and Bournemouth simply were not interested in hardbacks, and Hodder was ill-equipped to compete with specialist firms like Penguin, Corgi and, indeed, Pan. The Hodder paperbacks were, Attenborough recognised, 'very scruffily produced'; the cover images were usually taken from old editions of women's magazines, and he concluded 'we couldn't just go on slapping a lozenge on *Women's Own* artwork'. Michael Attenborough formed an alliance with a member of the Collins family – he told me their traditional rivalry was put aside in the interests of resisting some of the upstart newcomers on the publishing scene – and with his help came up with a fresher and more appealing look for the books. In 1966 Hodder Paperbacks were rebranded as a separate imprint, Coronet Books.

The real challenge, however, was persuading the best authors that Hodder was up to handling their paperback editions – they were not, Michael Attenborough concedes, 'showing the same volume' as the specialist paperback firms. It took a couple of spectacular pieces of good fortune to show that Hodder & Stoughton could compete with the best in the modern mass market.

Robin Denniston was the kind of larger-than-life figure who attracts his own mythology, so perhaps it is no surprise that I have been given two quite different versions of how he secured the British rights to *Love Story*, the phenomenally successful Erich Segal book that came out as a film starring Ali McGraw and Ryan O'Neill in 1970. According to one version Denniston won an auction of the rights in New York because he was, true to form, wearing odd socks, and thus attracted the attention of the agent selling the book. Maggie Body's account has more detail and is therefore more convincing. 'Robin wasn't all upmarket fine writing and could recognise a Hodder mainstream novel when he saw one', she writes; 'he casually offered some paltry advance for the UK rights in Erich Segal's *Love Story* which he read in the New York office of an editor he was waiting to come back from lunch. (The editor hadn't looked at the script yet and accepted the offer.)'

The 'paltry advance' was, according to Michael Attenborough, £1,000, and he remembers that the firm very quickly received an offer of £25,000 to sell the rights on to another London publisher. But before accepting this tempting profit, 'One or two of us read it, and our wives read it, and' – he added this somewhat gruffly – 'started crying, and one realised that there was something in this curious little book.' Hodder decided to publish the British paperback themselves, producing one edition immediately and a second when the film came out. *Love Story* became a teenage craze, and Michael Attenborough recalls 'whole classes of schoolgirls buying a copy each at Waterloo station'. It was the firm's first million-copy seller in paperback, and he says it 'Did us a huge amount of good because we were noticed'.

Attenborough himself can claim a main part in the other great paperback success story of the era. Since the early 1950s Hodder & Stoughton had been publishing what he called 'bread and butter stuff' by a now largely forgotten novelist called Hermina Black. By the early seventies she had, it seems, fallen on hard times, and was, according to Michael Attenborough, constantly pestering Paul Hodder-Williams for floats. Michael was eventually despatched on a diplomatic mission to her home in Winchester to sort things out. He took a dim view of her literary talents – he described her to me as 'an expert in the doctor/nurse category' – and set off from Waterloo feeling depressed about the day ahead.

In the hope of cheering himself up he took a book that had been published in hardback by Hamish Hamilton – without making any great waves – but had been repeatedly turned down by paperback firms. Attenborough spent the journey in 'absolute fits of laughter', and the following day made an offer for the paperback rights to David Niven's 1972 autobiography *The Moon's a Balloon*. With no other hats in the ring (Pan, the only firm to show an interest, had offered to publish on the condition that Niven cut the 'terribly boring' section on Hollywood), Hodder picked up the book for a song; an advance of £750 and royalties of seven and a half per cent.

David Niven proved immensely energetic in the promotion of the book, travelling the country and charming everyone he met. He was, Attenborough remembers, 'One of those people who made you feel you were the only person in the world who really mattered.' He was also a television natural, and in those days of three terrestrial networks (BBCs One and Two and ITV) appearing anywhere on television meant that you were likely to be seen by a very high proportion of the British population.

The *Parkinson* chat show, a format that usually included three fifteen-minute interviews, was tailor-made for him, and he told some of the best stories in the book with the economy and comic timing of a true raconteur. Some of them were, by the standards of the day, extremely risqué, and definitely would not have passed an 'MC' test; David Niven described, for example, how he had fallen in love with a prostitute as a teenager and invited her to watch cricket matches at his public school, Stowe. But part of Niven's charm was that he seemed such a gent, and he got away with a great deal that might have been condemned in a less suave performer.

When Niven appeared on *Parkinson* three years later after the publication of his second volume of autobiography (*Bring on the Empty Horses*), Michael Parkinson introduced him thus: 'If you were an author and you had a first novel coming out this week you could expect to sell 250 copies in hardback. If you were an established author with a bit of form you might expect to sell between six and seven hundred hardback copies. My special guest tonight wrote a book once – it was his first effort. It sold 200,000 copies in hardback and a staggering four million in paperback, which isn't bad for a beginner, and certainly not for a book described by the author as the sort of book people like to read on the loo.' It was said that David Niven changed the record of his occupation in his passport from 'actor' to 'writer'. And Hodder did so well out of *The Moon's a Balloon* that a couple of years after publication, as the paperback sales approached the two million mark, a senior editor rang Niven's agent out of the blue and volunteered a *retrospective* increase in the royalty rate to ten per cent.

Hodder & Stoughton was flourishing on its traditional turf too. In 1966 the firm recruited Edward England to revive the firm's religious list. England was a journalist by training and at the time of his recruitment he was running a large religious bookshop; he approached his specialist field with the kind of energy that Robin Denniston had brought to the general list.

There was widespread public concern in the West about the persecution of Christians in the Soviet Bloc, and England championed the cause of Richard Wurmbrand, a Romanian pastor who had been imprisoned and tortured for fourteen years before fleeing to the United States. Wurmbrand's *Sermons in Solitary Confinement* sold two million copies in twenty-three languages. In a departure from the firm's strongly evangelical tradition, England also published the autobiography of Cardinal John Heenan, the Roman Catholic archbishop of Westminster.

John Attenborough writes that 'Edward England's first journey to America penetrated the Bible Belt as old Matthew Hodder had a hundred years earlier', and 1968, Hodder & Stoughton's centenary, provided the opportunity for ancestor worship. Edward England organised an exhibition at Stationer's Hall, home of the Worshipful Company of Stationers since the seventeenth century, dedicated to 'One hundred years of Christian publishing'. It would, as Attenborough pointed out, 'have gladdened the founders' hearts'.

Those hearts would have been rather less gladdened by what Michael Attenborough calls 'the awful business' of *The Sacred Mushroom and the Cross: A Study of the Nature and Origins of Christianity Within the Fertility Cults of the Ancient Near East*, a book that set Hodder & Stoughton's two religiously minded editors, the Evangelical England and the Anglo-Catholic Denniston, at odds with one another. The author, John Allegro, argued that Christianity had its roots in fertility cults and that Jesus was a mythical figure dreamt up by cult members high on magic mushrooms – it involved a re-translation of the Dead Sea Scrolls in which, as Michael Attenborough put it, 'words like Yahweh turned out to mean penis'. Denniston, whose publishing flair had an iconoclastic streak, backed the book enthusiastically, and so upset the religious books editor that England wrote to *The Times* to dissociate himself from the project.

The firm continued to be, as Maggie Body puts it, 'good at the outdoors'. In the 1960s the veteran adventurer Francis Chichester turned his attention from aviation to yachting, winning the world's first single-handed transatlantic yacht race at the beginning of the decade. His first couple of books were published by Allen and Unwin, who paid an advance of £200 and what the agent George Greenfield described as 'modest royalties'. When the firm offered the same deal for Chichester's autobiography Greenfield dug his heels in.

In a telephone call to Philip Unwin, nephew of one of the firm's founders, he made a bold gesture: 'If I can't get someone else to put up ten times as much – £2,000 – within one week from now,' he said, 'you can have the book at your price. Okay?' He then rang Robin Denniston at Hodder, and – to his great delight – got a call back within forty minutes; 'We were in business. He had talked it over with "the family", who were prepared to back his judgement,' Greenfield recalled later. He recorded that *The Lonely Sea and the Sky*, Chichester's memoirs, sold over '70,000 copies in hardback and several hundred thousand copies in paperback'.

The following year, 1966, Chichester set off from Plymouth in *Gipsy Moth IV*, securing his place in history by becoming the first person to achieve what was regarded as a true circumnavigation of the globe on his own – and he managed it in just 226 days. He was duly knighted and the chairman himself, Paul Hodder-Williams, rolled up his sleeves to get involved in the book project that followed. *Gipsy Moth Circles the World* sold 100,000 copies.

As well as acting as Francis Chichester's publisher, Hodder was also publishing his wife Sheila, and Maggie Body reports that the couple were fiercely competitive. 'Once we were rash enough to allow them each to have a book on the go at the same time', she writes, '. . . fortunately their son Giles was doing a holiday job at Hodders at the time so I could slip him his mother's proofs and tell him to tell her that if she got them back corrected not too heavily by next week she would be ahead of Francis on the production schedule.'

The optimism of the era is reflected in a 1966 document drawn up by Paul Hodder-Williams to explain his plans for restructuring the Hodder group: 'The demand for books will increase,' he wrote, 'and we must plan for controlled expansion wherever public demand leads us, anywhere in the world.'

The only real complaint Maggie Body makes about this happy and energetic publishing decade relates to the habits of General Sir John Glubb – Glubb Pasha, as he was nicknamed for his work in training the Jordanian army. She describes him as 'our most irritating author' because he 'kept writing vast books about Arab history, demanding lots of maps, and would spell the place names differently on each one, trying to explain it away by informing us there were no vowels in Arabic, so you could take your pick'. Maggie Body and the firm's map-maker, who had drawn maps for Montgomery during the desert campaigns of the Second World War, were 'never convinced'.

15

Snowballs and Wicked Ladies

In the middle of the break-up of his first marriage, David Cornwell – much better known, of course, as the novelist John le Carré – wrote to his psychiatrist describing his ideal relationship. He added that he had found 'a mistress who might very well provide me with the happiness I speak of . . . In the time we have been together – admittedly never long – I have been content, and have written a great deal. When this last book was in shreds it was she who helped me piece it together and make something of it. I find her compassionate, understanding, and remarkably intelligent.'

The subject of this encomium was Jane Eustace, who worked at Hodder & Stoughton first as a publicist and later as foreign rights manager. She was to become – and remains – David Cornwell's second wife, and the relationship brought her then-employers one of their most famous and profitable authors.

David Cornwell's progress towards Hodder & Stoughton was crab-like – he came sideways to the firm. The journey began with a change of agents. Cornwell's first literary agent was Peter Watt, a scion of the family we've often met before in the Hodder story, and he had also relied heavily on his accountant to manage his affairs. But his international success in the mid 1960s meant he needed more high-powered representation.

Before working at Hodder, Jane Eustace had been a secretary to George Greenfield, the literary agent who introduced Francis Chichester to the firm, and she brought her old boss and her lover together for dinner one evening. Since the relationship was still secret, Greenfield was surprised when Cornwell opened the door of Jane's flat, but the evening passed off successfully. The following week the three of them enjoyed an epic lunch washed down with 'various glasses of malt whisky, three bottles of Corton Clos du Roi and a *marc* or two to round things off', and as they waited for their car afterwards Cornwell asked Greenfield to be his English-language agent (he had a separate one for worldwide rights).

Cornwell was also becoming unhappy with his British hardback publishers, Heinemann. He later complained about the 'shoddy' production values of the firm's edition of *The Looking-Glass War*, which came out in 1965, and his biographer, Adam Sisman, reports that he was disappointed by the £22,000 advance Heinemann offered for his next book, *A Small Town in Germany*, which was published in 1968. Sisman also notes that he had been in dispute with Heinemann over paperback royalties; in the days when most paperback publishing was done by separate specialist firms it was normal for hardback publishers to take as much as fifty per cent of the paperback royalties when they sold a book on, and Cornwell wanted to 'break the system'.

Hodder featured on a shortlist of possible new publishers that Greenfield offered to his client, and Sisman writes that the firm was attractive in part because of the 'resurgence that would make it one of the most powerful forces in British publishing by the early 1980s'. Robin Denniston had by now taken over as the managing director of Hodder & Stoughton. With his cleverness and cultivated shabbiness Denniston could, as Sisman notes, 'almost have been a character out of a le Carré novel himself', and he had a natural affinity for the murky world of espionage. Maggie Body records in her memoir that he had 'an intriguing line in retired spies because his father [Commander Alastair Denniston, head of the Government Code and Cypher School] had once run Bletchley Park'. She recalls an episode when

Denniston asked her to send proofs to the Cambridge spy and
Cold War defector Donald Maclean 'c/o the Central Post Office
Moscow' (Maclean duly returned them 'in good time').

The deal was done – again in the best publishing tradition –
over a meal at Boulestin, the venerable French restaurant in St
James's, and John le Carré joined the increasingly impressive list
of Hodder & Stoughton authors. But the first offering he brought
the firm was, in Michael Attenborough's view, 'an extremely
difficult book'.

Cornwell had made his breakthrough in 1963 with *The Spy
Who Came in from the Cold*, a Cold War classic and the foundation of the le Carré brand. But there are no spies in *The Naïve and
Sentimental Lover*; the book, a more domestic drama of infidelity,
is very clearly rooted in Cornwell's own experience, and it came
out in 1971, the year of his divorce from his first wife.

It was not especially well received. Cornwell wrote later that
'British critics fell gleefully on it, welcoming it almost with one
voice as the proof, if proof were needed, that I should stick to the
"genre" novel and not aspire "to real literature".' That was over-
stating things a little, but some of the criticism was damning: *The
Times Literary Supplement* called the book 'a disastrous failure' and
the *Listener* declared that the 'narrative limps along'.

Michael Attenborough is full of praise for the way Robin
Denniston handled the book; he was 'brilliant, absolutely brilliant, in the way he saw *The Naïve and Sentimental Lover* through
publication,' Attenborough told me. And Denniston's nurturing
of John Cornwell's relationship with the firm soon paid dividends. The next le Carré, *Tinker, Tailor, Soldier, Spy*, marked a
real return to Cold War form; George Smiley, who had appeared
in the author's first published novel, *Call for the Dead*, was back as
the star of the hugely successful 'Karla Trilogy', the three books
in which Smiley takes on the Moscow spymaster of that name.
Tinker, Tailor, Soldier, Spy became a BBC television series with
Alec Guinness in the lead role; the plot was sometimes

bewilderingly complex, but it was compulsive. The viewing figures were helped by the happy coincidence of that all-out ITV strike, which took the network off the air for over two months. The audience hit eight and a half million, with a further three million watching the repeats.

But by the time *Tinker, Tailor, Soldier, Spy* was published in 1974 Denniston himself had left Hodder & Stoughton. His departure is one of the last episodes covered in John Attenborough's *A Living Memory*, but the book is oddly coy about the reasons behind it. John Attenborough writes that Denniston 'had often contemplated new directions, ranging from the calling of a parish priest to a quiet life on his small-holding near Worcester. Clearly by the end of 1972 the title of managing director of Hodder and Stoughton was not a final goal for Robin.' And he pays somewhat ponderous tribute to the way Denniston had 'helped to rescue the firm from the fuddy-duddy Establishment image derived not so much from the books it published as from a misinterpretation of tradition which could only be eradicated by an editor unencumbered by it'.

But John Attenborough's son Michael was blunter about the reason for Denniston's departure in his interview with me. It was, he said, 'the old glass ceiling' that limited promotion in what was, despite all the modernisation, still very much a family firm. The top job of running the wider Hodder & Stoughton group was reserved for a member of the clan. 'He [Denniston] wanted to be the boss,' Michael Attenborough told me, 'Paul [Hodder-Williams] said, "You are not going to be boss."'

Denniston, Attenborough added, 'felt he was still quite young', and off he went, accepting an offer to be deputy chairman to George Weidenfeld at Weidenfeld & Nicolson. He was later hired for a senior job at Oxford University Press, and at the end of his career he did indeed become a vicar, taking over the beautiful medieval church at Great Tew in Oxfordshire. The publisher John Mitchinson, now of the Unbound imprint, moved there in

1997 and remembers Father Denniston as 'fabulously eccentric and messy' and much loved by his parishioners. Denniston somehow raised the money for a swimming pool to be built at the Rectory, and would join the villagers in the water wearing 'moth-eaten swimming trunks'. When he discovered John's profession he would send him advice – sometimes obscure but always sound – 'scruffily typed and thrust into recycled envelopes'.

The strong sense of a continuing family tradition at Hodder was reflected in the weekly routine of St Paul's House; even in the early 1970s members of staff called Attenborough or Hodder-Williams would – no matter what their level in the firm – gather for a Friday family lunch on the top floor. The meal was cooked by the wife of one of the warehouse staff, and she favoured roast chicken – Paul Hodder-Williams especially enjoyed the ritual of carving the bird – or steak and kidney pudding. There was a glass of sherry beforehand, and coffee was served with mint-flavoured Turkish delight. Michael Attenborough remembers the weekly ritual with great affection, and regretted its passing when the firm finally sold St Paul's House and followed the rest of the publishing world to Bloomsbury. But it is difficult to imagine that these exclusive gatherings were not at least a little alienating to senior staff – like Robin Denniston – who were not included.

Michael Attenborough was, at thirty-three, promoted to fill Denniston's shoes as the managing director of Hodder & Stoughton. His father, John Attenborough, retired that same year (1973), and Paul Hodder-Williams stood down as chairman of the group in 1974. The guard changed in accordance with family tradition. Paul was succeeded by Michael's older brother Philip, so the two Attenborough brothers were running the firm between them. Their cousin Mark, Paul's son, who had joined in 1961, was in charge of developing modern computing and distribution systems and a new warehouse operation on land the firm had bought at Dunton Green in Kent. There was, however, a concession to modern etiquette: Philip decided to abolish the habit of referring to members of the family as 'Mr' followed by their Christian names.

And the board was refreshed by the appointment of one significant outsider – Eric Major – who was pinched from Collins for the job of publicity manager. Major went on to run the firm's general publishing for fifteen years, and presided over the publication of a remarkable mix of books, ranging from popular and literary novels to mountaineering (he enjoyed climbing himself), religion and cooking. Sometimes these passions made for unlikely combinations. Major was an enthusiastic Delia Smith promoter, and both were Roman Catholics; he published her devotional work *A Journey into God* on the firm's religious list as well as her immensely successful cookery books.

Michael Attenborough told me he was, despite the experience he had built up in turning round the paperback business, 'terrified' when he took on the managing director's job at such a young age, and he concedes a couple of terrible mistakes in the early days. In the year he took over Hodder & Stoughton this most respectable imprint published a book called *My People Shall Live: the Autobiography of a Revolutionary* by Leila Khaled, a member of the Popular Front for the Liberation of Palestine, who had become famous – perhaps notorious would be a better word – after taking part in two plane hijackings in 1969 and 1970. And Michael also discovered he had inherited a contract to publish a book by the Holocaust-denying historian David Irving; *Hitler's War*, a revisionist account of the Second World War from the Führer's perspective, duly came out in 1977, and provoked widespread controversy. Michael Attenborough now says that he wishes 'we hadn't been involved in any way', adding that 'We were all incredibly innocent.'

The firm's perennial habit of looking forward and backwards at the same time was reflected in the management of its new purpose-built distribution warehouse at Dunton Green, which opened in 1975. The era of the company sports days was over

– the last was held in 1968 – but something of the old YMCA spirit survived; a squash court was included in the building plans, and Mark Hodder-Williams played the opening match. Tony Brown, who was very much involved in planning the new plant and became head of distribution, remembers it as a 'small village', and recalls a Sevenoaks taxi driver who picked him up from the station with the words: 'Off to the Happy Hodders Holiday Camp then!'

Tony Brown painted me a picture of a company that retained a sense of family – in the broader as well as narrow sense – that would have been recognisable to Matthew Hodder and Thomas Stoughton. The Dunton Green location had been chosen so that the firm would be able to retain many of those who had worked at its old warehouse in Brockley. The staff association organised football and cricket matches, and there was an annual staff dinner; divisional directors and staff with at least twenty-five years of service were allowed to bring their wives to the occasion. Junior staff at the Dunton Green warehouse who excelled were recognised with the Leonard Cutts Award – a Parker pen and pencil set engraved with their initials.

And life at the warehouse was enlivened by author visits; stars of the Hodder list like David Niven, Cliff Richard, Henry Cooper and Susannah York trooped down to Kent to enthuse the sales and distribution teams. The new chairman, Philip Attenborough, used to arrive at the warehouse at the wheel of a Morris 1100; Tony Brown discovered this modest motoring style was creating rumours that the firm was 'up the spout' financially, and persuaded his boss to upgrade to a more expensive car.

Tony Brown himself was recruited as the result of a conversation at a cricket match. He played for the Bickley Park Second XI, and after a game one afternoon he complained to his captain, an old friend, that he was dissatisfied with his job at an engineering firm in Sidcup. The captain was Mark Hodder-Williams, who duly responded by offering him a job in the family firm.

There was no personnel department at the time. The man who eventually set one up in the mid-1970s, Tubby Tyas (a figure fondly remembered by many Hodder veterans), was a pre-war recruit who had come to Hodder & Stoughton as the teenage son of Percy Hodder-Williams' gardener.

This benignly nepotistic and paternalist culture seems to have thrived despite the increasingly unionised industrial scene of the 1970s. The acronyms SOGAT (Society of Graphical and Allied Trades), NGA (the National Graphical Association) and NUJ (the National Union of Journalists) made many employers tremble in the mid-1970s, but Tony Brown, who became responsible for union relations, remembers most difficult issues being resolved over a drink or, in one instance, during a break in formal negotiations for a visit to the urinals.

While Tony Brown and Mark Hodder-Williams were enjoying the thwack of leather on willow on the playing fields of Kent, Eddie Bell was flogging pre-bottled ladies' cocktails around the bars of Glasgow. He had trained as a whisky distiller but moved into the world of sales because he could not afford a car, and a set of wheels came with his first salesman's job at a greetings card firm. He 'got back into booze' with a line in 'Snowballs, Wicked Ladies and Baby Bubbly', but he hated the work. Women, he pointed out to me, scarcely went into pubs in the Scotland of the early 70s, so shifting the goods was that bit tougher; he was tasked to sell twenty-four cases of these evil-sounding concoctions a day, and it meant starting with the off-licences in the morning and working right through until closing time at the clubs. When he bumped into an acquaintance from his greetings card days in Glasgow's Buchanan Street one day in 1973 he poured out his woes.

The result was an introduction to Hodder, who were looking for a sales rep at the time. The new job brought him a new love in the manner the French call a *coup de foudre*; 'For me it was enlightenment,' he told me, 'it was transforming. It was the most amazing thing. I wasn't a great reader – I became a great reader. And I loved writers – I still love writers . . . It changed my life totally.' Thinking back to the glory days when Thomas Stoughton came north to fish for talent and William Robertson Nicoll was a power in the land, I asked him whether the Hodder & Stoughton he knew in the 70s was conscious of its Scottish heritage. 'Only,' he replied, 'in the way the Queen was.'

Some of the work was almost as difficult as persuading canny Scottish publicans that they really needed to stock up on pre-mixed Wicked Ladies. One of the first books he had to sell was R. F. Delderfield's *God is an Englishman*, not an easy title in central Scotland. He also experimented with a tour to promote the 1973 cookbook *How to Cheat at Cooking* by the then relatively unknown Delia Smith. He managed to fill the window of WHSmith at Edinburgh airport with copies of her book to impress her on her arrival, and then contrived that the same books followed her round on the tour to other bookshop windows. Her agent Deborah Owen writes that 'Delia remembers that at her first book signing she didn't sell a single book and ended up buying three herself.'

But after his 'horrible job' Bell 'really got stuck in', and revenue rose 'dramatically'. Within two years he was asked down to London to take a job in sales.

The firm's quirky paternalism struck him even more forcefully as an outsider. 'It was kind of based on gentlemen and players,' he said. 'It was run on the rules of cricket, which was quite difficult for a boy from central Scotland to get his head round.' He was, he added, left in no doubt that he was a player, not a gentleman. But he responded to the warmth that was also part of the family firm ethos. It was, he told me, 'just tremendously civilised – with civilised people and great things to sell'.

He explained to me that the key to successful sales then lay in what he called 'locomotives' – powerful big sellers that would pull the 'carriages' of the other books on the list behind them.

'And we had massive locomotives at the time,' he said proudly. 'A tremendous array of authors. Every month there was a lead title on your list.' He cited James Clavell's 1975 *Shogun* as an example of the kind of book that would persuade a buyer to up his order for all the other Hodder titles too.

Eddie Bell was, by his own account, very much a paperback man and, despite all that Michael Attenborough had achieved in the field, Hodder & Stoughton still saw itself as a hardback publisher first. Paperbacks, Bell says, 'were a bit like moving from test cricket to twenty-twenty – accepted as a necessary new departure but not quite the thing'. And he challenged the plans for Dunton Green; 'I asked the question why seventy per cent of the shelving in the plant was dedicated to hardcover books and thirty per cent to paperback,' he told me, 'when the distribution figures showed it should have been the other way round.'

The agent George Greenfield, partly responsible for the le Carré coup, also played a big role in keeping the firm's adventuring list refreshed, and his 1970s offering was the mountaineer Chris Bonington. After bringing out books with Victor Gollancz and Cassell, Bonington moved to Hodder & Stoughton in 1973 for *Everest South West Face*. Unlike most agents Greenfield became heavily involved in raising the sponsorship that made his clients' expeditions possible; he negotiated flat fees for Bonington, and royalties on the books were used to repay the sponsors. The model proved successful, and Bonington stayed with the firm for the two most productive decades of his climbing and writing life.

By the time he wrote *Everest the Hard Way* in 1976, Maggie Body had taken over the 'the traditional Hodder mountaineering list' from Elsie Herron, and she managed the book. Chris Bonington is – and this is unexpected in someone who has regularly stared death in the face in the high Himalayas – nervous about his writing skills. 'As soon as I finish a chapter I have to get it off to my editor,' he told me; 'I need that reassurance.' Maggie Body would send the material back with her suggestions marked in pencil, and he says he usually accepted ninety per cent of them. Sir Christopher (as he now is) described Maggie Body to me as 'an unbelievably brilliant editor', and she stayed with him throughout his time at Hodder. The warm feelings are reciprocated. 'I wouldn't have missed knowing and loving my climbers for the world', Maggie Body wrote in her memoir, and the two of them still see one another.

Bonington was less complimentary about Hodder's production values – at least in the early days of his association with the firm. He told me that in the 1970s there was a tendency for publishers to underestimate the importance of design in adventure books, and to 'chuck the pictures in at the end'. His wife Wendy was an illustrator, and was so horrified by the initial design for *Everest the Hard Way* that, he says, she took over and redesigned the whole thing. Bonington describes the result as a 'fabulous-looking book' that 'sat at the top of the bestseller list for about four months'. He said Barclays, who Greenfield had roped in to sponsor the expedition behind the book, were handsomely repaid, and Bonington believes that Hodder learnt an important lesson about the value of good design in books of this kind.

And even as a writer he was struck by the family atmosphere that was still such a marked characteristic of the firm. 'They were just very nice people,' he told me. He added that he found the Attenboroughs 'slightly distant characters' – he remembered Michael Attenborough as 'urbane' – and was much closer to the senior outsider in the hierarchy, Eric Major.

The decade that began with the le Carré coup ended with the addition of another locomotive to the Hodder list. The firm had published the British paperback of Jeffrey Archer's first book, *Not a Penny More, Not a Penny Less*, and Archer was persuaded to move to Hodder for the hardback of his next book, *Kane and Abel*, which came out in 1979. Eddie Bell had done a stint in the United States, working closely with Simon & Schuster, and had admired the latest innovations in book packaging. For the *Kane and Abel* cover he pushed – successfully – the idea of a 'foil on foil book cover', something that had never been done in Britain before.

'We flooded the market with *Kane and Abel*,' he told me. It was a good call; the book features on lists of the top one hundred all-time bestsellers, with world sales in the tens of millions. Jeffrey Archer was impressed by the way Hodder handled the book, and even more impressed by Eddie Bell's marketing techniques. In an interview for this book he said, 'The shock came when Eddie Bell was in charge of the campaign, and the softback sold one million copies in the first week and two million by the end of the year. This year [2017] the book has had a hundred printings. Only *To Kill a Mockingbird* has had over a hundred printings.'

If *Kane and Abel* marks a thumping new chapter heading in the Hodder & Stoughton story, *One Man's Inheritance*, which the firm also published in 1979, is more of an intriguing footnote. After completing *A Living Memory*, his history of the firm, John Attenborough tried his hand at fiction. In his *Publishing and Bookselling in the Twentieth Century*, F. W. Mumby notes a certain symmetry between the two books: 'John Attenborough wrote not only an excellent history of the company,' he observed, 'but also a novel about a family of not unsuccessful business people living in Kent (the Attenboroughs lived in Kent).'

In fact, the Mortimer-Wottons, the family at the centre of *One Man's Inheritance*, are landowning grandees rather than business people, but there is a good deal in the book that reflects the Hodder story. One member of the family abandons his inheritance for the sake of gay love and beauty in the way Cecil Stoughton seems to have done, and the central figure, Philip Mortimer-Wotton, fights a Second World War very much like John Attenborough's own, with service in the Western Desert and the Italian campaigns. And the central dilemma that engages his energies on his return from service is very like the challenge the Attenboroughs and Hodder-Williamses faced at the family firm; how do you preserve the ethos of an inherited institution while making it fit to face the modern world?

There is an intriguing twist at the end of *One Man's Inheritance*. The estate goes to a bright young man called Alex, who is married to Philip's niece Susan and seems just the right person to carry it forward into the second half of the twentieth century. He is also – though this is unknown to the wider world – Philip's illegitimate son, conceived in a moment of youthful passion with a local girl before her marriage. Secure in his knowledge of this dynastically satisfying denouement, Philip dies peacefully while resting during a post-prandial walk on a sunny afternoon, his faithful Labrador Carla by his side.

16

Nice girls worked at Hodder

One hot Beverly Hills day in the autumn of 1980 the Australian writer Thomas Keneally set out from his hotel to find 'a modestly priced briefcase' – an unpromising mission in such a fabulously moneyed area. Opposite a hamburger chain restaurant on South Beverly Drive he spotted a shop called Handbag Studio, which was offering reduced prices in its 'Fall Sale', and he allowed himself to be persuaded through the door by the owner, who 'had a stocky Slavic look . . . a touch of Tartar in the cheeks, a barrel chest, powerful arms, a wrestler's neck'.

He bought a briefcase, and while an assistant phoned to check his credit card – what a very different world it was then – the store owner introduced himself as Leopold Page, a name, he explained, he had taken at Ellis Island when he arrived as an immigrant; his original Polish name of Poldek Pfefferberg had been judged too challenging for regular Americans. And when Leopold/Poldek learnt that his customer was a writer (there was, conveniently, a review of one of Keneally's novels in that week's edition of *Newsweek*) he took him into the back office and, from two metal filing cabinets, produced a sheaf of documents. They told the extraordinary story of Oskar Schindler, the Second World War German Nazi who used his forced labour factories as a way of helping hundreds of Jews (Leopold/Poldek among them) to escape the death camps.

Keneally was persuaded to hang around while his host, the briefcase now almost forgotten, escorted him to the local bank, where they waited in a queue to get the documents photocopied – again, what a very different world it was. When he finally made it back to his air-conditioned hotel room he began to read with half an eye on the television set because Notre Dame, once his great-uncle's university team, were playing an American football game. But he found his reading material 'instantly engrossing'.

It was the genesis of *Schindler's Ark*, a book that was, over the next decade and a half, to bring glory and money to both Keneally and his publishers, Hodder & Stoughton. And it is a story to gladden everyone in the publishing and writing games; a striking example of the serendipity that sometimes brings us our best material, and a reminder that patience is one of the great creative virtues. Leopold/Poldek's long battle to draw the world's attention to the way he and his wife, and so many others like them, survived the Holocaust is also a humbling illustration of the power of the storytelling compulsion.

And the episode has a moral that is likely to be welcomed by most writers but to puzzle some publishers: despite all the evidence that safe formulas drive sales, readers sometimes love the unexpected, the ambiguous and the complex. Schindler was a womaniser and a drinker, a 'ruined Catholic hedonist', as Keneally puts it. And that, as Keneally understood, is exactly why he made a compelling hero. 'Paradox is beloved of novelists', he wrote. 'Most writers spend their lives writing about unexpected malice in the supposedly virtuous, and unexpected virtue in the supposedly sinful.'

Keneally, in midlife and feeling that some of the early shine had come off his writing career, was invigorated; 'To have a tale before you which you believed, with whatever degree of self-delusion, that the world needed to hear, was a splendid, euphoric, ever-renewing experience,' he wrote. Before sitting down to write he travelled across Israel, the United States and his native Australia in search of other Schindler survivors, and visited south-west Poland, where Schindler ran his businesses and bargained for his Jews.

While Keneally did homage at Yad Vashem and soaked up the atmosphere in Krakow, his London publishers were preoccupied with a very different kind of novel; in 1981 Hodder & Stoughton bought the New English Library, or NEL, a mass-market paperback publisher that specialised in romance, mystery, science fiction and adventure. 'We needed more volume, and it was there for the taking,' Michael Attenborough told me.

Hodder & Stoughton was now settled in offices in Bedford Square, and its respectable image seemed unshakeable. In *The British Book Trade – An Oral History*, a collection of publishing reminiscences of the period, Diane Spivey, who was working as a rights manager at the firm, notes that the Bedford Square office 'was right in the heart of old-fashioned publishing', with firms like Chatto & Windus, Edward Arnold and Thames & Hudson as its neighbours. It was, she remembered, 'quite a smart place to be . . . and there seemed to be quite a lot of debby young girls who wore pie-crust collars, coloured tights and print dresses, and cycled in from Fulham on bicycles with big baskets on the front, which they left chained to the railings in Bedford Square. Nice girls worked at Hodder.' But one of the consequences of the NEL acquisition – which no one seems to have given much thought to at the time – was the death of MC, the moral censorship that had played such a big part in the life of the firm since its earliest days.

Because one of NEL's biggest sellers was Harold Robbins, the king of 'sex and shopping' beach-blockbusters. 1981 also saw the first publication of his *Goodbye, Janette*, an erotic novel celebrating sadomasochism and high fashion; the idea that Hodder & Stoughton could be a guarantor of wholesome family reading was clearly no longer sustainable. As Eddie Bell observed, 'Dear old Harold wouldn't have had a look-in in the old Hodder and Stoughton days.' The NEL, he says, brought a whole range of authors to Hodder who might be regarded as 'kind of questionable', and, he added, 'we embraced them dearly'.

Michael Attenborough describes the NEL as 'good backlist publishing', and says the 'contracts forward were not very exciting'. The acquisition did, however, come with one very big name indeed. Attenborough remembers a 'hair-raising time' while he and his colleagues wondered whether Stephen King would sign on the dotted line, but he did, and he has remained one of Hodder & Stoughton's most loyal stars ever since. The first of his books that Hodder moved from the New English Library imprint to the Hodder list illustrates his enduring appeal: *It* was first published as a horror novel in 1986, and when Warner brothers based a film on the story in 2017 the book climbed back to the top of the bestseller lists, more than thirty years after the novel was first launched.

Schindler's Ark came out the following year – it was published in the United States under the title *Schindler's List* because the American publishers believed that American Jewry was sensitive about the suggestion that Jews had been passive during the Holocaust, and 'the *Ark* implied passivity, the prisoners entering two-by-two'. When Keneally arrived in London on the eve of the 1982 Booker ceremony he was surprised to find that Ladbrokes had his book as the second-favourite, just behind William Boyd's *An Ice Cream War*. There was some dispute about whether *Schindler's Ark* could really be considered a novel at all – since it was so heavily based on real events – but that does not seem to have bothered the judges.

Keneally's initial response to his Booker victory was to feel 'momentarily electrocuted; an electric pulse of disbelief as direct as an arrow'. Then he settled into a writer's dream; 'Every morning new stocks, printed the day before and rushed up from Kent, cluttered the marble lobbies of Hodder's beautiful eighteenth-century headquarters in Bedford Square,' he remembered. 'Salesmen got there early so that they could pick up enough copies to satisfy the bookshops they served. What a heady and extremely rare time for a writer, when demand could not quite be served.'

Behind that heady state lay some hard graft and fancy foot-work by the Hodder production team, which was then being run by Jamie Wilson, another senior manager who had first joined as a result of family connections (his father had been Paul Hodder-Williams' GP). A Booker prize was, he told me, worth an increase of five- or six-fold in sales, but 'you are not going to press the expensive green button [for extra copies] until your author actually wins', and in those pre-digital days 'just-in-time manu-facturing did not exist'.

The day after the Booker dinner, Wilson summoned the relevant staff (those responsible for 'paper, printing, binding, jacket printing, jacket paper') to a lunch and told them they had forty- eight hours to produce new copies – a process that would usually have taken up to six weeks. By the end of the meal they had worked out new ways to dovetail their roles in the production process, and within the required two days the first of the new run were on their way to Bloomsbury to glad-den the author's eyes, in good time to capitalise on the Booker publicity.

Three years later Hodder claimed the Booker again – with Keri Hulme's New Zealand novel *the bone people* ('always lower case', according to one of those involved in the book's original publication). This complex, sometimes violent story, with its underlying meditation on the interplay between Western and Maori culture, defied publishing formulas even more emphat-ically, and the book's journey from the shores of the South Pacific to the Guildhall is itself a great romance.

It was written over a twelve-year period and was at first rejected by almost every publisher. Eventually a small feminist collective in New Zealand called Spiral brought it out in a first run of 2,000 copies. That sold out almost immediately, and when the second run did the same Spiral looked for a bigger publisher. Hodder's senior editor in New Zealand, Bert Hingley, was a champion of New Zealand fiction, and the book seemed a gift to his campaign to establish an accepted canon of New Zealand writing. There was an additional twist of serendipity: Keri Hulme liked chess, and Hodder lore has it that the chessmen colophon played its part in her decision to publish with the firm. Hodder & Stoughton brought the book out in New Zealand but not, initially, in London.

Jamie Hodder-Williams, one of Mark Hodder-Williams' sons, was doing a gap-year stint in the New Zealand office, helping out with the files and photocopying. Bert Hingley gave him a copy of the manuscript, and Jamie remembers the two of them discussing the book on a long drive down to a Gallipoli memorial ceremony at a military base on North Island. When he got back to London Jamie pressed the case for a British edition with Eric Major, the senior non-family executive in the firm at the time, and he published extracts from *the bone people* in a literary magazine at university.

Major himself visited the New Zealand office just after the publication of the local edition, and took a copy to read on the long flight home. He said later that if he had had anything else to turn to he might have put the book to one side after a few pages but – as his obituary put it – 'he persevered and by page 40 he realised that here was something "rather special"'.

The first order for the British market was still tiny; 1,500 copies. When *the bone people* made the Booker shortlist Philip Attenborough himself sent a congratulatory telex (this was long before the age of emails) to Keri Hulme and the New Zealand team, but she was still regarded as an outside punt; Iris Murdoch, Peter Carey, Jan Morris and Doris Lessing all had books on the shortlist too. And the decision to award the prize to Keri Hulme was controversial even among the judges. One of them, Marina Warner, wrote later that among her fellow judges Nina Bawden opposed it 'very strongly' because of the child-beatings it included, while Joanna Lumley favoured Doris Lessing's *The Good Terrorist*. However Lumley, according to Warner's account, did not turn up to the final judging session because of a rehearsal, and the chair of the judges, the former arts minister Norman St John-Stevas, 'unexpectedly championed' *the bone people* throughout.

Keri Hulme was not even in the country to hear St John-Stevas announce her win on the night – three members of the Spiral collective, two of them in traditional Maori dress, received the prize on Hulme's behalf, singing a Maori praise song as they approached the stage. When Keri Hulme was telephoned with the news in the United States – where she was lecturing – the author responded with the words 'Bloody hell'.

Jamie Hodder-Williams told me that the Booker win made this 'the perfect publishing story'. He said 'it made me realise the thrill of discovering a manuscript that you wanted to bring to a wider public and taking it all the way to the top'. Like his great-uncle Ernest he had discovered 'the joy in the game', and he joined the family firm soon after graduating.

The Booker winners were followed by the establishment of a separate paperback imprint for literary fiction: Sceptre was launched in 1986, and evolved into the imprint for hardback and paperback editions of authors like Keneally.

Keneally's original editor there was Ion Trewin, a former literary editor of *The Times,* who joined Hodder in 1979 and also brought Melvyn Bragg to the company (although Bragg had previously published in paperback with Coronet, the firm's paperback imprint). Bragg's first novel for Sceptre, *The Maid of Buttermere*, was launched with what the publicity department called a 'big push', including an author appearance at the Fish Inn on Lake Buttermere itself, where the book's heroine lived. It sold more copies than any of his previous books, and he was to become one of the anchors of the literary list, publishing with the firm for more than thirty years – at the time of writing his Hodder tally is nine novels and seven works of non-fiction.

So by the mid-1980s Hodder & Stoughton was, if anything, becoming even more respectable – and pulled off that trick at the same time as it enjoyed commercial success through its paperback operation. That provided a measure of protection against the change that was shaking so much of the business world in the 1980s, and in many ways the firm was still run on the principle that publishing was, as Eddie Bell would have put it, a game for gentlemen, not players.

Mark Barty-King, who was hired by Transworld in 1984 to set up Bantam Press, its hardback imprint, remembers ringing up Hodder for advice. 'I said, "Look, we're coming into this business – we're going to be your competitors – and we don't know a damn thing about it. Could we have a look at your warehouse and distribution operation at Dunton Green?" And they said, "Oh, do. Come and look around, tell us what you want to see. We'll give you lunch." They knew we would be in direct competition with them, but that was the sort of business it was in those days.'

But the Attenboroughs might have done well to play closer heed to the message of one of their own books – the latest iteration of Anthony Sampson's evergreen *Anatomy* series. *The Changing Anatomy of Britain* – which described itself as 'The Handbook for the 1980s' and was dedicated to Robin Denniston 'who really invented it' – painted a vivid picture of the way business was undergoing a revolution in the Thatcher years, and it includes a chapter on 'Entrepreneurs' with the prescient subtitle 'The Outsiders Come Inside'.

Sampson chose a quotation from the eighteenth-century philosopher David Hume to introduce these new beasts of the business jungle: 'Avarice, spur of industry'. Their true home, he wrote, was 'the world of anthropology, or even zoology, as if they belonged to a different species from a strange habitat. While ordinary workers and managers move in their well-worn sheep tracks, the entrepreneurs swing above them like chimpanzees, jumping from tree to tree and only occasionally dropping to ground level.' And he cites, as he fills out his picture of the new breed, the example of Robert Maxwell, who at this stage of his career had bounced back from being declared (by the Department of Trade) unfit 'to exercise proper stewardship of a publicly quoted company' and was busy restoring the fortunes of the British Printing Corporation, which later became Maxwell Communications.

And Hodder & Stoughton was being closely watched by one of Maxwell's entrepreneurial young lieutenants. Tim Hely Hutchinson was hired by Maxwell in 1982 as sales director of his Macdonald Futura imprint; he was still in his twenties, and was promoted to managing director within six weeks of joining the firm. He remembers Hodder as a formidable competitor; 'Imagine,' he said to me, 'I had to persuade agents to bring their authors to us despite the spectre of Robert Maxwell, and [we were] up against Hodder which was like the Bank of England in terms of respectability ... when Michael Attenborough was firing on all cylinders and focusing on the trade side of the business they were really the most desirable house to go to ... They had a raft of top-selling authors.'

The first real sign that, however respectable, Hodder & Stoughton might not be quite as solid as the Bank of England came in 1985, and it was a nasty shock for the Attenborough brothers. Eddie Bell, who was very much aware of the way business was changing, was approached by Collins with the offer of a senior job. He put the position to his employers and was thoroughly unimpressed by what they came up with as an inducement to stay; 'They thought they were offering the kingdom,' he said, 'but it was many layers below [that].' Eddie Bell decided to go.

Michael Attenborough was so angry that he did what he now describes as 'a terrible thing'. He confronted Bell and 'I suddenly thought I was a merchant banker and told him to clear his desk and get the hellside out.' There was worse to come; many of Eddie Bell's sales team followed him out of the door and joined Collins, and so did one of Hodder & Stoughton's most profitable authors. In an interview for this book Jeffrey Archer said, 'I sort of stayed with Eddie – in publishing what really matters is people.' And he added that 'The Attenboroughs were old-fashioned, old-school traditionalists, Eddie was a breath of fresh air, quite mad with a touch of genius.'

Tim Hely Hutchinson, who watched this drama unfold from his berth in the Maxwell empire, is brutally clear in his conviction that Eddie Bell's departure reflected the weakness of a management structure built on family ties. Linking it with the departure of another senior Hodder & Stoughton executive, Alan Gordon Walker, he told me, 'They [the Attenboroughs] had refused to put them on the board just because they didn't like the cut of their jib. They were snobbish about them in some way.'

The way the publishing industry was changing was elegantly summed up in a speech given by Ian Chapman, the chairman of Hodder's old rival Collins, to the Royal Society of Arts in 1984. 'Until the middle of this century,' he said, 'publishers were individuals who carried on their businesses with relative meagre financial resources at their own risk. The publisher was the proprietor, the shareholders were likely to be composed of members of family and, broadly speaking, he could publish what he liked so long as he remained solvent . . . he did not have to worry about his bottom line. His list was meant to look like his library. It was a reflection of his tastes.' But by the 1980s more and more publishing firms were merging with one another or taking each other over. Chapman pointed out that just eleven big publishers accounted for as much as sixty-five per cent of British book production. One reason for the merger mania was competition from big American firms in the British market; size became increasingly important to survival and, as George Greenfield put it, 'Security lay in strength.'

Mary Mouse was born of a wartime 'make do and mend' brainwave; Hodder's Brockhampton Press used *Picture Post* off-cuts to get round paper shortages.

And brought out a big pie. Look at them pulling the plums out of it one by one!

So when Mary put it on the dinner-table, and Mummy Doll cut into it . . .

1942 proved a bumper year for children's books; the first of *The Famous Five* series appeared, and Biggles flew his first mission for Hodder. *Biggles' Second Case* was published in 1948.

'Working for Robin [Denniston] was fun', according to one Hodder veteran, 'You never knew what might happen next'.

ANATOMY OF BRITAIN TODAY

Anthony Sampson

The first *Anatomy* came out in 1962, the last in 2004. The early endpapers reflected the concept of a 'deep state' in Britain.

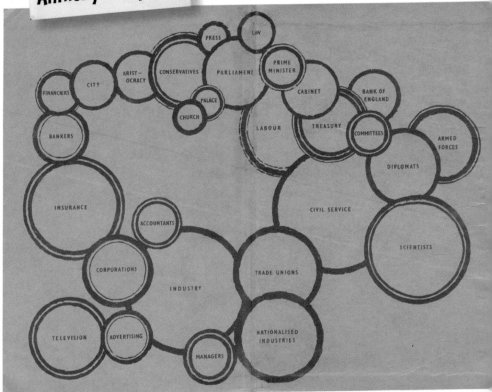

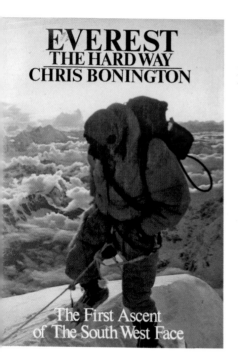

Hodder has long been, as Chris Bonington's editor put it, 'good at the outdoors'.

The Ascent of Everest, 'a success so great it transformed the firm'.

Sir Francis Chichester with Mark Hodder-Williams.

A family affair; Paul Hodder-Williams, chairman, front left, and his cousin John Attenborough, deputy chairman, front right, watch the Dean of St Paul's, the Very Reverend W R Matthews, laying the foundation stone of the new St Paul's House in 1963.

Philip Attenborough with two stars of the 'raft of top selling authors' Hodder could boast in the glory days – David Niven…

…and Jeffrey Archer

The rights to *Love Story* were bought for a 'paltry advance' before the film came out.

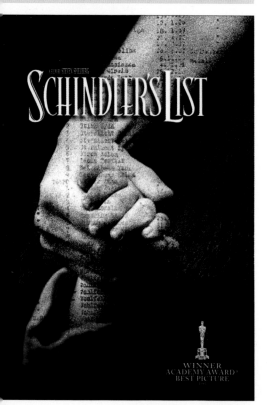

Thomas Keneally's Booker Prize winner was published in Britain as *Schindler's Ark,* but American publishers felt that the title suggested 'that Jews had been passive during the Holocaust'. Under its American title the story became a Spielberg blockbuster and cleaned up at the Oscars.

The success of *Taken on Trust*, Terry Waite's account of his time as a Beirut hostage, allowed him to devote his time to writing, lecturing and charity work. It also inspired Tim Hely Hutchinson's assault on the Net Book Agreement.

The unlikely lads: Stephen King and Dickie Bird, Trent Bridge, 1998.

John Connolly promoting *The Black Angel* in the Sedlec Ossuary, 2005.

Rosamunde Pilcher by the Hodder wall of fame at the new Carmelite House headquarters, 2016.

Jodi Picoult boating on the Thames, 2015.

Carole Welch, Sceptre publisher, with two stars of the list – David Mitchell and Andrew Miller – at the Booker Prize dinner 2001, when both were shortlisted.

Alex Ferguson at his marathon signing in Manchester, 2013; 'people were sleeping in the long queue', he remembered.

St Paul's on the night of 29th/30th December 1940, when the Luftwaffe destroyed the heart of London publishing.

The same view from Carmelite House today –
cathedral and publishing house both still going strong.

Hodder had joined the 80s, but in a slightly half-hearted way. Measured by turnover, the biggest publishers in the British market in the mid-1980s were ranked as follows:

The Pearson companies, Longman and Penguin – £240
    million
Octopus – £150 million
Collins – £140 million
Reed – £95 million
OUP – £80 million
Associated Book Publishers – £80 million
Macmillan – £75 million
Hodder – £50 million.

Number eight on the list was an awkward place to be – the firm was too big to be nimble but, in money terms at least, it remained at the bottom of the First Division. 'We had', Michael Attenborough says, 'grown to be an uncomfortable size. We didn't know where we stood.'

There was still a hunger for new acquisitions, and in 1987 Hodder bought Edward Arnold, one of its Bedford Square neighbours. This had the happy side effect of adding the great novelist E. M. Forster to the roster of Hodder authors, but the main impact of the acquisition was a re-commitment to educational publishing. The deal coincided with the introduction of the National Curriculum and GCSEs in England, opening up a demand for new materials throughout the schools system. It also provided a springboard for the firm to expand in the then relatively neglected field of Further Education.

Perhaps the most successful textbook that came with the Edward Arnold deal was the catering manual *Practical Cookery*, first published in 1963 with a text by Victor Ceserani and Ron Kinton. When the book sold its one millionth copy, Lis Tribe, the head of Hodder education at the time of writing, and her predecessor Philip Walters took Ceserani and Kinton out to dinner in the Savoy. Walters remembers that at the end of the meal 'the doors of the kitchen were flung open and the chef followed by all his sous-chefs personally delivered the puddings to us. The chef then knelt down between Victor and Ron, kissed both their hands, and then swept back into the kitchen without a word.' Walters adds, 'That's what the best textbook publishing does . . .'

And in the mid-1980s Hodder could still make a splash. In 1986 they announced that they were paying a quarter of a million pounds to the advertising agency Saatchi & Saatchi to promote new novels by seven of their top-flight authors – Jeffrey Archer, Noel Barber, John le Carré, James Clavell, James Herbert, Stephen King and Morris West. Books appeared in television commercials for the first time. George Greenfield writes, in his publishing history *Scribblers for Bread*, 'The scheme appears to have worked well, although whether the £250,000 cost of the budget has been more than earned back through additional sales and turnover that would not have been achieved without the glossy campaigns is a secret that remains locked in accounting files on the south side of Bedford Square.'

Whatever the figures showed, the advertising campaign provided another boost to the firm's image within the industry. Tim Hely Hutchinson was mightily impressed; Saatchi & Saatchi was, as he put it, the 'hottest agency' of the day, still glowing from its association with Margaret Thatcher's election successes. His friend Martin Neild – the two started their careers at Macmillan, and Neild would later play a central role in the Hodder story – also recalls being struck by the boldness of the firm's move into television advertising; 'in marketing we were rather in awe of that,' he told me.

At around the time of what he regarded as this 'great coup' by Hodder, Tim Hely Hutchinson left Maxwell and set up his own publishing company, Headline. He and his team had transformed the fortunes of Macdonald Futura: in 1982 it was losing £1.5 million and three years later it had a pre-tax profit of £550,000, certainly the kind of performance that would have recommended Hely Hutchinson to the bankers who provided the necessary venture capital. The new project was, however, not entirely free of a flavour of family influence: George Greenfield observed that 'Tim Hely Hutchinson's father, the Earl of Donoughmore, was a well-known figure in the City, whose contacts no doubt proved most useful to the youngish entrepreneur.'

Sue Fletcher, who had been part of the team that turned around the fortunes of Macdonald Futura, followed Tim Hely Hutchinson to his new business. The company was, she told me, the first to be set up 'vertically'. Until then publishers had operated separate – and indeed duplicate – operations for their hardback and paperback books, and it was not unusual for a writer to be published in hardback by one imprint and paperback by someone else. 'Vertical publishing' is industry jargon for the integration of the hardback and paperback operations, which greatly increased efficiency and reduced staffing levels. 'We were aware that we had to be very fleet of foot because we were small and new,' Sue Fletcher says, 'we had to prove ourselves by doing better.'

They began to do things that are now regarded as standard practice, but at the time were radical innovations – reading a book the moment it was submitted, for example, and making an offer within a day. The new firm was also, according to Tim Hely Hutchinson's friend Martin Neild, 'absolutely focused on the consumer – what did the consumer want?' The older houses, he said, 'were never particularly worried about who the readers were'.

Tim Hely Hutchinson himself told the *Daily Telegraph* that part of his recipe for success was to take the lessons he had learnt from Maxwell and reverse them. 'Robert Maxwell used to pay his authors late to improve his cashflow,' he said in a 2006 interview. 'The same with staff. He would mess about with staff bonus rules and he was extremely secretive about giving out information. I thought we could turn it completely on its head and be the people's publisher.' Headline set out to woo its authors as a matter of policy, and this cheeky start-up began to make money almost immediately.

In creative terms Hodder & Stoughton still appeared to be going great guns. In 1987 the firm published the enduring best-seller *The Shell Seekers*, and the author, Rosamunde Pilcher, was to retain a prominent place on its list for many years to come. But the firm's big-name strategy was creating its own problems. Jamie Hodder-Williams, who joined that year, says that the company focused too much on nurturing their existing bestselling writers at the expense of new talent. It was also becoming more and more expensive to keep successful authors happy. Across the book trade as a whole, 'Money was being spent on authors' advances like it had never been spent before,' Jamie Hodder-Williams says, and that made life even more difficult for 'a medium-sized family firm competing with global conglomerates'.

In March that year Michael Attenborough sent his brother Philip and his cousin Mark Hodder-Williams a memo musing on the company's future – it was marked 'PERSONAL AND PRIVATE; TO BE OPENED BY ADDRESSEE ONLY'. He wrote that 'The English language world is no longer split into the two empires controlled from London and New York. On the one hand it is more fragmented, with publishing taking place locally in each of the main markets, USA, UK, Canada and Australia: on the other this very fragmentation is forcing unifica-tion with vast international corporations setting up in each centre.'

Attenborough offered his fellow family directors this *tour d'horizon* of the publishing scene: 'In the UK, Maxwell announced yesterday that BPCC sales were £480 million last year and he was looking for £1,000 million in '87 (profit to match). Heinemann with Octopus above and Pan below are major operators with huge resources on hand or immediately available to them. Century Hutchinson plan to go to the City in 1989, leaving the current owners either personally rich or with new resources to expand.'

He then floated – and this is the earliest document I have seen where this is suggested – the idea of ending Hodder & Stoughton's long run as an independent family business. 'So has the time for international partnership come?' he wrote, 'I think we must not bury our heads to the changing world. And there might be great advantages for the three of us if sensible deals can be struck. But not naturally for the next generation of the family – in this great publishing house at least.' The temptation to cut loose and realise the value locked up in their shares must have been strong.

The 'three of us' evidently kept up a discreet conversation between themselves. A memo circulated by Philip Attenborough in February the following year affirmed that 'We believe that it is in the company's interest to retain our independence and continue the development of H&S as a truly first class publisher.' But it also conveys a certain weariness about the challenge of keeping the ship afloat in such difficult seas; Philip Attenborough stressed the importance of 'bringing on the young, whether family or non-family . . . so that we can engineer the firm's greater success and reduce the immensely onerous executive burden we all currently carry.' In his interview with me his brother Michael confirmed the sense that they had all simply run out of puff: 'We'd been going hammer and tongs,' he said, 'and we kept losing people. Eddie Bell going, Alan Gordon Walker going. I think we all got a bit tired.'

Carolyn Mays, who is now the managing director of Hodder & Stoughton, joined the staff as a secretary that year. She never picked up any sense of impending financial catastrophe – she was, after all, a very junior member of staff – but she does look back with some wonder at the way the 'non-vertical' Hodder & Stoughton of those days was run. She worked for the publisher – as the senior editor was known – at Sceptre paperbacks, and she was part of a team of three. In addition to her secretarial work she was required to read books and write reports, and there was a junior editor immediately above her in the hierarchy whose duty it was to oversee the way the books on their list were published. However, there was very little editing to do since the books had already appeared as hardbacks, so her boss, the publisher, spent 'all day on the phone negotiating and having lunches and reading books'. There were similar teams of three in every area of paperback publishing, and the whole structure was replicated in the hardback operation. 'Where there were six people then there's one and a half today,' she says. And in those days, she added, 'almost all the bosses were men'.

Tim Hely Hutchinson turned to Hodder to sell Headline's books in overseas markets, so by the late 1980s he was able to make a good first-hand assessment of the firm's condition. 'Somehow,' he told me, 'they went a bit off the boil.' In 1989 Michael Attenborough was chosen for the prestigious role of Captain of the St Andrew's Golf Club; it was, as Tim Hely Hutchinson tells the story of those years, the moment when the weakness of a business run by gentlemen rather than players really became apparent. 'He went on a year-long sabbatical leaving nobody in charge,' he says, 'and I think it drifted from there on.' Michael Attenborough remembers things rather differently. 'No, I did not take a sabbatical during my period of R&A [Royal and Ancient] Captaincy from September 1989 to September 1990,' he says, '. . . I relied on the goodwill of my fellow main board directors.' He added, 'Working with an understanding family in a family firm was a huge plus for me.'

But Hely Hutchinson compared the comfortable habits at Hodder with his own lean operation at Headline: 'They started losing money – haemorrhaging cash,' he said. 'It was just loose management. The margins were wrong, the overheads were wrong, they kept their own paper, which most publishers don't do – so they had millions of pounds tied up in unnecessary printing paper. It was just sloppily managed in every department.'

The crisis that hit the firm in the early 1990s must have been bewildering for many of those who worked for it. On 5 January 1990 the *Dunton Green Gazette*, the in-house paper, ran a piece under the heading: 'Fiction Publisher of the Decade'. It reported that 'The last ten days have seen several newspapers reflecting on publishing and "the books of the 80s". Hodder and Stoughton scored quite extraordinarily, especially in the Fiction "top 10" listings.' *The Sunday Times* hardback list had the *Little Drummer Girl* (John le Carré) in at number five, *A Perfect Spy* (le Carré again) at seven and *First Among Equals* (Jeffrey Archer) at nine, and its top ten paperback fiction table included two other Jeffrey Archer books, *Kane and Abel* at number two and *The Prodigal Daughter* at nine. The *Daily Mail* listed the top thirty paperback fiction books of the decade, and nine of them were from Hodder or the New English Library, a higher score than that of any other publisher. 'And now for the new decade!', the piece ended triumphantly.

And yet that same year the Attenboroughs put Hodder & Stoughton up for sale and, according to Tim Hely Hutchinson, 'Nobody was interested except for us.' He put together a deal to buy the company and float it on the stock exchange, but Hodder & Stoughton's auditors refused to sign off the company accounts. A public offering with 'qualified' accounts – the accountants' way of signalling they cannot be quite sure what is going on in the books they are being shown – was impossible, and the deal collapsed.

The 1990 debacle prompted a fundamental restructuring of the company. In a letter to staff in March 1991 Philip Attenborough announced a plan to 'secure our future as an independent publisher'. It included, he told them, 'a necessary and substantial reduction in the size of the staff'; the UK-based workforce of 640 was to be cut by 120. Attenborough also announced that Hodder & Stoughton would be adopting the 'vertical' publishing model that had proved so successful at Headline; henceforth there would be a single team dealing with hardbacks and paperbacks in areas like marketing and publicity.

Jamie Hodder-Williams describes the restructuring of the firm as 'quite bloody, but also quite exciting, because a lot of us got more opportunities'. His father was one of the casualties; Mark Hodder-Williams' resignation left the Attenborough brothers alone on the bridge for this final chapter of Hodder & Stoughton's history as a family firm. 'It was difficult,' Jamie says, looking back, 'Michael Attenborough, Philip Attenborough and my father all went to school together, they all grew up together and they all joined at around the same time. I don't know how frank they were with one another.'

In October that year Hodder & Stoughton said goodbye to one of the last pieces of Ernest's legacy: the *Lancet* and its central London headquarters were flogged to raise badly needed cash. Philip Attenborough wrote to the paper's staff to say that 'After 71 years within Hodder and Stoughton – and 34 years of my own publishing career – I find it hard to say goodbye.' He enclosed a cheque for two weeks' salary with his letter by way of a goodwill gesture.

Tim Hely Hutchinson came back with a new offer in 1993. What he proposed was described as a 'merger' – a piece of flattery for Hodder, since the plan he put forward was much closer to a straight takeover. He flattered the Attenboroughs further by telling them he would call the new company Hodder Headline; 'When we said that it was as if we'd given them an extra ten million pounds,' he told me. 'It didn't cost us anything, but they really liked it.' Hely Hutchinson also said that everyone he dealt with at Hodder was 'very nice and very well-meaning', and his correspondence with Philip Attenborough in the run-up to the merger was extremely civilised. The takeover was a player's move, but the proper form required by publishing as a game for gentlemen was observed.

Hodder & Stoughton's shareholders met in June to consider the deal. Although the family's executive control of the company had always been concentrated in a small number of hands, the ownership had, unsurprisingly, become diffused along the branches of the family tree in the century and a quarter since it was founded. There were also non-family shareholders who had taken advantage of an Executive Share Purchase Scheme introduced in 1969. 'The shareholding was spread very widely,' Tim Hely Hutchinson remembers. 'There were over a hundred family shareholders. Philip in his negotiations with us had been saying, "I don't know whether I'll get this through . . . there's going to be a lot of unhappiness and so on."'

According to Tim Hely Hutchinson's enjoyable account of the denouement, he and his backers managed to 'infiltrate' someone into the shareholders' meeting that was to vote on the deal. 'To start off with there were quite a lot of people saying, "Oh, do we really want to sell our heritage – there was a bit of 'barbarians at the gate' attitude,"' their observer reported. 'And then a quite elderly and sensible shareholder at the back stood up and banged his walking stick on the floor. And he said, "My problem is that I can't see what the problem is!"' The shareholders had had to put up with a good deal during Hodder & Stoughton's difficulties, including one year when the company paid no dividend at all. 'They might as well have wallpapered the bathroom with their share certificates,' Hely Hutchinson said, 'and suddenly they realised that people with one per cent [of the company] were going to get half a million pounds.' Headline's offer was accepted with one hundred per cent shareholder support.

When the merger became public, Hodder & Stoughton found itself on the news pages instead of the book pages, and Tim Hely

Hutchinson was able to announce that for the first time ever *Publishing Weekly* had extended its deadline to cover the story. The papers especially relished the contrast between the firm's venerable history and the brash youth of its conqueror. 'Hodder and Stoughton, the 125-year-old publishing company which has John le Carré and Dorothy Sayers on its list, is to be merged with Headline, a far smaller company founded just 7 years ago', reported the *Daily Telegraph* on 4 June, and the paper's arts correspondent could not resist adding, 'Lurking on Headline's list are such titles as *Bride of the Slime, The Ultimate Frankenstein* and *The Art of Sensual Living*.' Even the *FT* ventured onto celebrity territory to bring the force of the story home: 'Authors such as TV personality Cilla Black and champion jockey Peter Scudamore are teaming up with Winston Churchill, John Buchan and John le Carré', the paper reported the same day. 'Such diverse talent is being brought together under one roof in a £48 million takeover by the 7-year-old upstart Headline Book Publishing of the stately 125-year-old Hodder and Stoughton.'

The *Guardian's* story was, in a similar vein, headlined: 'The Upstart and the Old Lady'. 'What got tongues wagging was the almost indecent age difference between the partners and the unusual power relationship between them,' the paper stated. 'The swallowing of Hodder is the most poignant sign yet that the era of independent family-owned publishers is all but over.' The *Guardian* added – waspishly – that 'at least one rival points out that although Headline is publicly quoted, its chairman, the Earl of Donoughmore, is Tim Hely Hutchinson's father.'

17

Sun, Sancerre and Sexual Tension

Carolyn Mays was so anxious about the new regime that she took up smoking again, and she has a vivid memory that suggests her new boss was nervous too: 'Tim gathered us all together in the boardroom and I remember sitting on the floor at his feet, and I could see he had these cards in his hands which he was reading from,' she told me. 'And – this is so unlike Tim – his hand was shaking as he read the speech.' He told his audience they were the chosen ones. 'We've tried to move very quickly, we've tried to be very clear,' she remembers him saying, 'you are the ones who I hope will stay here and go forward with us.' She recalls that he added – in what she calls 'a very Tim-ish way' – 'I love you all dearly.'

Those not numbered among the chosen left in three stages; the merger agreement stipulated that some senior managers must clear their desks before the new team from Headline moved into Bedford Square. Jamie Wilson, who had joined the firm through a family connection with Paul Hodder-Williams nearly thirty years earlier and overseen the accelerated production of the Booker-winning *Schindler's Ark*, was among them.

He refused to leave immediately because, he told me, 'I had a wonderful staff I had worked with for many years – they were like family.' He sat through what he called the 'charade' of a Monday morning board meeting in the full knowledge that his time with Hodder was over, and left a few days later. He had acquired an HGV licence through his training in the Territorial

Army and, in his late forties, spent some time driving lorries before buying into a small publishing company with his redundancy money.

Tim Hely Hutchinson put in a new team to implement the next stage of redundancies; Sue Fletcher, who had worked with Hely Hutchinson since his days with Robert Maxwell, took control of the editorial side of the business – her appointment meant that for the first time in Hodder's long history it was no longer true that 'the bosses were men' – and Martin Neild, Hely Hutchinson's old friend from his days at Macmillan, took over as the managing director of Hodder & Stoughton. 'We looked at it department by department using Headline as a benchmark,' Neild told me. 'In Headline we have four people in marketing doing x turnover – at Hodder you have sixteen people doing y turnover – the ratio is all wrong.'

A report in *The Times* laid out the cold contrast between the way the two companies had been performing: at Hodder, it recorded, '450 people ran a business with a worldwide publishing turnover of £55 million, or £122,000 a head. By contrast Headline last year generated publishing sales of £14 million with only 50 employees, £280,000 a head – 130 per cent more than Hodder.' Each head of department was told that he or she had to match the Headline benchmark; if they did not want to be part of the process of slimming down the company they were offered redundancy, if they did they were told, 'You need to say who in your department should stay and who should go.' In August the newly combined Hodder Headline made seventy-two redundancies.

At the same time the firm announced that a further 150 jobs would go with the closure of the Dunton Green operation in Kent. Hely Hutchinson told me he found they were employing several gardeners there, plus a staff of six in a photocopying department; 'if you wanted a photocopy – say three copies of a manuscript – you had to send it to Sevenoaks,' he said, '. . . and they would photocopy it when they got round to it, so it could easily take five or six days.' Photocopiers were installed on each floor of the Bedford Square headquarters, and the warehouse and distribution operations were merged with Headline's facilities in Abingdon.

The jobs cull was made easier by de-recognising the trades unions represented in the firm. There was no sign of a strike, Hely Hutchinson said, because 'the Father and Mother of the Chapel [as shop stewards are known in journalism and printing unions] were delighted to see a change in management. There was a very strong sense of an old-fashioned class system, so that junior and middle people weren't listened to. So a more merito-cratic management coming in was welcome.' The new team promised to review everyone's pay and introduce a new bonus system.

Jamie Hodder-Williams weathered this storm in his family firm. 'The great family fear was Maxwell or Murdoch,' he says. Collins had been taken over by Rupert Murdoch four years earlier, and the Hodder clan had at least avoided that. Jamie describes the Hely Hutchinson revolution as 'nerve-wracking and absolutely thrilling', and says he never considered leaving, although he was close to many of the senior people who did. His immediate boss was one of them, and Jamie was promoted to fill his shoes as marketing manager. His brother, Andrew Hodder-Williams, lasted for six months before deciding to go, leaving Jamie with a very strong sense of being the last family member still standing on deck. He told me he was made to feel 'incredibly welcome' and part of the new order.

And there was a 'thrilling' side to the revolution: Tim Hely Hutchinson was determined to eliminate obstacles to creativity in the way the company was run. His main bugbear was the meetings culture he found at Hodder. 'It was considered a lack of respect not to attend all the meetings,' he said, 'some of which took place in London and some of which took place in Sevenoaks.

So in addition to all their meeting time they [senior staff] had quite a lot of train time. So it really stopped them functioning properly.' Carolyn Mays remembers travelling down to Kent for weekly meetings, and she can even remember that one of her bosses would spend them eating digestive biscuits, but she no longer has any idea what they were about. 'We thought we would begin by cancelling the whole lot,' Hely Hutchinson told me; 'they loved it, because they could do their jobs rather than sitting in meetings saying everything was in hand – which it wasn't.'

The new regime also focused on streamlining decision-making. Like Matthew Hodder, Tim Hely Hutchinson 'detested dawdling and loitering'. Before the takeover the commissioning process involved an elaborate process of report-writing and colour-coded memos. 'If you wrote a report you showed it to your boss,' Carolyn Mays explained. 'If he decided it should go further you had to put a pink slip on it with the names of fifteen or twenty people – some of them in Dunton Green and some of them in Bedford Square. Each of these people read it and contributed to the discourse on it. Then you filed it. Everyone filed everything even if it had no relevance to the person who filed it at all.' The process could, she said, take 'aeons'.

Her first encounter with Sue Fletcher was an invigorating contrast; she had just received a submission from an agent for a novel she liked the look of, and mentioned it to her new boss. 'That sounds amazing,' Sue Fletcher said. 'You had better offer a hundred thousand pounds for it.' Sue Fletcher told me, 'We trusted the taste of the younger editors. We did not buy books by committee.'

Sue Fletcher made her own first acquisition for Hodder in similar style. Not long after the merger an agent sent her what she describes as a 'Big, fat, light-hearted Jilly Cooper-esque romance'. The manuscript was 500 pages long, and she left work early to read it – 'I am a fast reader,' she told me. The following day she offered a generous two-book deal to Fiona Walker, who had never published anything before and was still in her early twenties.

To market *French Relations*, a 'hilarious tale of sun, Sancerre and sexual tension' (to quote Hodder's own website), Jamie Hodder-Williams came up with the idea of offering a free pair of espadrilles with every copy. 'We had a great beach-read cover,' he remembers, 'and wanted to persuade the chains like Dillons to take dump bins, so came up with the idea of a free gift with every copy. It was quite unusual at the time. And I think we over-printed the espadrilles, which may still be in our warehouse somewhere, but it did get Fiona's career off to a big start.'

By the end of 1995 sales of *French Relations* were getting close to six figures, and at the time of writing the total stands at over 275,000. Listening to Sue Fletcher and Martin Neild talking about the episode, I heard an echo of the great Sir Ernest: 'Publishing is a gamble,' Sue says, 'you can't be frightened.' And Sir Ernest would surely have endorsed Neild's ambition that 'We wanted it to be fun – the fun had gone out of it.'

Sue Fletcher's first number-one bestselling novel for Hodder was not, however, a book that Ernest, still less Matthew Hodder or Thomas Stoughton, would have approved of. The review of *A Parliamentary Affair* in the *Independent* was characteristic of much of the critical comment. 'Anyone who supposes that Edwina Currie's amazing first novel is the usual sort of kill-an-hour-on-the-beach codswallop had better think again: it is much, much worse than that,' the paper declared. 'As a corny political saga it is not all that much worse than Jeffrey Archer, but it has huge hidden shallows and is a whole lot sleazier. Big-selling schlock-busters such as this usually want adjectives for the paper-back, so here are a few: breathless, stupid, vain, petty, shrill, self-indulgent, cynical, vulgar and insulting. Will they do?'

For all that, the book made money. In its first publication year nearly 130,000 copies were sold, and 78,000 were shifted over the following twelve months. Carolyn Mays told me that Sue Fletcher had been determined from the first that it would reach number one, adding, 'and I remember the thrill when that was achieved. She was very clear in her strategy.'

The book enjoyed an intriguing afterlife when Edwina Currie revealed – in 2002 – that it was based on her relationship with the former prime minister John Major. By that time the author had, as Carolyn Mays delicately put it, 'moved on' from Hodder, but the firm's records show a healthy spike in sales of *A Parliamentary Affair* in the year of Currie's revelation.

The final stage of the Hely Hutchinson revolution – achieved some six months after the merger – was a move from gracious Bloomsbury to a tower block on the Euston Road. Hodder & Stoughton had occupied two buildings in Bedford Square, and they were configured so that staff working on the top floor of number 46 had to go via the basements if they wanted to see someone on the top floor of number 47. The offices were full of character, and some of them evoked the publishing romance of Matthew Hodder's days; Carolyn Mays and Jamie Hodder-Williams shared what she describes as a 'garret', with tiny windows and sloping floors that made their pencils roll off the desks. The layout of the buildings did not, however, encourage communication between departments; the lifts were temperamental, and Jamie recalls spending a good deal of his day climbing stairs.

Euston Road came as a shock; Carolyn Mays says 'it seemed way out in the boon docks' and that there was 'nothing round there of any interest at all'. But the entire staff was housed on a single floor (the fifteenth), and the eccentric arrangements that had kept different bits of the business apart at Bedford Square disappeared; the sales department was, for example, just a few feet away from the editorial teams. The result was 'a huge difference in terms of company spirit,' Carolyn Mays says; 'it immediately made it feel as if we were on the same side.'

Tim Hely Hutchinson says it is wrong to see his revolution as simply turning Hodder & Stoughton into Headline. 'We professionalised [Hodder],' he argues, 'but I don't think it was any less the Bank of England in terms of respectability.' There was a lunching campaign to convince the big names that that was the case. Sue Fletcher remembers 'taking Ros Pilcher out to lunch and feeling quite nervous', only to find that she was 'thrilled to have a younger editor'. Their lunch meeting *à deux* was followed by a team meal at Le Manoir aux Quat'Saisons. 'The publicity suggested it was "barbarians at the gate",' says Martin Neild; 'we had to show that we weren't completely uncivilised, and knew how to order a decent bottle of wine.'

But there were wobbles. The Headline merger coincided with the publication of John le Carré's *The Night Manager*; Jeffrey Archer's first book with HarperCollins, *Honour among Thieves*, came out at the same time, and easily outsold le Carré's novel. 'David was irked by a succession of minor problems,' le Carré's biographer Adam Sisman writes, 'which he felt had damaged sales.' Le Carré wrote to Hely Hutchinson complaining that 'I cannot remember an unhappier publication. I don't honestly know whether I can muster enough conviction for the future to remain with Hodder's.' To steady the ship, Hely Hutchinson for a while took on personal responsibility for the firm's relationship with le Carré.

Carole Welch, who runs Hodder & Stoughton's literary imprint Sceptre, remembers the merger as an 'unsettling and worrying' time, and says that it was 'sad to witness the end of a family-run, independent company'. The transition to the 'vertical' model of publishing created particular challenges for the literary imprint; it had set out as paperback operation, and when it began to publish in hardback it was competing with firms associated with the great names of twentieth-century literary fiction; 'it wasn't always easy to persuade agents (and sometimes authors) to take Sceptre as seriously as other long-established publishers of original fiction in hardback like Cape, Secker and Faber,' Carole Welch says, but she adds, 'although Headline seemed relatively "downmarket" in its publishing, it was evidently run by people who cared about books and knew how to publish them well.'

Some Hodder traditions did fade, although that may have owed as much to changing tastes as it did to the new regime. Religious publishing had once been at the heart of the Hodder & Stoughton mission; Martin Neild regarded it as 'an interesting niche business that was profitable', a verdict, surely, to set Matthew Hodder and Thomas Stoughton spinning in their graves. There was a push to move some religious books onto the general list so that they would reach a wider audience, and the firm still retains an important Bible publishing contract: NIV, or New International Version, remains the world's most popular Bible translation. Tim Hely Hutchinson, however, takes the view that religious publishing will now always be limited by the fact that 'we are basically a pagan country'.

Mountaineering and exploration had once defined the Hodder & Stoughton brand; now Chris Bonington's new agent Vivienne Schuster (she took over from George Greenfield on his retirement) found that the firm's interest in the field had waned, and she took her client to Weidenfeld & Nicolson instead. 'The great period of major expeditions on the 60s/70s and 80s had passed,' she writes, 'and into vogue came books about survival.'

Hodder was still 'good at the outdoors', in Maggie Body's phrase, but the firm's focus turned to sport rather than epic adventures like the ascent of Everest. Roddy Bloomfield's recruitment to build up a sporting list coincided with the merger, and he had the odd experience of being interviewed first by Michael Attenborough (Roddy numbered some prominent golfers among his sporting contacts, and believes that may have helped to secure him the interview) and then, a few weeks later, by Sue Fletcher and Martin Neild.

Bloomfield, educated at Harrow and Oxford, says he came to sports publishing because he grew up keen on sport in a house full of intellectuals and their books – when I interviewed him he produced, with a fine flourish, a copy of a novel his father published with Hodder & Stoughton in 1923. He left Hutchinson after a long career there because his quirky – or, to use his own word, eccentric – publishing style no longer fitted with the company ethic, and he also felt the firm had lost all interest in his subject. In his new publishing home he found, by contrast, that 'everyone was interested in sport', from the young Jamie Hodder-Williams to the veteran Maggie Body (Welsh rugby).

Over the next two and a half decades Bloomfield would bring Hodder some of the most successful sporting biographies and autobiographies of all time; he was also responsible for Michael Parkinson joining the Hodder family. Twenty-five years later, at the time of writing, he has, in his eighties, yet another Christmas bestseller out in the shape of a memoir from the cricket commentator Henry Blofeld.

And his last venture before leaving Hutchinson had been a happy lesson in the virtues of quirkiness. In the mid-1980s the newly privatised British Telecom (BT, as we now know it) ran a television advertisement for the *Yellow Pages*, the chunky telephone bible of goods and services we all used before the internet made such things redundant, which featured an elderly gent walking round bookshops looking for a second-hand copy of *Fly Fishing* by one J. R. Hartley. After a vain search on foot his daughter hands him the *Yellow Pages*, and when he finally tracks down a copy over the phone he reveals that he is himself the author. 'Good old *Yellow Pages*,' intones the actor Joss Ackland, as the benign old body hangs up the phone, smiling contentedly, 'we don't just help with the nasty things in life, like a blocked drain . . .' The ad acquired a kind of cult status.

Roddy Bloomfield was inspired to turn this television fantasy into a real book, and recruited his friend Michael Russell together with a first-class fly fisherman to provide the know-how. The result – surely the first book to be promoted by an advertising campaign that was paid for by someone else and run before the text was even written – was a bestseller, although no one was sure which chart it should appear in as, according to Bloomfield, 'it was listed in some as fiction and in others as autobiography'. When British Telecom put J. R. Hartley on the links with a follow-up ad, Bloomfield repeated the trick with *Golfing by J. R. Hartley* for Hodder. Michael Parkinson, who, after many years of collaboration, thinks of Roddy Bloomfield as a friend, believes his editor's life has been so 'fascinating' that he should turn writer and produce an autobiography of his own.

18

You've sent us the French edition

Even without the Headline merger, 1993 would have been a big year for the firm; the final months were dominated by two memorable creative events related to the pre-Hely Hutchinson era.

Steven Spielberg's film *Schindler's List* came out that winter, to almost universal popular and critical acclaim, and reflected further glory on Thomas Keneally's Booker-winning novel. Like Keneally, Spielberg was drawn to the story 'because of the paradoxical nature of the character'. The film is widely regarded as his masterpiece, features prominently on most lists of the greatest films of all time and won no fewer than seven Oscars, including Best Film and Best Director.

Hodder's ability to capitalise fully on the film's success was nearly compromised by the fact that the Hely Hutchinson revolution took time to reach every outpost of the Hodder & Stoughton empire. When *Schindler's List* was released in Australia the new management there was not yet in place, and the Australian office had no copies of the book available. This was of course before the digital era, and an intern had to be flown out from London carrying what was known as the 'film' of the book – not the Spielberg movie, but the prototype that would allow the book to be printed locally.

And the Hodder & Stoughton title doing brisk business in the shops that Christmas is still cited by Jamie Hodder-Williams and others as an example of the kind of book that has always defined the firm's ethos. Terry Waite had childhood memories of Hodder & Stoughton as the publisher of the *Biggles* books and Enid Blyton, but he took his account of the four years and ten months he spent as a hostage in Lebanon to the firm for sound commercial reasons; Hodder won a bidding war for *Taken on Trust* against HarperCollins (that old rivalry again).

The writing and editing process was unusual. Waite had written the book in his head while he was in captivity, and he explained to me that he wanted the structure to move backwards and forwards in time to reflect the way he 'might at one moment be reliving my childhood, and then be brought up to the present with a jerk because someone comes into my cell and my life is threatened'. It was an unconventional way to put together a memoir, and the challenge of managing the manuscript was made greater by the way Terry Waite committed the book to paper.

He was awarded a fellowship by Trinity Hall, Cambridge, and spent his weekdays in college writing in the rooms he had been assigned. There was a telephone in the corridor outside, and every three days he would break and ring his editor at Hodder, John Curtis, to read over the material. The editing process was done during these telephone calls, and the book took a year to complete. Terry Waite believes that *Taken on Trust* reflects Hodder's religious tradition because 'you can discern faith as the bedrock running through the book'.

Terry Waite had good reason to feel delighted with the book; 'It's been in print for twenty-three years and sold around half a million copies,' he told me. It allowed him to fulfil his post-hostage ambition to leave salaried employment and make his living by writing and lecturing, devoting much of his spare time to charity work.

Tim Hely Hutchinson, however, looked at the immediate sales figures and drew a rather different lesson from the episode. 'I remember Terry Waite's very, very successful memoir of his time in captivity was number-one bestseller all the way through

Christmas [1993],' he says, 'and I think it sold about forty thousand copies. Today a bestseller of that status would sell three or four hundred thousand copies.' In fact, the records show that the total hardback sales of *Taken on Trust* were nearly 230,000, but Hely Hutchinson says that Terry Waite's book was one of the factors that inspired him to take on the near-sacred publishing institution known as the Net Book Agreement.

The Net Book Agreement – or NBA – was as old as the century. It came into force on 1 January 1900 as a means of allowing publishers to fix the price at which books were sold. It was enforced by what we would today describe as a cartel; the big publishers agreed that they would all boycott any bookseller who tried to sell books at a discount. But for decades it was generally held to be a benign influence on the book trade, encouraging publishers to bring out a wide range of books and protecting the margins enjoyed by booksellers. Its great champion was the Publishers Association, an organisation in which past generations of Hodder-Williamses and Attenboroughs, including Philip Attenborough, the last family head of the firm, had often played a prominent role.

Tim Hely Hutchinson says he decided to challenge the system because of the contrast between the British and American markets. 'We observed that bestsellers in Britain were selling in tiny quantities compared to America,' he says. 'If you took someone like Stephen King, twenty or thirty times fewer books were sold in Britain compared to America.' And he saw the NBA as an obstacle to the publisher's basic duty of getting books to readers. 'We have the job on behalf of the author to get the books read by as many people as possible, and it was terribly frustrating that this agreement prevented price being used as a marketing weapon, and that we were selling so little,' he says.

In the spring of 1995 Hodder Headline announced that it would allow retailers to sell its books at a discount. It was not the first publisher to abandon the NBA, but it was the biggest, and the move marked the beginning of the end for the Agreement. The attack on the system that had been a cornerstone of the publishing trade for so long was, however, initially resisted by the Publishers Association, and Philip Attenborough, who had kept a seat on the Hodder Headline board after the merger, resigned in protest, finally cutting his ties with his old family firm.

Hodder's decision to pull out of the NBA coincided with the publication of the latest John le Carré, and Hely Hutchinson decided to use *Our Game* as the spearhead of his assault on the Agreement. 'Asda special offer: cut price le Carré', was the headline in the *Daily Mail* on 1 May 1995; 'New novel by John le Carré goes on sale at half price in 203 ASDA stores today', the paper reported, 'Safeways, Sainsburys, Dillons and John Menzies also plan to discount the book, *Our Game*, in one of the biggest attacks yet on the NBA'.

WHSmith was sniffy about the move, and their order for the new book was low; 'I can't really see the point of backing a book that will be sold more cheaply by other groups,' their buyer said. 'As for le Carré himself, I wonder what he thinks about being treated as a mass-market author, being sold in supermarkets and service stations? Not a lot, I should think.' The combative Hely Hutchinson retorted, 'the author would like as many people as possible to read his stories. He is very keen to reach beyond a literary or a committed book-buying elite in order to embrace a new readership. He is supporting everything we do.' That in turn provoked a fax from le Carré himself to Hely Hutchinson, complaining about being 'dragged into this battle' and declaring, 'You really do not have my authority to say you have my blanket support, nor to represent my views.'

The Hodder Headline sales team were, meanwhile, greatly enjoying the mayhem and the publicity it generated. 'It was amazing, it was suddenly like the Wild West,' Martin Neild remembered. 'We were doing deals . . . we were riding a bucking bronco.' Dealing with buyers who were accustomed to ordering vast quantities of food and household goods came as a shock, even for publishers who took pride in being commercially minded. 'The supermarkets had highly trained negotiators,' Neild says, 'and they were not interested in books. One rang up the sales department and said, "There's been a mistake, you've sent us the French edition – le Carré, it must be the French edition."'

Three weeks after publication Neild was congratulated by John le Carré on 'a splendid sales performance'. The hardback went straight to the top of the bestseller list in Britain, and within a year the huge advance – £550,000 – had been all but cleared.

Our Game did not kill the NBA on its own. The main resistance to ending it altogether came from booksellers, especially smaller firms who were ill-equipped to compete with selling-machines like the supermarkets. 'The vast majority of UK booksellers do not believe that discounting will result in a sufficient number of additional copies being sold to compensate for lower profits on discounted titles,' argued Tim Godfray, the Chief Executive of the Booksellers Association. 'Selective price cutting would inevitably lead to compensatory increases in the price of other books and independent bookshops would be unable to compete with supermarkets which will undoubtedly claim bigger discounts from publishers to fund the price cuts. The customer would therefore end up with a restricted choice of titles at higher prices, in fewer shops . . .'

But even before the Hodder move the Agreement had come under pressure from some of the big bookshop chains – like Dillons and Waterstones – which were beginning to dominate the British market, and although Amazon was in its infancy (the company was founded in 1994), more and more books were being imported from the United States, beyond the reach of the NBA.

Hely Hutchinson believes that a shakeout was inevitable. 'In the end Britain was terribly over book-shopped,' he says. And he is unsentimental about the independent bookshops that went to the wall. 'The thing about the independent booksellers at the time is that the majority of them were terribly bad – not even in a characterful way sometimes,' he declares. 'They were just dismal places which provided a very poor service and very poor stock, and were not part of any modern retail environment that normal customers would want.'

In September 1995 Eddie Bell, now chairman of HarperCollins, said that the move by his old employers had made it 'increasingly difficult to support' the NBA, adding, 'From where I am sitting the NBA is just not going to make it. It's not got a chance.' HarperCollins and then Random House and Penguin pulled out later that month, and at a meeting on 29 September the Publishers Association decided that it would no longer administer or try to enforce the Agreement. The Association did not formally kill off the NBA, but three years later, not far short of the Agreement's one hundredth birthday, the Restrictive Practices Court ruled it illegal.

Some of those who attended the PA's decisive meeting predicted dire consequences: 'The war is now going to start,' said one. 'There's going to be bombing and torpedoing and a lot of people are going to lose their livelihoods.' Tim Hely Hutchinson welcomed a decision that he said would 'stimulate interest in books', and the marketing director of Dillons, Stephen Dunn, supported him, declaring confidently that 'It's good news for book lovers, good news for booksellers and good news for literature.' Hely Hutchinson argues that their bullish optimism has been justified by events. 'For ten years after that it helped to increase the size of the book market,' he told me, 'so while other markets are still going down – magazines, monthly magazines and particularly newspapers – books went up every year because the public appreciated the new pricing.'

Carolyn Mays' big adventure of the mid-1990s was what she calls her 'leap of faith' in Charles Frazier and his novel *Cold*

Mountain, the American Civil War story of a wounded Confederate soldier who deserts from hospital and undertakes an epic journey to return to his first love, Ada, who is running the family firm on the eponymous mountain in Tennessee. Carolyn heard about the book from a contact at a small publisher in New York. 'It wasn't finished,' she says, 'quite a lot of it was written, but we didn't know how the love story was going to end. And it was very literary. It was written without quotation marks – beautiful literary writing but not one of those books that's actually easy to read, you had to work quite hard at it. It was about the American Civil War, which everyone knows never sells any books.'

She told me she paid £30,000 for the British rights, a figure that does not sound huge today but 'at the time seemed a lot of money for a literary novel'. She took satisfaction in having 'snatched it out of the jaws of Robert McCrum at Faber' and says that she and her team felt like 'the bright young things who were going to steal it away from the old people'. The book initially attracted very good reviews but failed to take off in the shops.

Hodder then handed out cards to booksellers that carried a column of single-word quotes from the reviews – 'amazing', 'fantastic', 'brilliant', 'genius' etc. The cards were placed on top of the piles of books, and the stock started shifting. Like Thomas Keneally's *Schindler's Ark*, *Cold Mountain* was turned into an immensely successful film, and sold millions of copies round the world; that £30,000 turned out to have been extremely well spent.

Life at the firm in the 1990s must sometimes have felt like being caught up in a permanent revolution. In May 1999, Hodder Headline announced another takeover: WHSmith bought the merged company for £185 million. 'As management we weren't mad about the deal, we weren't expecting it and it came out of the blue,' Tim Hely Hutchinson told me, '. . . the reason we accepted it was because it was a fantastic deal. The price was so high that I knew that if any shareholders were in the room as we discussed it they would have said you can't turn it down.' Investors who had paid one pound per share when the company was originally floated were now being offered five pounds a share.

The marriage did not last very long and its end after five years is remembered with little regret by those I have spoken to for this book. 'We survived,' is the way Hely Hutchinson sums up the Smiths episode. He did, however, have to expend more energy smoothing the ruffled feathers of his star British author. John le Carré judged the takeover 'an unattractive alliance', and told Hely Hutchinson that he regarded Smiths as 'a dismal house, an ailing giant . . . Their banality has been a curse on the industry.' Once again, the threat that the great man might take his books elsewhere hung over the firm.

Roddy Bloomfield, in the meantime, had played something of a blinder in the campaign to keep relations sweet with Hodder's American star, Stephen King. King is a baseball fan, and took Martin Neild to see a Boston Red Sox game while the Hodder & Stoughton managing director was visiting New York. Neild was trying to persuade Stephen King to promote his latest book with a British tour, so when it emerged that the author's interest in ball games extended to curiosity about cricket, he promised a meeting with the great umpire Dickie Bird.

Bloomfield, who had been the midwife to Dickie Bird's highly successful 1997 autobiography, was roped in to make the meeting happen. He tracked the great man down to a county game at Trent Bridge, and arranged for the American novelist and his Hodder entourage to be bussed up to Nottingham, only to find that the wicket was so soaked with rain that there were 'ducks wandering round the middle'.

Bloomfield says Dickie Bird had 'no idea at all' who Stephen King was, and the Yorkshire miner's son turned cricket celebrity is not famous for being generous with his time or conversation.

But he rose to the occasion. Once the game had been formally called off he spent four hours looking after the visiting American. 'He took him to the pavilion, showed him all the pictures, showed him what a stump was, showed him how the game was played, introduced him to the Nottingham Team,' Bloomfield remembers. 'He's never done anything like that in his life before.'

The incident had an enjoyable postscript. Some months later Dickie Bird was the subject of the *Life in the Day* column in *The Sunday Times,* and when asked to name his current book he replied with Stephen King's *Bag of Bones.* The book is a dark thriller based around an author with writer's block shacked up by an isolated American lake. Roddy Bloomfield seems to have some doubt about whether Dickie Bird has actually read it – he says it was certainly the only non-cricket book in the umpire's house.

The biggest name in Bloomfield's 1990s bag, Alex Ferguson, published the first version of his autobiography in 1999. To secure the rights, Bloomfield was required to submit a proposal and an offer for an advance not to a literary agent, but to the accountancy giant KPMG. 'I heard nothing, and thought "That's it", and put it out of my mind,' he remembered. 'Three or four weeks afterwards I got a call from this man, who was very much like an accountant, and he said, "The Ferguson book's yours" – just like that.' The manner of his first meeting with his new writer was altogether alien to the long-lunches way in which publishers have traditionally wooed authors; Bloomfield was instructed to turn up at the Cliff, Manchester United's training ground, at 7.30 in the morning.

Managing My Life was co-authored by the respected sports writer Hugh McIlvanney. Bloomfield says it was a complicated process because although Ferguson was 'a good writer', he would often scribble material during plane trips and send pages in to be deciphered and woven into the narrative. The result has never been out of print, and Ferguson did three more books for Hodder.

Bloomfield would not tell me how much Hodder paid for *Managing My Life* – a figure of a million has been reported in the press – but he did volunteer that, for the first and only time during his career with the company, he was required to discuss the proposed advance with Tim Hely Hutchinson in person.

19

Men in tight breeches

In the summer of 2001 Martin Neild telephoned Jamie Hodder-Williams from his house in Italy and asked him to come and stay for a couple of days. 'I didn't know what it was about,' Jamie says, 'but thought it would be fun, and I knew there were some other publishing friends of Martin's there.' Tim Hely Hutchinson was also in the party.

When Jamie turned up the other guests were sent off to an early dinner in the ancient Umbrian town of Bevagna, ostensibly so that the Hodder team could 'write an urgent marketing plan for le Carré'. Instead Martin Neild offered his guest the job he had always wanted: Jamie Hodder-Williams was to take over as the managing director of the firm his great-great-great-grand-father had founded.

'Tim took me to dinner straight afterwards at a beautiful hotel overlooking the Umbrian hills,' Jamie remembers, 'and we talked about what we could do to renew Hodder, to boost the literary publishing in particular, to bring in some new talent, and to increase Hodder's reputation for marketing its authors with energy and flair. We went back down to Martin's house and drank grappa on the terrace while we welcomed back the other publishers from their dinner . . . It was all a big surprise, and of course I knew my father would be (very quietly) thrilled, and that meant a lot to me.'

At the same time Carolyn Mays took on Sue Fletcher's editor-ial responsibilities; she and Jamie had come up through the firm as something of a double act, and she says, 'it felt that we were inheriting it'. She describes the manner of Jamie's appointment as 'so elegant and such a perfect way to do it', adding that 'I think that's quite a Hoddery thing.'

This fairy-tale beginning to the new millennium was followed by several years of what she describes as 'the era of entertainment'. In the early 2000s it was commonplace to spend large amounts of company money wooing everyone involved in the business of writing, buying and selling books. Carolyn remembers 'enormously fun, expensive days and nights' at luxury spa hotels like The Grove, Champneys and Cowley Manor.

Twenty or so buyers from the big retailers would be entertained with massages and treatments or, for the more energetic, clay pigeon shooting and archery, and in the evening a group of selected Hodder authors talked about their books over dinner. They were usually writers of commercial fiction, and their task was to 'make the retailers feel warmly toward our books and understand the specialness of our authors'. The general idea was that once a buyer had 'met Santa Montefiore at the massage table and decided they liked her' they would choose Hodder books for their promotions.

Sometimes the junketing involved glamorous foreign trips. Jean Auel's prehistoric novel *The Shelters of Stone*, published after a gap of twelve years since her previous book, is set in south-west France; the heroine is credited with the discovery of the Lascaux caves, and her people are said to have created the famous paintings there. So the book's 2002 publication was marked by three days of press conferences and sightseeing for journalists and booksellers in the Dordogne.

John Berendt's Venetian investigation *The City of Falling Angels* was also regarded as a major publishing event because, like Jean Auel's book, it followed a long period of silence from the author. When it came out in 2005, Hodder flew a group of authors including Kate Adie and Tracy Emin to soak up the atmosphere in La Serenissima. Tracy Emin is reported to have taken on the persona of a cat during the trip; she 'made it very clear to us that she only talked in cat language after midnight', according to Martin Neild.

And when John Connolly used the Sedlec Ossuary as a plot device in *The Black Angel*, the bookselling caravan rumbled on to the Czech Republic to see the chapel's bone chandeliers and garlands of skulls. 'As an industry we were trying to learn from film and music,' Jamie Hodder-Williams said, 'to learn the most effective media techniques – so that you can demonstrate to your authors that they are getting the best market reach.'

Connolly is cited by Hodder as an example of an author who understands the need to find new ways of connecting with his readers. His books, described as 'quality crime thrillers', are mostly set in Maine (Sedlec notwithstanding) and have a supernatural dimension that echoes Stephen King's style. He was one of the first authors to develop his own website, allowing him to 'meet' his fans in the virtual world. He also has a reputation for putting in time and mileage to promote his books in more conventional ways, heading off on road trips to give bookshop readings.

Carolyn Mays remembers the early 2000s as a period 'about making authors feel special and wooing them, petting them really'. The 'era of entertainment' gravy train hit the buffers with the financial crisis, and the archery and the clay pigeon shooting stopped as retailers began to demand ever larger sums to promote individual books; money that might have paid for a massage at Champneys or The Grove went into more conventional promotional expenditure. But author-petting has never entirely died. 'We still try to do that,' Carolyn Mays says.

Jodi Picoult's thank-you presents have included a visit to Chatsworth, a fancy-dress party with 'men in tight breeches' and an English springer spaniel ('I mean, who has a publisher that brings them a puppy!' the author remarked in an email for this book). She is cited by Hodder as another author who has earned the firm's admiration and gratitude by the hours she puts in to promote her work.

Picoult had been published in America for more than ten years before Hodder picked her up in Britain; until then her work had been consistently turned down by British publishers, perhaps on the grounds that her signature mix of issue-based stories and courtroom drama would not appeal to a British readership. Carolyn Mays, working with the Hodder publicity director Kerry Hood and the sales director Lucy Hale, developed a long-term strategy for introducing her to the British market. When Mays bought *My Sister's Keeper* she prepared the way for the book by first publishing one of Picoult's earlier works (*Plain Truth*), and then sending out thousands of reading copies across the country. Her efforts paid dividends when *My Sister's Keeper* was picked for the inaugural edition of the *Richard and Judy Book Club* on Channel 4. It was, she says, 'the perfect book for this new form of televisual discussion about books – it was accessible, entertaining, but packed with issues for "sofa chat", including a controversial ending that the real readers who came on the show could debate in their book clubs.'

Hodder followed up on the success of *My Sister's Keeper* by buying Jodi Picoult's entire backlist. However the firm resisted the temptation to indulge in binge publishing; instead of bringing all the books out at once it released them at a rate of three a year, 'giving the readers a new novel almost as soon as they finished the last one'. Hodder describe the strategy as 'an intense publishing schedule reminiscent of the rapid-fire launches of the Hodder Yellow Jacket era of the twenties and thirties', and Mays says, 'We were always looking for new ways to let the public know about the novels, with advertising in coffee shops, partnerships with record companies and new types of advertising on Facebook and the internet.'

Jodi Picoult herself worked hard for those thank-yous. As well as the sometimes gruelling book tours – with signings, readings and discussions – she responds swiftly and personally to reader messages on social media. The publication of her novel *Small Great Things* was marked by a digital twist to the traditional technique of trying to generate market interest with advance proof copies. Unconscious prejudice is one of the book's central themes, so Hodder sent out proof copies without any title, author name or final cover, and asked the recipients to post their reactions online. Thousands did.

In 2002 Hodder Headline bought the venerable family firm of John Murray, publishers of Jane Austen, Lord Byron and Charles Darwin. Two years later the company went through yet another corporate transformation when it was bought from WHSmith by the Paris-based group Hachette, which already owned two other British publishers. And two years after that Hachette expanded into the United States by buying Time-Warner's publishing division. Because some of the Time-Warner business – Little, Brown UK – was based in Britain, Hachette became, for a while, the biggest publisher in the United Kingdom. Tim Hely Hutchinson was appointed the chief executive of Hachette UK when it took over Hodder Headline.

The publishing challenges of the digital environment have thrown up an irony. In 2014 Hachette USA was involved in an ill-tempered dispute with Amazon over pricing. Hachette UK's former chief executive – Tim Hely Hutchinson retired in 2017 – recognises that Amazon's power to dictate prices is a natural consequence of the process that began with the destruction of the Net Book Agreement in 1995 for which he, of course, was partly responsible. Tim Hely Hutchinson still sometimes asks publishers whether they would like to reinvent the NBA. 'Not a single person has campaigned to get it back,' he says, 'despite the fact that there is one crucial strategic problem it has introduced, which is the growth of the non-traditional booksellers. Initially it was the supermarkets, and more recently it's been Amazon.'

Amazon, he concedes, 'does a fantastic job' and so, 'from a consumer point . . . is a good thing.' But he adds a caution about the future: Amazon's 'own success has created a huge market share . . . Their combined share of our UK business [physical and digital sales] is about forty per cent. That of course puts them in a position to be bossy about terms . . . As their market share rises every year you wonder where it might all end up.' Amazon has already killed off those marketing junkets to the Dordogne and Prague, probably for good; marketing in the digital age is, as Jamie Hodder-Williams puts it, much more 'to do with metadata and the right cover', which sounds rather less fun.

Hodder & Stoughton's absorption into the vast Hachette empire was part of a more general trend in the publishing industry, and Jamie Hodder-Williams says the firm 'couldn't ask for a better owner'. Hachette, he believes, under its French chief executive Arnaud Nourry, takes a long-term view of publishing and is willing to invest time in developing authors. But the way his family firm has gone through such a whirligig of acquisitions and mergers since the clan shareholders voted out the old order in 1993 must surely raise a question about what is left of the character of the original company. What, to put it another way, does the name Hodder & Stoughton now really mean?

Jamie believes part of the answer to that question is – and there is another irony here – a sense of family. He shies away from the word because of his own association with the idea of a family firm, but he believes Hodder & Stoughton nurtures a particularly close relationship between its authors and the people who edit, publish and sell their books. He says that at the heart of the firm are 'say a hundred people who feel close to them [the authors] and are desperate for their next book', and he argues 'that's what a really good publishing company has; a core of authors and a core of staff who intersect. They don't intersect every year or all the time, but across the writer's career they are joined together. And the Hodder team has been very, very stable since the Headline acquisition.'

Jamie Hodder-Williams cites Andrew Miller and David Mitchell as writers who have become part of that family 'core'. Miller published his first book (*Ingenious Pain*) with Hodder's Sceptre imprint in 1997; Carole Welch read the book over a weekend and, even though Miller had no previous track record, offered him a two-book deal for £50,000 immediately after the Tuesday editorial meeting. 'We knew little about Andrew at that point,' she says, 'or what he would write next, but he was evidently so talented that we were happy to commit to a two-book deal.' Twenty years later Miller is still with the firm, and Carole Welch describes him as 'a delight to publish'. Jamie Hodder-Williams includes the author's 2011 Costa Best Novel and Best Book of the Year awards (for the historical novel *Pure*) as one of the high points of his time as managing director.

David Mitchell also published his first novel with Hodder & Stoughton (*Ghostwritten*, in 1999) and, like Miller, has been with the firm ever since. He too is wary of the word 'family'; 'It's always a bit cringey when people talk about a company as a family – it's not,' he writes. But he recognises that the publishing process is more than mechanical; 'it all comes down to people,' he observes. 'There are dozens – hundreds, probably – of H&S employees involved in the business of turning my manuscripts into books and from books to numbers in my bank account, and I'm grateful to every single one. The number of "interfaces", of people who I email and interact with, is much smaller, however . . . but I've known some people at Hodder for two decades now, and they've become more than people at my publishers.'

In 2004 his novel *Cloud Atlas* was shortlisted for the Booker, and Hodder booked a bar in Soho for a party after the ceremony. The book did not win, and Mitchell turned up at the event with some trepidation. 'I was fine,' he remembers, 'it was only a 1-in-6 chance, but not winning the Booker gets psychically tiring because you have to spend days assuring well-meaning friends and acquaintances declaring "You was robbed!" – by the dozen – that you're fine.' He found Jamie Hodder-Williams nursing a pint at the bar. 'He read the situation and didn't try to console me or fortify my spirits,' Mitchell writes in an email exchange for this book. 'If memory serves he bought me a gin and tonic and we just chatted for a few minutes, not about the Booker, not about *Cloud Atlas*, probably just about our families. Fifteen years ago, this was, but I still remember his tact and restorative kindness.'

20

The Very Arteries of the Trade

A publisher is, of course, to a great extent defined by the books it produces.

Judged by sales figures, Hodder & Stoughton's claim on the religious heritage of its founders is slim; religion accounts for just five per cent of the business. But Hodder still has a commanding position in the Bible market that was such a huge and profitable feature of the publishing landscape when Matthew Hodder began his publishing apprenticeship; its New International Version has a market share of more than a third in the United Kingdom.

The tradition that began with Ernest Hodder-Williams' early forays into educational publishing is also still alive: in 2017 the group was able to claim nearly a quarter of the educational market. And, in a pleasing piece of symmetry, recent years have seen a revival of the dog literature Ernest also pioneered; nearly a hundred years after the publication of *Where's Master?* the firm brought out the monster bestseller *Marley and Me* by John Grogan. The book has sold more than a million copies in the English-language edition alone.

But the glamorous parts of the business remain the province of the novelists, popular and literary, and the big-hitting non-fiction writers – in that respect publishing today is just as it was in the era of J. M. Barrie, John Buchan and Fisher Fever. When I asked the senior Hodder figures whether there is still an identifiable 'Hodder & Stoughton book', they all focused on these publishing fields, but each gave a slightly different answer.

Tim Hely Hutchinson says the firm stands for a certain quality of book; 'whether it is a romance, a crime novel or a literary novel, it will be of a high standard, and it will be well produced, well edited and well marketed,' he says. There should, he argues, 'be nothing tacky' on the firm's list. He describes Hodder & Stoughton as a 'liberal' publisher with political red lines. When we met he had recently been asked about publishing biographies of Nigel Farage and Donald Trump; 'I don't need to see the sums,' was his reaction to both proposals, 'the answer is no.'

Carolyn Mays cites the example of David Nicholls' *One Day* to define her 'perfect Hodder book', by which she means one that 'tells a wonderful story, it moves you, it makes you laugh, and has meaning. It is not difficult but you don't feel you are slumming it when you are reading it either.'

One Day benefited from an especially memorable cover: a graphic image of two people facing one another. It proved so popular that one Hodder staffer saw the image reproduced at the 'One Day Café' in Beijing. But Nick Sayers, who worked as Nicholls' editor on the book, believes 'it would have been just as big a bestseller with a lousy jacket'. He writes, 'I think you are privileged as a publisher if you have that feeling even once in your career, when you know you are holding pure gold in your hands.'

Nicholls is a professional scriptwriter as well as a novelist, which allowed the marketing director Auriol Bishop to experiment with new ways of selling the book. 'We created a series of book trailers and audio snippets (what would now be called podcasts)', she writes. 'We worked with him on scripting them, and worked with an up-and-coming film-maker to create them, so they had a real filmic feel to them. We then advertised the films in a teaser campaign, driving people to watch them and hooking them into the story without even really telling them it was a book.' The strategy evidently worked; Sayers recalls the satisfaction of 'days when I would see several people in one tube carriage reading the paperback'.

Jamie Hodder-Williams' ambitions for the firm's list are democratic. 'The really big books have been those big adventure, sporting hero books where we reach hundreds of thousands of people who don't buy many books in a year – in some cases it's probably the only book they buy,' he says. He is especially fond of citing the example of Alex Ferguson's second memoir, *My Autobiography*, which came out in 2013; according to figures from Bookscan, the current mechanism for measuring sales, the book has been – and at the time of writing remains – the biggest-selling autobiography in Britain ever. Ferguson himself has vivid memories of its publication: 'I'll never forget the signing session for the book in Manchester,' he writes. 'It began early in the day and lasted for 12 hours. People were sleeping in the long queue and I was very amused at the number of small children to whom I was introduced, whose parents had named them "Alex"!'

Ferguson is full of praise for Hodder and the 'total professionalism' of his main editor, Roddy Bloomfield. Bloomfield's disciplined style clearly appealed to the legendary Manchester United manager. 'He regularly came up to the training ground for our meetings to explain the various processes in the book's production,' Ferguson recalls. 'He cannily prefaced his requests for meetings when I was busy by saying, "Don't worry, I'll have a taxi waiting in the car park so I won't be able to stay with you for long"!'

Hodder had a rather different relationship with the author of another highly successful autobiography, Russell Brand. He was, like Ferguson, expensive; Jamie Hodder-Williams and Nick Davies, who worked in the non-fiction division, had to seek an audience with Tim Hely Hutchinson to make their case for the advance. Hely Hutchinson agreed to the 'substantial' figure, even though he 'didn't know much about a relatively undiscovered Russell at that point'.

It was a race to meet the agent's deadline for offers, and another race to get the book done in time for the Christmas market. Russell Brand had to be sent to a villa in Umbria along with his agent and editor to get the work done (William Robertson Nicoll once despatched J. M. Barrie to a villa by the Thames to get him to finish a manuscript in similar style). *My Booky Wook* – a title that, says Rowena Webb, Hodder's non-fiction publisher, 'we needed to sit with for a while when Russell decided on it' – did spectacularly well at Christmas 2007; the firm had to print 100,000 copies a week to keep up with demand and, Webb remembers, 'Russell was like a pop star to his screamingly passionate followers, and his public events were heaving with ecstatic fans.'

Rowena Webb also has vivid memories of another popular author who could be difficult, or, to quote her view of the late Clarissa Dickson-Wright more precisely, 'fearless, irascible, fragile'. Clarissa, whom I knew a little, was one half of the television cooking duo *Two Fat Ladies* (the other being the militantly Catholic Jennifer Paterson) and can best be described as a force of nature. 'Publishing her could make for hairy moments – but we loved her,' writes Rowena Webb. 'Her publicist Kerry Hood and I enjoyed our Chinese meals at her favourite and unpretentious Crispy Duck restaurant in Chinatown, where we tried to avoid most of the dishes of innards and duck's feet she ordered.' The strategy did not always work; 'Eating was always a bit of a challenge with CDW,' according to Kerry Hood, 'I remember feeling I had to try all sorts of things that went against my nature – razor clams being one . . . she stared at me hard as I ate a couple.' Clarissa Dickson-Wright was a ferocious champion of fox-hunting, and the Hodder team feared she might end up in jail because of her campaign against the hunting ban; 'It was a close-run thing,' says Rowena Webb.

Webb cites Dickson-Wright as one of the 'strong women' she says have been a 'theme' of the firm's non-fiction list – she also mentions the BBC's Kate Adie, the former Irish president Mary Robinson and the comedian Miranda Hart.

The latter's first book, *Is It Just Me?*, was written 'in character', but Hodder's market research showed that most of her readers thought they were reading a real autobiography. To market the book Hodder used Twitter to appeal to Hart's fans for their own embarrassing stories, and the responses were collected in an e-book that, according to the sales director Lucy Hale, 'stimulated huge early ordering of the new book'. The concept of book publishing as a kind of 'conversation' with the readers is of course one of the defining changes of the digital marketplace, but in spirit it is perhaps not so very different from Ernest Hodder-Williams' efforts to market Lord Fisher's memoirs on the basis of the dinner party conversations they would generate.

Webb's roster of male 'national treasures' includes an impressive list of actors (Paul Eddington, Nigel Hawthorne and Michael Caine among them) and my colleague John Humphrys, whose company she enjoyed in unexpectedly cuddly form 'sitting around his table enjoying home-made nettle soup'. She also oversaw the publication of several volumes of autobiography from the television gardening guru Alan Titchmarsh; 'The nation's favourite gardener with heart-throb status would have long queues of women at his book signings clutching pots of home-made jam and home-crafted gifts for him,' she reports, 'some of them weeping gently as they arrived at his desk.'

Jamie Hodder-Williams believes that most of those who work with him are, in part at least, motivated by an old-fashioned faith in the power of books. 'There is a desire from our staff and the company as a whole that the books we publish do good in the world,' he says. 'It certainly doesn't apply to every book we've published, but I think it does underpin everyone's purpose in coming to work. They believe there's a wider good in reading and books, and that there's a cultural benefit to the nation. If you read fiction you tend to be more open to other people's views of the world, and you tend to be more empathetic.'

Over lunch – some publishing traditions never entirely die – I asked Jamie Hodder-Williams to reflect on the way the trade had changed since the days of his great-uncle, Sir Ernest. 'I suspect Ernest took on a book without overtly saying to himself, "I am going to make money from this book",' he replied. 'He probably thought "This book could be a success", but he probably wasn't calculating a profit and loss sheet.' And he believes that missionary sense of the cultural value of books was stronger in Sir Ernest's day. 'Ernest was absolutely involved in every nook and cranny of the business, and with the cultural life of the country, and almost towards the politics of the country,' he says, 'and I think that connectivity between the industry and the nation can be lost in commerce.'

But listening to him describe some of the adventures of his own time running Hodder & Stoughton, I was struck by how many echoes there were of the firm's earlier history.

Timing and technology remain as decisive as they always have been, especially for non-fiction books. In 1919 Sir Ernest and his team pulled off a production miracle to capitalise on 'Fisher Fever'. In 2005, when England won the Ashes for the first time in eighteen years, Hodder brought out three cricketing autobiographies – by Michael Vaughan, Andrew Strauss and Freddie Flintoff – immediately after the series. The Flintoff book was almost ready to go before the final test; the last chapter was written over two days, and Roddy Bloomfield had the book in the shops within a week of England's series victory.

And 'commerce' has not killed Ernest's sense of the 'joy in the game'; many of the Hodder editors who have contributed to this book have enjoyed the moment of excitement that comes with the discovery of a new talent. Carole Welch recalls the lunch at which a literary agent produced 'a manuscript in a plastic bag and gave it to me with no preamble, saying, "Read this". It just had the name of the author on it.' The name, which at the time meant nothing to Welch, was Siri Hustvedt. She has since become one of the firm's most successful authors; *What I Loved* has, at the time of writing, sold more than 300,000 copies, a remarkable figure for a literary novel.

In 2006 Jamie Hodder-Williams, with an eye to the firm's traditions, tried to reinvigorate the religious publishing that had been the foundation of his great-great-great-grandfather's partnership with Thomas Stoughton. He recruited Wendy Grisham, the sister of the bestselling American writer John Grisham, and she brought in a book called *The Shack* by William Young. It tells the story of a man who loses his daughter to a serial killer and then has an encounter with the Holy Trinity. God the Father, it turns out, is an African American woman, God the Son is a Middle Eastern carpenter and God the Holy Spirit is an Asian woman named Sarayu.

The book was initially self-published, but it proved formidably popular and became a huge commercial success. Jamie Hodder-Williams believes it was probably the firm's 'biggest-selling religious book – aside from the Bible – since Matthew Hodder set up shop next to St Paul's.' Quite what Matthew and Thomas Stoughton would have made of the book's unusual theology is another matter. Wendy Grisham's recruitment was eventually followed by the seduction of her brother John; she returned to the United States, but Hodder took on John Grisham's editor Oliver Johnson, who, over time, brought several of his authors with him, including the bestselling master of the legal thriller.

The long – and so often fractious – relationship with John le Carré finally came to an end in 2009. David Cornwell decided that he would publish his next book in hardback with Penguin Viking, and would move his backlist to Penguin over time. He seems to have been motivated above all by the desire to see his books in the company of the literary classics that the imprint could claim as its own. 'My reasons are primarily to do with my posterity, such as it may be,' he wrote to his editor at Hodder, 'and the prospect of seeing my work included on a classic and enduring list.' He had been with Hodder & Stoughton for thirty-eight years, and his message to Jamie Hodder-Williams must have been painful to swallow: 'Increasingly I have felt over the last few years that I was not a natural feature of the house,' he wrote. He added that 'my standards were becoming egregious by comparison with those of other authors', though precisely what he meant by 'egregious' in that context is not clear.

The loss of le Carré still rankles at Hodder, but that debit in the ledger is more than offset by the continued success of another of the firm's star authors, Stephen King. King is a little younger than le Carré/David Cornwell, but he enjoys a similar status as a colossus on the literary landscape, and, like le Carré, he is one of those rare writers who combine big sales with literary reputation. King once described himself as 'the literary equivalent of a Big Mac and fries', but the editor and writer Robert McCrum wrote more recently of him as 'a sophisticated literary craftsman' whose 'work anatomises, with folksy charm, the social fabric of small-town American life'. McCrum's piece in the *Observer* continued, 'It also plumbs, with unnerving accuracy, the hopes and fears of an entire nation.'

Philippa Pride, King's editor, writes about him with awe, calling him 'a legend . . . a delight to work with, wonderfully creative and innovative as well as the most incredible storyteller who attracts generation after generation of new readers.' As well as novels his range extends to the short story, which he has memorably described as a 'kiss in the dark from a stranger'. He published his first novel in 1973, the year the first mobile phone call was made, and nearly two decades before the creation of the World Wide Web. Hodder marked his seventieth birthday with 'a day-long celebration of his writing across social media'. To encourage his fans to join in, hourly 'events' were created, starting in Australia and then unfolding through Asia and Africa and back to the United Kingdom. King himself tweets about his corgi, Molly, which perhaps makes him a suitable digital heir to the Hodder & Stoughton tradition of mixing literature, royalty and dogs.

In 2015 Hodder & Stoughton, along with the rest of the Hachette empire, moved into a gleaming new building at Victoria Embankment. Tim Hely Hutchinson says, 'For me, it was a publishing deal more than a property transaction.' He believed the 'stunning roof terrace and river views would help us recruit and retain the best colleagues, who would in turn attract the best authors.'

The headquarters is a new development, but the building's name, Carmelite House, evokes the area's deep religious history: in the mid-thirteenth century it became home to a community of Carmelites, a monastic order founded on the slopes of Mount Carmel in the Holy Land during the years of the Crusader states. Because they wore white cloaks over their brown scapulars, the monks gave the name of Whitefriars to this stretch of the riverbank. And as the brochure the company had printed for the move noted, the site was for long years close to the heart of the publishing world. 'There may be no ghosts of writers and printers in these streets and buildings,' the brochure declares, 'but they have echoed to the rhythms of London publishing for centuries: the very arteries of the trade.'

One of the most striking views from the roof terrace that Tim Hely Hutchinson so much admires is the great dome of St Paul's. The Carmelite House space was formerly occupied by the offices of the *Daily Mail*, so when you stand on the terrace – perhaps with a cup of good coffee from Hachette's sleek canteen – you are looking at London's cathedral from the spot where the paper's photographer took that famous picture of the Blitz bombing that, in December 1940, wiped out the historic home of London publishing.

And perhaps, the official brochure notwithstanding, there is a ghost about. The building is, after all, just a step or two from where Matthew Hodder alighted when he arrived in Fleet Street on the stagecoach from Staines.

Acknowledgements

A I have referred to Sarah Harrison's research work in my Introduction, but I cannot overstate her contribution to this book; she was thorough, imaginative and always enthusiastic. I am also grateful to the following people for interviews and emails; Thomas Abraham, Jeffrey Archer, Michael Attenborough, Eddie Bell, Auriol Bishop, Roddy Bloomfield, Sir Chris Bonington, Tony Brown, Alex Ferguson, Sue Fletcher, Lucy Hale, Tim Hely Hutchinson, Jamie Hodder-Williams, Kerry Hood, Carolyn Mays, Ian Metcalfe, David Mitchell, John Mitchinson, Martin Neild, Deborah Owen, Michael Parkinson, Jodi Picoult, Philippa Pride, Nick Sayers, Vivienne Schuster, Lis Tribe, Terry Waite, Philip Walters, Rowena Webb, Carole Welch, Jamie Wilson. Maggie Body merits a special mention for her short memoir.

This book was written at some speed, and Maddy Price, my editor at Hodder and Stoughton, deserves great credit for the steady nerve she showed in managing a complex project. She was unfailingly supportive, and her suggestions significantly improved the text. I am grateful to her and everyone else who helped at Hodder – particularly Tanya Cowell, who always ensured that I felt welcome on my visits to Carmelite House. Juliet Brightmore did some inspired picture research and has curated some memorable images. The copyeditor, Sophie Bristow, tidied up the manuscript swiftly, precisely and with a light touch, and David Fleck has clothed the book beautifully.

I am also very grateful to my agent, Gordon Wise, for his

advice and guidance – the tight deadline for delivering this book made it especially important to have such a solid anchor. On the home front my wife Fiona acted as the editor of first resort, and was, as ever, a sharp and constructive critic. Finally, my thanks to Fig, the younger of our spaniels, who kept me at my desk by the simple expedient of sleeping on my feet while I wrote.

Note on Sources

Much of the material for this book was drawn from the extensive collection of Hodder & Stoughton documents, photographs and family records held at the London Metropolitan Archives, 40 Northampton Row, Clerkenwell, London EC1R 0HB (https://www.cityoflondon.gov.uk/things-to-do/london-metropolitan-archives/Pages/default.aspx).

Copies of the firm's magazines can be found at the British Library, 96 Euston Road, NW1 2DB (https://www.bl.uk/?ns_campaign=brand&ns_mchannel=ppc&ns_source=google&ns_linkname=The%20british%20library&ns_fee=0&gclid=EAIaIQobChMIg7GdkNbk2gIVipXtCh12aQ7REAAYASAAEgJTQPD_BwE).

Material relating to publishing and propaganda during the two world wars was drawn from the National Archives, Kew, Richmond, Surrey, TW9 4DU (http://www.nationalarchives.gov.uk/), and copies of Hodder & Stoughton's wartime propaganda pamphlets are held at the Imperial War Museum, IWM London, Lambeth Road, London, SE1 6HZ (https://www.iwm.org.uk/visits/iwm-london).

For the later chapters I have relied heavily on interviews and email exchanges with current and past members of Hodder & Stoughton's staff, and with some of the firm's authors. The text makes it clear where these sources have been used.

In addition, I have drawn on the published sources listed in the bibliography. I am grateful to the copyright holders of the books listed. My publisher and I have made every effort to obtain permissions to use copyright material and apologize for any omissions here. We will be pleased to make appropriate acknowledgement in any future addition.

Bibliography

Arlen, Michael, *The Green Hat: A Romance for a Few People*, W Collins Sons & Co, 1924

Attenborough, John, *A Living Memory, Hodder & Stoughton, Publishers, 1868-1975*, Hodder & Stoughton, 1975

Barnes, Trevor, *People with a Purpose*, Hodder & Stoughton, 2008

Barrie, J M, *The Little White Bird*, Hodder & Stoughton, 1902

Binfield, Clive, *George Williams and the Young Men's Christian Association – a Study in Victorian Social Attitudes*, Heinemann, 1973

Bradley, Sue (ed), *The British Book Trade, An Oral History*, The British Library, 2008

Chaney, Lisa, *Hide-and-Seek with Angles: a Life of J M Barrie*, Hutchinson, 2005

Charteris, Leslie, *Trust the Saint*, Hodder & Stoughton, 1962

Chesterton, G K, *Autobiography,* Hutchinson & Co, 1936

Cox, Geoffrey, *The English Churches in a Secular Society: Lambeth 1870-1930*, Oxford University Press, 1982

Darlow, T H, William Robertson Nicoll; life and letters, Hodder & Stoughton, 1925

Doran, George, *Chronicle of Barabbas*, Methuen and Co, 1935

Feather, John, *A History of British Publishing*, Routledge, 2005

Fogazzaro, Antonio, *Il Santo, The Saint*, Hodder & Stoughton, 1906

Gedye, G. E. R., *Fallen Bastions – the Central European Tragedy*, Gollanz, 1939

Greenfield, George, *A Smattering of Monsters: a Kind of Memoir*, Little, Brown and Company, 1995

Greenfield, George, *Scribblers for Bread*, Hodder & Stoughton, 1989

Haste, Cate, *Keep the Home Fires Burning*, Allen Lane, 1977

Hodder & Stoughton wartime pamphlets

Hodder Williams, J E, *One Young Man*, Hodder & Stoughton, 1917

Hodder Williams, J E, *The Life of Sir George Williams*, Hodder & Stoughton, 1906

Hodder, Edwin, *Life in London; the Pitfalls of a Great City*, Hodder & Stoughton, 1890

Hodder–Williams, Ernest, Where's Master, the King's Dog, Hodder & Stoughton, 1910

Holman, Valerie, *Print for Victory, Book Publishing in England 1939-45*, The British Library, 2008

Howsam, Leslie, *Cheap Bibles: Nineteenth Century Publishing and the British and Foreign Bible Society*, Cambridge University Press, 2002

Hunt, Sir John, *The Ascent of Everest*, Hodder & Stoughton, 1953

Jones, J D, *The Power to Endure*, Hodder & Stoughton, 1940

Keene, Derek; Burns, Arthur and Saint, Andrew (eds), *St Paul's, the Cathedral Church of London*, Yale University Press, 2016

Keneally, Thomas, *Searching for Schindler*, Sceptre, 2008

Lane, Margaret, *Edgar Wallace: the biography of a phenomenon*, Heinemann, 1938

Lefanu, Sarah, *Rose Macaulay: A Biography*, Virago, 2003

Liefde, J B, *The Beggars; the Founders of the Dutch Republic*, Hodder & Stoughton, 1868

McEvoy, Sadia, *The Construction of Ottoman Asia and its Muslim Peoples in Wellington House's Propaganda and Associated Literature, 1914-1918*, King's College London, 2016

Norrie, Ian, *Frank Mumby's Publishing and Bookselling in the Twentieth Century*, Bell and Hyman, 1982

Partington, Wilfred, *Forging Ahead, the true story of the upward progress of Thomas J Wise*, G P Putnam's Sons, 1939

Sampson, Anthony, *The Changing Anatomy of Britain*, Hodder & Stoughton, 1982

Sapper, *Bulldog Drummond*, Hodder & Stoughton, 1920

Sisman, Adam, *John le Carre, The Biography*, Bloomsbury, 2015

Stoddart, Jane, My Harvest of Years, Hodder & Stoughton, 1938

Stoney, Barbara, *Enid Blyton; a biography*, Hodder & Stoughton, 1974

Swann, Annie, *My Life*, Hodder & Stoughton, 1934

Tangye, Nigel, *Teach Yourself Flying*, Hodder & Stoughton, 1938

Tebbel, John, *Between the Covers: the rise and transformation of book publishing in America*, Oxford University Press, 1987

Temple, William, *A Conditional Justification for War*, Hodder & Stoughton, 1940

Tuchman, Barbara, *The Guns of August*, The Macmillan Company, New York, 1962

Various, *The Queen's Book of the Red Cross*, Hodder & Stoughton, 1939

Index

Sources of illustrations